The Dynamics of Creation

By the same author

The Integrity of the Personality
Sexual Deviation
Human Aggression

ANTHONY STORR

The Dynamics of Creation

SECKER & WARBURG

LONDON

First published in England 1972 by
Martin Secker & Warburg Limited
14 Carlisle Street, London W1V 6NN

Copyright © Anthony Storr 1972

SBN: 436 48755 1

Printed in Great Britain by
C. Tinling & Company Limited
London and Prescot

TO C.L.S.

Acknowledgments

I want warmly to thank Elizabeth Macdougall for her patience and her typing.

I want also to thank the Bollinger Foundation for a grant which enabled me to devote time to the preparation of this book.

My publishers and I gratefully acknowledge permission from the following to quote copyright material: George Allen & Unwin Ltd, Humberto Nagera, *Vincent Van Gogh* (International Literary Management); Bertrand Russell, *Portraits From Memory* (Simon & Schuster Inc.). The Bodley Head Ltd for *Prometheus: The Life of Balzac* by André Maurois, translated by Norman Denny (Harper & Row). Cambridge University Press, R. B. Onians, *Origins of European Thought*. Jonathan Cape Ltd, Desmond Morris, *The Human Zoo* (McGraw-Hill Book Company). Chatto and Windus Ltd, Sigmund Freud Copyrights Ltd, The Institute of Psycho-Analysis, The Hogarth Press Ltd, *The Standard Edition of the Complete Psychological Works of Sigmund Freud*, revised and edited by James Strachey (Basic Books Inc., W. W. Norton & Company Inc., Liveright Publishing Co.). Chatto and Windus Ltd, M. Proust, *Remembrance of Things Past*, translated by George Scott Moncrieff (Random House Inc.). The Hogarth Press Ltd, Dr K. R. Eissler (ed.), *Searchlights on Delinquency* (International Universities Press Inc.); Mrs Katharine Jones, E. Jones, *The Life and Work of Sigmund Freud* (Basic Books Inc.). William Collins Sons & Co. Ltd, C. G. Jung, *Memories, Dreams and Reflections* (Pantheon Books Inc.). Faber and Faber Ltd, Terence McLaughlin, *Music and Communication*; Herbert Read, *Icon and Idea* (Harvard University Press); Eric Walter White, *Stravinsky. The Sonnets of Michelangelo*, The Folio Society, published for its members in 1961. Victor Gollancz Ltd, Ernest Newman, *Wagner as Man and Artist*. Grune & Stratton Inc, Hélène Deutsch, *The Psychology of Women*. Harvard University Press, A. Copland, *Music and Imagination*; S. K. Langer, *Philosophy in a New Key*. Indiana University Press, A. C. Kinsey, etc., *Sexual Behavior in the Human Female*. Methuen & Co. Ltd, S. Brodetsky, *Sir Isaac Newton*; Desmond Morris, *The Biology of Art*. Phaidon Press Ltd, E. H. Gombrich, *Art and Illusion*. Routledge & Kegan Paul Ltd, *The*

Acknowledgments

Collected Works of C. G. Jung, Vols VII, XVI, XIII (The Bollingen Foundation at Princeton University Press); Mary Douglas, *Purity and Danger* (Praeger Publishers Inc.); H. Hartog (ed.), *European Music in the Twentieth Century*; Johan Huizinga, *Homo Ludens*; Ari Kiev (ed.), *Social Psychiatry*, Vol. I (Science House Inc.); Suzanne K. Langer, *Feeling and Form* (Charles Scribner's Sons). Tavistock Publications Ltd, D. W. Winnicott, *Playing and Reality* (Basic Books Inc.). The Trustees of the Estate of Albert Einstein, *Out of My Later Years*. George Weidenfeld & Nicolson Ltd, Alex Comfort, *Nature and Human Nature* (Harper & Row).

Contents

			page
Introduction			xi
CHAPTER	1	The Ambivalence of Freud	1
CHAPTER	2	Creativity as Wish-Fulfilment	14
CHAPTER	3	The Conscious Motives of the Artist	29
CHAPTER	4	Creativity as Defence	40
CHAPTER	5	Creativity and the Schizoid Character	50
CHAPTER	6	New Models of the Universe	61
CHAPTER	7	Creativity and the Manic-Depressive Temperament	75
CHAPTER	8	Creativity and the Obsessional Character	92
CHAPTER	9	Creativity and Play	113
CHAPTER	10	Play and Social Development	127
CHAPTER	11	Is Art Adaptive?	137
CHAPTER	12	Man's Inner World: Origin and Function	151
CHAPTER	13	Divine Discontent	163
CHAPTER	14	Disposable Passion	175
CHAPTER	15	The Creative Ego and Its Opposites	188
CHAPTER	16	Genius and Madness	203
CHAPTER	17	The Quest for Identity	217
CHAPTER	18	Symbols of Integration	229
Index			243

Introduction

The third edition of the Shorter Oxford English Dictionary does not acknowledge the existence of the word 'creativity'. It is an omission which should be remedied, since the word is in common use, and the subject one of widespread interest. Creativity has been defined, simply and concisely, as 'the ability to bring something new into existence';[1] and this definition will serve our present purpose well enough. Fortunately, it does not imply that the 'something new' need be new to everyone, or, indeed, new to anyone else save the person who creates it. The child who links together in his mind two ideas which have hitherto been separated, and who produces a third as a result of the fusion, may find, disappointingly, that he has not been as original as he had supposed when his teacher points out that someone else has had the same idea before him. None the less, he has been creative in that he has produced for himself something which is new to *him*; and the manner in which this process of creation comes about has been found so enthralling that many millions of words have been written about it.

No single human being can possibly know enough to produce a comprehensive study of all that can be comprised under the heading 'creativity'. The particular aspect of the subject with which this book is chiefly concerned is that of motive. What drives an artist or scientist to engage in his creative activity is a question of great interest, but one which has been somewhat neglected in academic studies of creativity. There are many possible answers to the question, ranging from mundane statements like 'the need for money' to complex metaphysical speculations. Since many creative people pursue their avocations with passionate intensity, one might suppose that psychoanalysis, or some other variety of dynamic psychology, would long ago have solved the problem; for the emotional drives of man are the special concern of such approaches to human nature. But such is not the case. Even Freud's most enthusiastic admirers have long recognized that his interpretations of works of art, and his remarks on the nature of artists, are often unsatisfactory. Indeed, dissatisfaction with psychoanalytic writings upon art has been one spur prompting the writing of this book.

It is not my intention to disparage Freud, whose ideas, even when incomplete or limited, are invariably stimulating. But no point of view is all-embracing; and even the ideas of a man of genius like Freud are bound to reflect the limitations of his own interests. Freud was a cultured man, devoted to literature, interested in history, and a collector of antiquities. But he had little aesthetic appreciation, as his biographer points out; and, even in the field of literature, of which he had an extensive knowledge, was not really concerned with what makes a work of art. Lionel Trilling deeply admired Freud, but he wrote of him: 'But he is always, I think, outside the process of litera-ture. Much as he responds to the product, he does not really imagine the process. He does not have what we call the *feel* of the thing.'[2]

Freud's followers have often been less modest than he was in their approach to artists and their works. Indeed, many psychoanalytic writings on such subjects appear to be a Procrustean effort to fit obstinate facts into a bed of psychoanalytic theory which is both too short and too narrow to accommodate them. It seems improbable, for example, that Leonardo's interest in water took origin from his suffering from enuresis in childhood; yet this interpretation has been confidently advanced. Perhaps the author has never seen a baby playing in a bath, nor himself appreciated the shifting, flashing sparkle of water in sunshine.[3]

In any event, psychoanalysts have principally been concerned with the content of creative products, and with explaining content in terms of the artist's infantile past. They have paid less attention to examining why the artist chooses his particular activity to express, abreact or sublimate his emotions. In short, they have not made much distinction between art and neurosis; and, since the former is one of the blessings of mankind, whereas the latter is one of the curses, it seems a pity that they should not be better differentiated.

Although some creative people may be impelled by neurosis or incipient psychosis to engage in their particular pursuit, not all appear to be thus driven. Nor is it necessarily convincing to assume that the creative impulse is a simple derivative of the more primitive drives of sex and aggression. Perhaps creativity is more closely bound up with what might be called a 'dynamic of the normal' than with psychopathology: and maybe one weakness of current psychoanalytic thinking is a failure to make sufficient distinction between normal and neurotic in this context as in others.

REFERENCES

1. BARRON, Frank. 'The Psychology of Creativity', in *New Directions in Psychology II* (London: Holt, Rinehart & Winston, 1965) p. 3.
2. TRILLING, Lionel. 'Freud: Within and Beyond Culture', in *Beyond Culture* (London: Secker & Warburg, 1966) p. 92.
3. EISSLER, K. R. *Leonardo da Vinci: Psychoanalytic Notes on the Enigma* (London: The Hogarth Press and The Institute of Psycho-Analysis, 1962).

1

The Ambivalence of Freud

All over the world, solemn-faced business executives are abandoning rational thought, allowing imagination free rein, abstaining from critical comment upon their own or their colleagues' ideas, and engaging in so-called 'brain-storming'. By thus summoning the irrational, they hope that inspiration will discover a 'creative' solution to whatever problem is taxing them, even if this be of no more import than the invention of a new can-opener. In schools and colleges, courses in 'creative thinking' are multiplying rapidly. Teachers hope to detect and foster creativity in their pupils. Psychologists construct tests to measure it; institutes and foundations are devoted to it; and there is a publication called the *Journal of Creative Behaviour* which, on its first appearance in 1967, immediately attracted five thousand subscribers. Creativity has in fact become fashionable; and fond parents, instead of modestly hoping that their children will be bright enough to succeed academically, anxiously examine them for evidence of creativity, which they have been taught to suppose is only tenuously connected with mere intelligence.

But why is creativity so highly regarded? One might have supposed that parents would be relieved to discover that their children had none of it, since a number of creative people profess themselves driven to create by distress, rather than by any excess of joyful vitality. Simenon, for example, in spite of being one of the most prolific and financially successful authors of all time, alleges that 'Writing is not a profession, but a vocation of unhappiness. I don't think an artist can ever be happy.'[1] And it is not difficult to match his statement with similar utterances from other creative persons. Moreover, in his 23rd Introductory Lecture on Psycho-Analysis, Freud writes of the artist in terms which might make any parent thankful to find that his child possessed no creative gift.

'An artist is once more in rudiments an introvert, not far removed from neurosis. He is oppressed by excessively powerful instinctual needs. He desires to win honour, power, wealth, fame and the love of women; but he lacks the means for achieving these satisfactions.

1

Consequently, like any other unsatisfied man, he turns away from reality and transfers all his interest, and his libido too, to the wishful constructions of his life of phantasy, whence the path might lead to neurosis.'[2]

If this conception of creativity is correct, it would surely be better to have none of it; for reality is generally to be preferred to phantasy, and it must be a sad state of being to 'lack the means for achieving' any of the gratifications which Freud catalogues.

However, in spite of Freud and the statements of writers like Simenon, it continues to be currently assumed that creativity is a 'good thing'; and an enormous amount of research and speculation has been devoted to examining how the creative process takes place, rather than paying attention to the motives of the creator himself. This, for example, is true of Arthur Koestler's vast and erudite book *The Act of Creation*.[3] Although he does devote a couple of chapters to the motivational drives of the scientist and the artist, the bulk of the book is concerned with elaborating his notion of 'bisociation', the way in which ideas are combined to produce new insights; and with his valuable exposition of the hierarchical structure of mind and nervous system.

Similarly, when creative persons are studied by psychological tests, interviews, questionnaires and the like, traits are discovered and listed which are of great interest as being characteristic of such persons. But the enumeration of such traits does not necessarily throw much light upon what it is that impels the potentially creative to make productive use of their endowment. We all know gifted people who have made but little use of their gifts; and there are also some who struggle endlessly to produce original work, but who lack the innate ability to do so.

Psychoanalysis, being fundamentally concerned with drive and motive, might have been expected to throw more light upon what impels the creative person than in fact it has. Many psychoanalysts, including Freud himself, have produced detailed studies both of works of art and of the artists themselves. Such studies are often of compelling interest. In examining the productions of a creative individual, it is often possible to detect recurrent themes and preoccupations which reveal a good deal of his psychopathology. Bernard C. Meyer's psychoanalytic biography of Conrad[4] is a particularly convincing example. The author is able to demonstrate that Conrad had many fetishistic preoccupations; that he tended to regard women

2

as dominant, 'phallic' creatures; that his preoccupation with strong, silent heroes was related to the fact that, as a child, he was sometimes seriously ill and never robust; and that his mother's death when he was seven years old had far-reaching effects which can be plainly detected in both his life and his writings. Conrad's psychopathology is of fascinating interest; and no student of his novels can now afford to neglect the psychoanalytic approach to them.

But the relation between Conrad's psychopathology and his adopting the profession of writer is by no means clear. Many people have a similar psychopathology and do not write. The quotation from Freud's Introductory Lectures given above suggests an explanation which, taken alone and out of context, appears almost naïve. It simply will not do to assume that the artist is a man who can only achieve satisfaction for his instinctual drives in phantasy, however true this may be as a partial explanation. The achievements of a Beethoven or a Tolstoy are not to be put upon the same level as a masturbatory phantasy, however much it may be true that the sexual drive enters into these achievements. As has been often pointed out, the weakness of psychoanalytic interpretations of works of art is twofold. Psychoanalysis neither distinguishes between bad art and good; nor, more importantly, between a work of art and a neurotic symptom.

Freud, of course, realized this; and nothing is more revealing of his uneasy ambivalence towards artists than his own statements, which vary from denigration to adulation with few connecting links between these opposing points of view. Compare, for example, the quotation already cited with the following passage from 'Delusions and Dreams in Jensen's Gradiva':

'But creative writers are valuable allies and their evidence is to be praised highly, for they are apt to know a whole host of things between heaven and earth of which our philosophy has not yet let us dream. In their knowledge of the mind they are far in advance of us everyday people, for they draw upon sources which we have not yet opened up for science.'[5]

Freud's own interest in the arts was primarily engaged by poetry, and Ernest Jones points out that when Freud wrote about 'artists' 'he had predominantly in mind creative writers', in spite of the fact that his most famous studies of artists are his paper on Michelangelo's Moses and his short book on Leonardo da Vinci, rather than his paper on 'Dostoevsky and Parricide' and his writings on Shakespeare

3

and Ibse ... than one place that psycho-
analysis ... 'It can do nothing towards
elucidatir ... nor can it explain the means
by which ... nique.'[6] So he wrote in his
'Autobio ... per on Dostoevsky opens
thus: 'Fo ... in the rich personality of
Dostoevsk ... otic, the moralist and the
sinner. H ... one's way in this bewildering
complexity?

'The creative artist is the least doubtful: Dostoevsky's place is not
far behind Shakespeare. *The Brothers Karamazov* is the most magnificent novel ever written: the episode of the Grand Inquisitor, one
of the peaks in the literature of the world, can hardly be valued too
highly. Before the problem of the creative artist analysis must, alas,
lay down its arms.'[7] Yet Freud did not really lay down his arms to
the extent which he professes. Although he may not have attempted
to explain artistic technique, he certainly conceived that works of
art were the product of sublimation; and derived, therefore, from
primitive sexual, and possibly aggressive, instinctive impulses for
which they were ultimately substitutes. Sublimation is the process by
which energy, originally instinctual, is displaced and discharged in
ways which are not obviously instinctual. Thus, the primitive wish
to exhibit the body, and more especially the genitals, may be 'sublimated' into more socially acceptable ways of 'showing-off'; by making
public appearances or speeches for instance, or by producing works
of art which can be exhibited instead of the person of the artist.
Anna Freud, in her book *The Ego and the Mechanisms of Defence*,
defines sublimation as 'the displacement of the instinctual aim in
conformity with higher social values'.[8] She also states that sublimation 'pertains rather to the study of the normal than to that of
neurosis'.[9] This latter remark is one to which I shall return.

The uneasy ambivalence of psychoanalysis towards creativity is
again reflected in what Ernest Jones wrote about the vexed problem
of whether psychoanalysis is likely to impair or to enhance artistic
achievement. In the chapter of his biography of Freud in which
he discusses the latter's attitude to art, he writes as follows:
'Many artists, both first-rate and second-rate, have now been analysed, and the results have been unequivocal. When the artistic
impulse is genuine the greater freedom achieved through analysis
has heightened the artistic capacity, but when the wish to become an

artist is impelled by purely neurotic and irrelevant motives the analysis clarifies the situation.'[10]

Is it really so easy to distinguish 'neurotic' and 'genuine' artistic impulses? One may venture to doubt it. Of course, as we implied earlier, there are a number of persons with little or no talent who both envy artists and attempt to imitate them in a futile way. Such people may, if analysed, abandon their efforts to become what they are not. As Freud himself wrote to a correspondent: 'It is not out of the question that an analysis results in its being impossible to continue an artistic activity. Then, however, it is not the fault of the analysis; it would have happened in any case and it is only an advantage to learn that in good time.' We may certainly agree with this; although Freud fails to mention the opposite phenomenon, which may be at least as common. This is the fact that there are also those with potential gifts, artistic and otherwise, whose talents have remained unrealized for lack of recognition or because of active discouragement. It is likely that such people are as numerous as those who think that they possess such gifts but do not in reality do so. Freud goes on to write: 'When, on the other hand, the artistic impulse is stronger than the internal resistances analysis will heighten, not diminish, the capacity for achievement.'[11]

This is an interesting statement on at least two separate counts. The term 'resistance' is generally used in psychoanalysis to describe the opposition put up by the patient to the analyst's interpretations. Most people are reluctant to recognize the extent to which their conduct takes origin in primitive, and often in infantile, sexual and aggressive impulses. The first point about Freud's remark is, however, that it seems to imply that the artistic impulse is something *sui generis*. By referring to it as sometimes stronger than the internal resistances, he is putting it on a par with instinct, or at least refraining from trying to reduce it to an infantile sexual or aggressive origin. And yet, as we noted above, he is in no doubt that works of art are the product of sublimation; and it necessarily follows from this belief that the artistic impulse must be reducible to instinctual origins. It is true that these instinctual origins are generally thought to be infantile: that is, 'pregenital' oral, anal, and phallic impulses which could not easily find direct expression in civilized adult life in any case. Some degree of sublimation is a requisite of 'normality' in Western civilization; hence Anna Freud's remark which I quoted above. Yet, according to Freud's point of view, the artist must

5

presumably suffer from some unusual overemphasis of his infantile sexuality, or some degree of failure to attain 'genitality' (sexual maturity), or why would he need the special sublimation implicit in the artistic impulse?

Since one of the objects of psychoanalysis is to help people rid themselves of their infantile sexuality, and attain satisfaction by the integration of these remnants of childhood under the supremacy of the genital drive, it is hard to see why the artistic impulse, in successfully analysed artists, should escape analytic dissolution. Fenichel, for example, is explicit in stating that sublimations are at least partially abolished as a result of psychoanalytic treatment. 'Quantitatively, however, sublimations play a lesser role in the adjustment of the instinctual economy of the former neurotic than does adequate sexual satisfaction.'[12] Freud's statement does not make it clear why, even in the 'genuine' artist, psychoanalysis should heighten his capacity for artistic achievement. On the theoretical grounds which he and other analysts advance, one would expect that it would be diminished.

Freud's ambivalent attitude to sublimation, and consequently to the activity of the artist, is further exemplified by the following passage from 'Civilization and its Discontents', itself a revealing title.

'Another technique for fending off suffering is the employment of the displacements of libido which our mental apparatus permits of and through which its function gains so much in flexibility. The task here is that of shifting the instinctual aims in such a way that they cannot come up against frustration from the external world. In this, sublimation of the instincts lends its assistance. One gains the most if one can sufficiently heighten the yield of pleasure from the sources of physical and intellectual work. When that is so, fate can do little against one. A satisfaction of this kind, such as an artist's joy in creating, in giving his phantasies body, or a scientist's in solving problems or discovering truths, has a special quality which we shall certainly one day be able to characterize in metapsychological terms. At present we can only say figuratively that such satisfactions seem "finer and higher". But their intensity is mild as compared with that derived from the sating of crude and primary instinctual impulses; it does not convulse our physical being. And the weak point of this method is that it is not applicable generally: it is accessible to only a few people. It presupposes the possession of special dispositions and gifts which are far from being common to any practical degree. And even to the few who do possess them, this method cannot give complete protection from suffering. It creates no impenetrable armour against the arrows of fortune, and it habitually fails when the source of suffering is a person's own body.'[13]

As Freud himself was notably creative, and, moreover, at the age of forty-one, wrote to a friend that 'sexual excitation is of no more use to a person like me',[14] one can only feel regret that, for the subsequent forty-two years of his life, his pleasures should have been so unexciting to him. Enthusiastic though he was about literature, and, to a hardly lesser extent, about sculpture and architecture, it is clear that he rates the enjoyment to be obtained from the arts, either as creator or appreciator, at a very much lower level than that of orgasm. This is, of course, implicit in the assumption that such pleasures are substitutes for 'the real thing', or part-aspects of it, which ought, somehow, to find more direct expression either in the sexual act itself, or else in the foreplay leading up to it: the latter being the conventional psychoanalytic repository for 'pregenital' impulses. As has often been observed, Freud's conception of civilization is essentially negative. It is an unwelcome, albeit necessary, restraint upon the natural man which interferes with his pursuit of happiness; rather than, as might be alleged, providing him with a choice of paths to enjoyment in addition to sexuality. Moreover, to restrict even the limited satisfaction which Freud admits to 'an artist's joy in creating . . . or a scientist's in solving problems' is to impose restrictions which are surely too severe for what Freud had in mind. One need not belong to the very small class of original creators to gain considerable satisfaction from many things which would undoubtedly rank as sublimations in Freudian eyes. The vicarious enjoyment of sport, for example, is enormously important to many people who are far from being creatively gifted. So is the release which the young find in pop music; a release which is so obviously partially sexual that it does not require a psychoanalyst to affirm it. Of course a satisfactory sexual life is an extremely important source of human happiness; but sex, like patriotism, is 'not enough'; and one of the themes of this book is that, because of the influence of psychoanalysis, we have come to expect too much of it.

The contradictions already noticed in our brief glance at what Freud had to say about the analysis of the artist are not resolved by Ernest Jones's remarks on the subject of aesthetic appreciation.

'They [the artists] are right in maintaining that the source of artistic appreciation lies deeper than any unconscious fantasy, and that it is more remote from our instinctual life than any other human interest, with the possible exception of pure mathematics: in other words, it represents the acme of de-sexualization. Remoteness, however, need not connote impenetrability. When one considers the material used in the five arts—paint, clay, stone, words, and sounds—any psychologist must conclude that the passionate interest in bringing an orderliness out of chaos must signify at the same time an extraordinary sublimation of the most primitive infantile enjoyments and the most extreme denial of them. In psychoanalytical terms that passionate concentration represents a fixation on a stage of "preliminary pleasure".'[15]

And so the artist, according to this account also, is sublimating his infantile sexuality in his art: yet both Freud and Jones deny that making him conscious of his conflicts around infantile sexuality, and thus at least opening the door to a more mature sexual expression, will impair his creativeness. It might be argued that psychoanalysts, in their heart of hearts, do not really believe that any human being can attain so high a degree of sexual maturity that he has no residue of pregenital sexuality which must needs be sublimated; a conception with which one would have considerable sympathy. But if any do hold this point of view, they do not state it unequivocally. The assumption that all infantile conflicts can be solved, or ought to be solved, and that all man's emotional problems are dissipated by the whirlwind release of repeated, regular orgasm, dies hard. The possibility that man is designed in such a fashion that his fulfilment is not wholly, or even appropriately, obtainable in this way is never admitted.

It is not disputed that creative persons may indeed be sublimating their pregenital sexuality in art. As an example of how psychoanalysts apply their insights to creativity, we may cite Dr Humberto Nagera's study of van Gogh. The author alleges that van Gogh made an 'unconscious equation between painting and masturbation'. 'Unconsciously he seems to think that it is masturbation that has ruined him as a man, ruined his mind and his ability to create a family as well as his sexual potency. Painting is an attempt at sublimation of his masturbation conflicts and sexuality generally, and at the same time a substitute and a symbol for them . . . Painting is a particularly suitable vehicle for Vincent because it can embody the essential components of his sexuality, not only his phallic creative strivings but also the strong anal components with which in his case they are contaminated. The media of oil painting form a traditionally well-known outlet for the gratification of otherwise forbidden anal impulses; the consistency, the strong smells, the messiness are highly enjoyable for the anal personality and allow for the non-conflictive gratification of the impulses to touch [the faeces], to enjoy the strong and diverse smells, to mess, etc. Such tendencies were particularly marked in Vincent who used his hands as a brush quite freely in order to create particular effects.'[16]

All this and much else of a similar kind may be true of van Gogh. But if it is, why is it that Freud and Jones are so sure that analysis would not destroy the creative impulse in such a person? If van Gogh had been subjected to analysis, would not Freud have hoped that he would lose his guilt about his infantile sexuality, about masturbation, and about sex in general? And if he had done so, and attained a fully satisfactory adult form of sexual life, why, according to Freudian theory, would he then have wanted to go on painting or even, as Freud suggests in the letter quoted above, have painted more or better?

Dr Nagera suggests, with good reason, that van Gogh looked upon sexuality and painting as incompatible alternatives. Moreover, he agrees with him. 'Similarly, his perception that a more frequent and freer sexual life than the very methodic, at best once a fortnight sexual outlet that he allows himself, will drain him of his creativity and ability to paint, is quite correct. The energy for his paintings is modified sexual energy and if he expends it on the one activity it will not be available for the other.'[17] According to Dr Nagera, it was because van Gogh abandoned any thought of women, marriage and a family that he was able to produce such a very large number of paintings during the last two and a half years of his life.

This negative correlation, which could be simply expressed as 'the more sexuality, the less art', is open to a number of objections. Quite a number of creative people have led rather active sexual lives without apparently diminishing their artistic production. But, for the moment, this interesting problem must be laid on one side. The passages and views that I quote above show that psychoanalysts, including Freud himself, are uneasy about the interpretation of artistic activity, and find it difficult to fit it into their scheme of things, which is essentially one of interpreting all human activity in terms of sexuality and (albeit reluctantly) aggression or the death instinct. In Freud's view, there were only two groups of instincts: 'the erotic instincts, which seek to combine more and more living substance into ever greater unities, and the death instincts, which oppose this effort and lead what is living back into an inorganic state. From the concurrent and opposing action of these two proceed the phenomena of life which are brought to an end by death.'[18] Freud believed that aggression was a redirection of the death instinct towards the external world, a concept which has been discussed elsewhere,[19] so that if, in this context, the word 'aggression' is used as a shorthand to describe Freud's 'death instincts', it is fair to say that sexuality and aggression are the two basic drives from which all else, in the Freudian view, is derived. One purpose of this enquiry is to demonstrate that this conception is inadequate when the artistic impulse is examined.

One psychoanalytic writer has attempted to circumvent the problem of the relation of psychopathology to creativeness by postulating that the psychopathology of genius is in a special category. 'Therefore I would with a grain of salt say that in the genius all psychic processes that support sublimatory processes are ego-syntonic and belong to a special category of psychopathology which is essentially different from all other forms of psychopathology as set forth in textbooks of psychiatry. This is the psychopathology of genius, which is not amenable to criteria derived from the non-genius.'[20] By 'ego-syntonic', the author, K. R. Eissler, means that the processes to which he refers are acceptable to, or compatible with, the genius's own conscious conception of himself. However, to postulate a 'special category of psychopathology' is surely an evasion of the problem. In addition, the notion offends against the principle of Occam's Razor: 'Entia non sunt multiplicanda praeter necessitatem.'

This idea of Dr Eissler's springs partly from his recognition that psychoanalysis finds it hard to distinguish between a work of art and a neurotic symptom. He recognizes that the achievements of genius are derived from a substratum of 'psychopathology'; yet, since he rates these achievements so highly, he cannot tolerate putting them in the same class as symptoms. Hence the 'psychopathology' has to be 'special'.

The same dilemma in which he finds himself is evident when he writes: 'It is no longer disputed that in the study of genius a surprisingly large amount of psychopathology is encountered. The question, however, has not been answered what connection exists between the genius's psychopathology and his achievements. Psychopathology, in general, is looked upon as defect, though most forms of psychopathology have a useful function in so far as they spare the psychic apparatus a damage that would be greater than that caused by the psychopathology (primary gain). Observation of the genius, however, suggests the possiblity that psychopathology is indispensable to the highest achievements of certain kinds.'[21] The way out of this dilemma is surely to reconsider what should be regarded as 'pathological'; but this apparently offends too much against orthodox psychoanalytic theory. Ultimately, the difficulty springs from the assumption mentioned earlier, that all psychopathological problems are, or ought to be, solved by the attainment of 'genitality', and the consequent channelling of infantile and 'pregenital' impulses into a fully mature relation with a person of the opposite sex.

That Dr Eissler shares with Dr Nagera the conviction that the attainment of such a relationship is incompatible with the production of works of art is abundantly clear.

'In the case of the genius, however, as far as one can reconstruct it, it does not seem possible that he would be capable of his extraordinary creations if his libido were gratified in an adequate object relation. The energy flow into the object relation would be diverted from the artistic process. Consequently, only the blockage of a permanent object attachment can produce that intense hunger for objects that results in the substitute formation of the perfect work of art.'[22]

But as we shall see later, the evidence that all great artists were incapable of mature relationships with the opposite sex ('an adequate object relation') is not forthcoming. Some were, and some were not. It is on this account that psychoanalysts should re-examine their own assumptions. It may be quite legitimate to suppose that artists are, in their work, resolving certain problems connected with childhood conflicts. There may, in addition, be many ways other than that of the artist to deal with the same problems. But we ought not necessarily to assume that mature interpersonal relationships, and, more especially, mature sexual relationships, are so much the be-all and end-all of human existence that all the emotional problems implicit in being human are solved by their consoling power. If we drop this assumption, we can also drop the idea that the work of art is *necessarily* a substitute for anything else. However, this is not to say that it is *never* a substitute. Accordingly, the next chapter is devoted to a consideration of Freud's notion of creative activity as wish-fulfilment, and to the provision of some examples which support the partial validity of this theory.

REFERENCES

1. *Writers at Work*. The Paris Review Interviews (London: Secker & Warburg, 1958) Vol. 1, p. 132.
2. FREUD, Sigmund. 'The Paths to the Formation of Symptoms', Lecture XXIII in *Introductory Lectures on Psycho-Analysis* (London: The Hogarth Press and The Institute of Psycho-Analysis, 1963), Standard Edition, Vol. XVI, p. 376.
3. KOESTLER, Arthur. *The Act of Creation* (London: Hutchinson, 1964).
4. MEYER, Bernard C. *Joseph Conrad: A Psychoanalytic Biography* (London: Oxford University Press, 1967).
5. FREUD, Sigmund. 'Delusions and Dreams in Jensen's Gradiva' (London: The Hogarth Press and The Institute of Psycho-Analysis, 1959) Standard Edition, Vol. IX, p. 8.
6. FREUD, Sigmund. 'An Autobiographical Study' (London: The Hogarth Press and The Institute of Psycho-Analysis 1959), Standard Edition, Vol. XX, p. 65.
7. FREUD, Sigmund. 'Dostoevsky and Parricide' (London: The Hogarth Press and The Institute of Psycho-Analysis, 1961) Standard Edition, Vol. XXI, p. 177.
8. FREUD, Anna. *The Ego and the Mechanisms of Defence* (London: The Hogarth Press and The Institute of Psycho-Analysis, 1968) p. 52.
9. Ibid, p. 44.
10. JONES, Ernest. *Sigmund Freud* (London: The Hogarth Press, 1957) Vol. III, p. 445.
11. FREUD, Sigmund. Letter to Maria Thoman, quoted in Ernest Jones' *Sigmund Freud* (London: The Hogarth Press, 1957) Vol. III, pp. 445-6.
12. FENICHEL, Otto. *The Psychoanalytic Theory of Neurosis* (London: Routledge & Kegan Paul, 1947) p. 573.
13. FREUD, Sigmund. 'Civilization and Its Discontents' (London: The Hogarth Press and The Institute of Psycho-Analysis, 1961) Standard Edition, Vol. XXI, pp. 79-80.
14. BONAPARTE, Marie (Editor). *The Origins of Psychoanalysis* (London: Imago, 1954) p. 227.
15. JONES, Ernest. *Sigmund Freud* (London: The Hogarth Press, 1957) Vol. III, p. 445.
16. NAGERA, Humberto. *Vincent Van Gogh* (London: Allen and Unwin, 1967) pp. 145-6.

17. Ibid, p. 147.
18. FREUD, Sigmund. 'Anxiety and Instinctual Life', Lecture XXXII in *New Introductory Lectures on Psycho-Analysis* (London: The Hogarth Press and The Institute of Psycho-Analysis, 1964) p. 107.
19. STORR, Anthony. *Human Aggression* (London: Allen Lane The Penguin Press, 1968).
20. EISSLER, K. R. *Leonardo da Vinci: Psychoanalytic Notes on the Enigma* (London: The Hogarth Press and The Institute of Psycho-Analysis, 1962) p. 287.
21. Ibid, p. 283.
22. Ibid, p. 287.

2

Creativity as Wish-Fulfilment

In his paper on 'Creative Writers and Day-Dreaming' Freud compares the writer's activity with that of the child at play. 'The creative writer does the same as the child at play. He creates a world of phantasy which he takes very seriously—that is, which he invests with large amounts of emotion—while separating it sharply from reality.'[1] The only difference which Freud points out between phantasy and play is that the child 'likes to link his imagined objects and situations to the tangible and visible things of the real world'.[2] When the child stops playing, he 'gives up nothing but the link with real objects; instead of *playing*, he now *phantasies*. He builds castles in the air and creates what are called *day-dreams*.'[3] Later in the same paper Freud writes: 'We may lay it down that a happy person never phantasies, only an unsatisfied one. The motive forces of phantasies are unsatisfied wishes, and every single phantasy is the fulfilment of a wish, a correction of unsatisfying reality. These motivating wishes vary according to the sex, character and circumstances of the person who is having the phantasy; but they fall naturally into two main groups. They are either ambitious wishes, which serve to elevate the subject's personality; or they are erotic ones.'[4] In other words, creative productions are nothing but surrogates; inferior substitutes for what the author is unable to obtain for himself in reality.

Many critics have attacked Freud's formulation, with good cause. In thus dismissing creative writing as 'nothing but' phantasy, Freud is omitting any reference to aesthetic considerations. Are dreams, day-dreams and works of art all to be bundled together in the same category, without any attempt to distinguish between them? Is there no difference between *Anna Karenina* and the sexual phantasies of an adolescent? Of course there is; but Freud, in this context, will go no further in admitting this than to write: 'We are perfectly aware that very many imaginative writings are far removed from the model of the naïve day-dream; and yet I cannot suppress the suspicion that even the most extreme deviations from that model could be linked with it through an uninterrupted series of transitional causes.'[5]

But, however incomplete Freud's explanation may be, there are

14

certain literary productions to which it may be fruitfully applied. These do not generally rank very high in the hierarchy of literature, although there are exceptions. One novel which belongs to the latter class, since it is highly rated by at least some critics, is *Hadrian VII* by Frederick Rolfe.[6] This curious work is now familiar to a large public, since it was recently converted into a successful play, and has, for a number of years, been available as a paperback. It is both ironical and characteristic of Rolfe that his only notable success should be posthumous. During his lifetime he earned nothing at all from *Hadrian VII*, since his publishers specified that there should be no royalties on the first six hundred copies, and the sales of the book had not attained this figure at the time of his death. It would be hard to find a better example than *Hadrian VII* of Freud's first group of wish-fulfilling phantasy, the 'ambitious wishes which serve to elevate the subject's personality'. For *Hadrian VII* is the story of a Catholic aspirant to the priesthood, rejected from a theological college whilst still a student, who, nevertheless, twenty years later, is reinstated by ecclesiastical authority, and actually comes to be elected Pope. The rejected candidate for the priesthood is, of course, Rolfe himself. He was, in reality, dismissed from the Scots College in Rome as being quite unsuitable for the priesthood, and everything which was discovered about him by his indefatigable and sympathetic biographer, A. J. A. Symons,[7] confirms the correctness of this decision. Rolfe was homosexual; but this disability need not debar a man from being a conscientious and valuable priest. Indeed, it is a condition rather frequently encountered amongst those who seek to embrace a celibate way of life. But Rolfe was not only homosexual; he was also a psychopathic personality of a markedly paranoid variety who invariably turned upon all those who tried to help him, and who remained, to the end of his days, querulous, egocentric, suspicious and misanthropic.

Like many psychopaths, Rolfe adopted an air of superiority which made him enemies; and he also attempted to give the impression of being an expert in all sorts of subjects of which his grasp was actually minimal. Thus he dabbled in music, pretended to a knowledge of Greek and other languages with which he had in fact but a nodding acquaintance, claimed the title of Baron Corvo on the grounds that he had been given it by an Italian Countess, dropped vague hints as to the grandeur of his ancestors, spent far beyond his means, said that the Kaiser was his godfather, and, in short, tried by every possible device to suggest that he was both more able and much grander than he was. It is characteristic of such persons to imagine that their gifts entitle them to avoid the drudgery of study, and so it was not surprising that Rolfe was actually a poor student who neglected his work. It is also typical of the narcissism of psychopaths that Rolfe was both particular and peculiar in his dress, not scrupling to order clothes for which he could not pay. Indeed, he was financially unscrupulous to an extent only matched by the criminal psychopaths who habitually make their living as 'false pretenders', and who exhibit the same total disregard for the pockets and the feelings of others. Whoever lent money to Rolfe was certain to incur his enmity rather than his friendship; for this was his invariable response to any effort to help him. Moreover, his allegations that he was persecuted by the Catholic clergy and others come very close to the paranoid delusions of the insane. In short, Rolfe was a textbook case: a paranoid psychopath of a variety well known to psychiatrists, to prison medical officers, and to the police. Such characters hover uneasily on the brink of insanity throughout their lives; and it is often impossible to tell how far they actually believe in their own phantasies. It may well be that it was the fact that Rolfe could write which kept him from becoming more of a criminal than he did. In his writing he found an opportunity of expressing his phantasies denied to those of similar personality who possess fewer gifts. And his writing, although peculiar, neologistic, and highly subjective, was at least an actual achievement in the real world which publishers printed, and which critics took seriously.

From rejected theological student to Pope is a leap which taxes the credulity of the reader, but Rolfe is able to make it more or less convincing. He imagines that the story of his hero's persistence in his vocation, in spite of twenty years' suffering, rejection and privation, makes such an impression of holiness upon the Cardinals who are in difficulty over electing a Pope that they finally settle upon this unknown, saintly Englishman. Nothing could, in reality, be more unlikely; but Rolfe is able to make this phantasy almost credible because of his own belief that he was an ill-treated genius for whom no recompense could be too much. It is well recognized that psychopaths who are false pretenders succeed in convincing others of the truth of the stories by which they obtain money from them because they half-believe in their own phantasies. The same mechanism was operative in Rolfe.

16

Rolfe's life was a tragic one. His invariable habit of savagely biting every hand which fed him, his arrogance, dishonesty and lack of scruple, finally caused him to be almost as rejected in reality as he had always supposed himself to be. He ended as a homosexual pimp in Venice, seducing boys that he might procure them to pander to the appetites of a wealthy patron in England with whom he corresponded, and who was in the habit of visiting Venice. Here is at least one example which bears out Freud's contention of an intimate connection between homosexuality and paranoia.

Rolfe provides an example of an extremely unhappy man whose phantasies, at least in *Hadrian VII*, are confined to ambition as a compensation for his actual failure in life and the pain of his rejection for the priesthood. The next example, though chiefly concerned with ambition, includes motivating wishes of the other variety which Freud mentions, namely erotic ones.

Ian Fleming, the creator of the enormously successful series of James Bond thrillers, was not nearly so disturbed a character as Rolfe. But his background and personality accord well with Freud's theory of creativity already outlined. (In what follows I am heavily indebted to John Pearson's excellent biography.)[8] Ian Fleming was born in 1908, less than a year after the birth of his elder brother, Peter Fleming, who later became a famous explorer and travel writer. His father was killed in the First World War, just before Ian's ninth birthday. Although he always said that he was unable to remember his father in reality, the latter was held up to him as a 'dead hero' model; a procedure which often creates psychological difficulties and a sense of inferiority. It is often hard enough for a boy to live up to a real father. How much more difficult it is to try to model oneself upon an absent hero, whose virtues are over-emphasized, and whose faults are forgotten or concealed. This is probably why Ian Fleming, all his life, remained a hero-worshipper. At school, according to his own account, his idol was his elder brother, Peter. Subsequent heroes were Sir William Stephenson, Lord Beaverbrook, Noël Coward, and Somerset Maugham. In his novels, Fleming's hero-worshipping propensity is strongly reflected in James Bond's attitude to his Secret Service chief, 'M'.

His mother was a formidable lady, rich, beautiful, energetic and self-willed. At the age of seventy-four she was involved in a bizarre legal action in which it was alleged that she had enticed the Marquess of Winchester away from his wife, and that she had later incited him to have his marriage annulled. She died less than three weeks before her son Ian's death in the summer of 1964. It was no doubt because of her influence that Ian Fleming avoided any really close involvement with women for most of his life, remaining a Don Juan who shunned intimacy. It was not until he was forty-three that he was able to commit himself to marriage. The first of the James Bond novels was finished six days before he finally took the plunge into matrimony.

There is a great deal to suggest that the creator of what is possibly the most ruthless and toughest hero in fiction did not himself possess the qualities with which he endowed James Bond, or at least believed that he did not. For a time, Fleming was actually trained in the techniques of a secret agent, and did very well until it came to the final test when trainees were required (as they thought) actually to shoot an enemy agent. Fleming balked at this. He couldn't bring himself to open the door of the room in which the ostensible agent sat, and pull the trigger. James Bond, the fictional hero who was a wish-fulfilling phantasy of what Fleming would like to have been, would have had no such inhibitions.

Ian Fleming's early life is a catalogue of disappointment and failure of a kind characteristic of boys who have been unable to identify with a real father, and who consequently develop little confidence in their own abilities, however considerable these abilities may be in reality. At Eton, Ian Fleming was outclassed by his brother Peter in every field except athletics. Peter carried off all the prizes, and was universally admired: Ian's response was to give up trying, except in the one field, athletics, in which he knew himself to be superior.

This pattern was to repeat itself when, at his mother's instigation, the attempt was made to turn Ian Fleming into a soldier. At Sandhurst, he again took no trouble with work and infringed the rules as he had done at Eton, with the result that his military career came to an end almost before it had begun. His next major failure was an attempt to enter the Foreign Office; but he came only twenty-fifth in the examination out of sixty-two applicants. He was so ashamed of this performance that he lied about it in later life, alleging that he came seventh in a year when only five candidates were accepted. After a brief interlude in journalism, he moved to a merchant bank. But this new endeavour lasted only two years, and he joined a firm of stockbrokers. Here he was not a success either. As in his previous efforts, he lacked application and staying power. One gets the impression that, at the first sign of failure, instead of making more effort, he simply retreated into phantasy.

Ian Fleming was notably successful with women, but only at a superficial level. Before leaving school he was already in trouble over girls, a pattern which was to repeat itself at Sandhurst. But, like other Don Juans, his success was more apparent than real. 'Men want a woman,' he wrote, 'whom they can turn off and on like a light-switch,' and this is how he generally behaved to them. He resolutely refused to become emotionally involved with the innumerable women with whom he slept. Interestingly, from the psychoanalytic point of view, he exhibited strong feelings of disgust about bodily functions, complaining that women did not wash enough, disliking nail varnish and lipstick, and disowning a girl who had attracted him because she had had the temerity to retire behind a rock on the beach at Capri in order to urinate. Such extreme distaste for anything to do with excretion suggests that Fleming was emotionally halted at what Freud called the 'anal-sadistic' stage of development; an hypothesis which is further supported by the many sadistic passages in the books. This particular 'pregenital organization' is the one which predisposes to the development of obsessional neurosis, in which the rituals and other symptoms of which the patient complains can regularly be shown to be defences against the emergence of both 'dirty' (anal) and hostile (sadistic) impulses. At forty-three he finally married Anne Rothermere. It was at her instigation that he began writing fiction, whilst they were waiting to get married, living in Fleming's house in Jamaica.

James Bond, Fleming's fictional wish-fulfilment, is ultimately as unlikely a figure as Hadrian VII. He is given many of Fleming's own characteristics, so many that he is unmistakable even in appearance. But he is much tougher and more ruthless, comparatively lacking in sensibility and much less imaginative. The sado-masochistic episodes which are so characteristic of the Bond novels are a not unexpected result of Fleming's own background and psychopathology. For sado-masochism is essentially the preoccupation of men who are predominantly concerned with power relationships. Although well-off by English middle-class standards, Fleming never lost the hope of attaining enormous wealth. Like many another Don Juan, his relations with women were power relations, not love relations; conquests, or proofs of masculinity, lacking both tenderness and involvement. The masochistic endurance of pain is something upon which many neurotics pride themselves. If one cannot succeed as a man, one can at least suffer like one. Although Bond, as he is bound to do, invariably emerges triumphant, it is Fleming's fictional villains who have the power and the wealth which he himself craved. They are also sadistic monsters who delight in cruelty for its own sake. The castration theme is overtly used in the first book, *Casino Royale*; and, in subsequent books, it crops up again and again in scarcely disguised form. Torture and the endurance of pain often appear to be dragged into the stories in a highly artificial way. In *Dr No*, for example, Bond is forced to participate in 'an obstacle race, an assault course against death'[9] which Dr No happens to have just finished constructing. The wicked doctor professes an interest in the capacity of the human body to withstand pain, and promises meticulously to examine Bond's remains when he has died as the result of his ordeal. These scenes of torture, with their threat of castration either explicit or implicit, reflect Fleming's own fear of being deprived of masculine power. It is clear that he was never confident in his own possession of masculinity, since he was over-concerned with proving it. Moreover, his persistent hero-worship demonstrates that he habitually believed other men to possess something which he himself did not, but which he envied; a belief which took origin in his childhood attitude towards his more successful brother and his dead, heroic father.

Interestingly enough, even quite small details reveal the compensatory nature of the Bond phantasies. Bond is an expert on firearms; a connoisseur of food and drink; a knowledgeable enthusiast of cars; a dedicated gambler. The books are famous for the meticulous detail in which all these subjects are treated. Yet Fleming himself knew very little of any of them. Noël Coward commented on the appalling food with which Fleming served his guests in Jamaica. He was not knowledgeable about wine and himself drank whisky or vodka. He was a cautious driver who never took risks. He misspelled three out of four of the names of the guns referred to in *Casino Royale* when he wrote to a gunsmith about them. Although he was fascinated by what went on in casinos, he left the actual gambling to others. As his biographer observes, Fleming was a born journalist who made excellent use of the experience of others in order to lend verisimilitude to his books, but himself lacked sufficient application to become an expert in any field. Expertise, therefore, became something which fascinated Fleming: something which he himself could not acquire, but which other men possessed.

Here then, is another example convincingly illustrating Freud's thesis that the writer 'desires to win honour, power, wealth, fame, and the love of women; but he lacks the means for achieving these satisfactions. Consequently, like any other unsatisfied man, he turns away from reality and transfers all his interest, and his libido too, to the wishful constructions of his life of phantasy.'[10]

Hadrian VII and the James Bond books are both instances which primarily illustrate Freud's category of ambitious wishes. Although erotic themes are prominent in Fleming's books, these are the conquest phantasies of a Don Juan who is hardly at all concerned with love in an adult sense. Indeed, whenever Bond does appear to become really involved with one of his mistresses, something violent or dramatic happens to interrupt the relationship. Power, therefore, rather than love, is the central theme of both these very different types of fictional phantasy: and, on this account, both tend to appeal more to men than to women. There is, however, a very different category of wish-fulfilling fiction which notably appeals far more to women than to men; and which also powerfully supports Freud's thesis.

When Kinsey and his team investigated what he calls 'psychologic factors in sexual response' he found that there were very marked differences between men and women in this regard. In general, men respond to, and are conditioned by, a far wider range of possible sexual stimuli than women, including some which appear at first sight rather remote from the sexual act itself. Thus, practically no females engage in voyeurism, whilst many males do so. There are no strip clubs for women; and pornography is very largely a male preserve. Women, in fact, appear to be more realistic about love than men; less prone to dissociate erotic feelings from actual physical contact; less obsessed with sexual phantasy; less easily aroused by any situation or stimulus in which they are not involved emotionally as whole persons. As Kinsey writes: 'Many females may go for days and weeks and months without ever being stimulated unless they have actual physical contact with a sexual partner.'[11] There are, however, exceptions to this general rule, one of which is relevant to our present enquiry. Here is what Kinsey writes:

'We have, then, thirty-three bodies of data which agree in showing that the male is conditioned by sexual experiences more frequently than the female. The male more often shares, vicariously, the sexual experiences of other persons, he more frequently responds sympathetically when he observes other individuals engaged in sexual activities, he may develop stronger preferences for particular types of sexual activity, and he may resort to a great variety of objects which have been associated with his sexual activities. The data indicate that in all these respects, fewer of the females have their sexual behaviour affected by such psychologic factors.

'It was in regard to only three of these items (moving pictures, reading romantic literature and being bitten) that as many females as males, or more females than males, seem to have been affected.'[12]

In a footnote to an earlier passage, Kinsey notes 'that the erotic stimulation which females derive from reading romantic stories or seeing moving pictures equals or exceeds that which is derived from those sources by males, is also recognized by: Friedeburg 1950:24'.[13]

Romantic literature, in Kinsey's use of the term, includes 'novels, essays, poetry or other literary materials'; and he states that erotic responses while reading such material 'may depend upon the general emotional content of the work, upon specifically romantic material in it, upon its sexual vocabulary (particularly if it is a vernacular vocabulary), or upon its more specific descriptions of sexual activity'.[14]

In Great Britain, the term 'romantic literature' is used only of literature which is indeed primarily concerned with love, but which specifically excludes the use of any sexual vocabulary or any description of sexual activity beyond kissing. Romantic novels are written by women for women. Erotic day-dreams are the very stuff of which they are composed, but they are erotic day-dreams of a special kind, which many males would hardly consider erotic at all. For the characteristic of these stories is that, although they are almost entirely concerned with love, any reference to the facts of sexuality is rigorously excluded. As a reader wrote in answer to a survey conducted by Mills & Boon, the principal publishers of romantic fiction, 'They are clean and wholesome without any unpleasant sexy stuff.'[15] Their appeal is mostly to housewives and others who live somewhat humdrum lives, and who require a literature which provides heroines with whom they can identify which will take them, in imagination, far away from the tedium of reality. These books are read by a large section of the community, larger than is generally admitted. For whereas educated and even intellectual men will freely admit to enjoying the James Bond stories, there is something of a stigma attached to the enjoyment of romantic fiction. Nevertheless, this survey disclosed that the readers of these books were by no means uneducated. Quite a number were from the lower professional or semi-professional grades. As the sociologist who conducted the survey points out: 'In a society in which the concept of "romantic love" is a part of the culture, the female is brought up to believe in ideas of courtship, and happy marriage, based on mutal attraction between two people. This type of society carries with it a certain male dominance, since romantic love itself carries with it the practice of the male pursuing the female (until she has finally caught him, the cynic might add).'[16]

Comparison of the world of romantic fiction with the world of James Bond entirely supports Kinsey's contention that, when it comes to sex, men and women are remarkably different, at least in their phantasy lives.

The romantic novel is generally based upon the Cinderella theme. The heroine, often of comparatively humble status, is shy, uncertain of herself, beautiful, yet unawakened. She usually has a good, old-fashioned name like Jane or Catherine or Elizabeth. She is often contrasted, favourably, with a more sophisticated 'fast' girl, who is skilled in the arts of seduction, dresses and makes up more obviously and less 'nicely', and who often has a somewhat outlandish, exotic name like Corinne Delamerie. In spite of, or rather because of, her lack of sexual experience or sophistication, the heroine succeeds in endearing herself to the hero of the novel, who is generally masterful, often rich, somewhat ruthless, yet possessing a need for love and tenderness of which the heroine becomes belatedly aware. The large series of romances in which the heroine is a nurse, secretary or receptionist, and the hero a doctor, illustrates the respective relationship of the protagonists. The outcome of the story is not in doubt; and such interest as it possesses depends upon the skill of the author in postponing the inevitable consummation by inventing various vicissitudes and misunderstandings which delay the lovers from finally falling into each other's arms. This last paragraph of a romantic novel is typical. 'Yesterday, thought Elizabeth, remembering the flowery bush outside the surgery—now it would be covered with flowers; yesterday had gone—was past; today was the happiest that she had ever known, and tomorrow—all the tomorrows—lay stretched out before her, full of promise. She had been given a good man, and whatever of joy, sorrow or trial life would hold for her, she would always have his support. She had shouldered her last burden alone. Breathing a prayer of gratitude, she slipped into bed and slept contentedly, waiting for tomorrow—all the tomorrows with John Allardyce.'[17]

Until very recently, any suggestion of premarital sexual relations was strictly tabu; and serious conflicts with parents were also out of the question. Moreover the characters portrayed bear very little relation to actual persons. Real human beings are complex: contradictory mixtures of kindness and cruelty, courage and cowardice, ruthlessness and compassion. But the heroes and heroines of romantic fiction need not bear any relation to real people. Their function is not to deepen understanding of human nature, but to provide entertainment and escape. Indeed, character studies in depth would be totally out of place in such novels, as out of place as would be the sado-masochistic phantasies of the Bond novels or the anatomic 'realism' of Henry Miller.

At first sight, the world of romantic fiction, so characteristically feminine, seems to indicate a paradox in feminine nature. For if we accept Kinsey's finding that women are, in general, less given to sexual phantasy, and more concerned with actual physical contact than are men, how is it that they are so enthralled by romantic fiction which is notable for its almost complete separation of love from the physical realities of sex? This discrepancy may be more apparent than real. As we have seen, Kinsey included under the heading of romantic literature a good deal of directly erotic writing which would be specifically excluded from this category in Great Britain. Moreover, the Kinsey interviewers may well have been skilful enough to include under the heading of 'sexual response' or 'arousal' reported by their subjects a number of answers to their questions which would not be regarded as indicating a sexual response by the subjects themselves. It is quite possible that a number of women say that they are 'thrilled' or 'excited' by romantic novels without acknowledging either to an interviewer or themselves that their response is, fundamentally, a sexual one. It is certain that many women who, in England at any rate, are ardent readers of romantic fiction, would be horrified if one told them that their interest in such fiction was sexual, as in the instance of the woman who delighted in such fiction because of the absence from it of 'any unpleasant sexy stuff'. Whatever the ultimate explanation of the Kinsey findings, it is certainly of interest to anyone studying the psychological differences between the sexes that 'twice as many of the females in the sample had responded to literary materials as had ever responded to the observation of portrayals of

24

sexual action, and five times as many as had responded to photo-graphs or other portrayals of nude human figures'.[18]

In considering romantic fiction in the English sense, another difference between the sexes is relevant. Whereas it is easy for men to recognize when they become sexually aroused, because of the phenomenon of erection, it is not so easy for women. Helene Deutsch, in the first volume of her book on *The Psychology of Women*, writes: 'In young girls, eroticism remains separated from awareness of sexuality for a longer time than in boys. This fact can be explained for the most part on the basis of anatomic differences. The erotic fantasies of boys are soon accompanied by obvious genital processes; they are, so to speak, discredited by these. Because of the temporal coincidence of the yearning for ideal love and the genital urge, it is difficult for the boy to deny the connection between the two.

'Girls, however, do not so easily discover that their genitals are the executive agents of their yearning for love, and, even if they have had orgastic emotions and have performed masturbatory acts, they still find it easier to keep their psychologic feelings and somatic tensions apart than do boys. Above all, masturbation can assume much more indirect and concealed forms in girls than in boys. The vaginal sensations cannot be compared with the pressure of the male organ, the tensions cannot always be exactly localized, excitation and relaxation can take place without conscious control on the part of the girl.'[19]

Sexual arousal, then, may mean something rather different and more difficult to define in women as compared with men; and one would like to know what the Kinsey researchers defined as 'arousal' when they reported a fairly frequent response in women to reading romantic literature.

To the psychiatrist, the world of the romantic novel resembles rather closely the world of the hysterical patient. In psychoanalytic terminology, hysterical patients have remained at a childhood pre-genital stage of development known as the 'phallic' phase. They have not been able to progress emotionally beyond the predominance of an attachment to the parent of the opposite sex; and, since sexual excitement really implies to them incest, they tend to repress physical manifestations of sex as much as possible. This has two results. First, they tend to be frigid in actual sexual intercourse; with the consequence that they fail to gain any physical satisfaction and also fail to develop the strong attachment to another person which is the

25

normal result of a repeated sexual satisfaction with that person. Second, they tend to intensify, and live in, a world of phantasy, because they are unable to find satisfaction in the real world. One would expect that romantic fiction would have a particular appeal to such persons, since it so closely corresponds to their own world of day-dreams: a world in which love is all-important, but only a love which acknowledges no 'nasty' sexual elements.

It has often been noted that hysterics, paradoxically, tend to 'sexualize' everything. That is, they tend to be preoccupied with the relations between the sexes to the exclusion of all else, to read sexual implications into casual remarks, to believe that men who are actually indifferent to them are in love with them, and to spend a disproportionate amount of time in making themselves look as seductive as possible. These attitudes and ways of behaving are, of course, compensatory. Many women who devote inordinate attention to their own appearance are in fact frigid. Incapable of loving anyone else, their concern is only with themselves, in spite of the fact that they are ostensibly obsessed with 'love'. To people living a normal sexual life, existence does not appear to consist of love relationships only. But to hysterics, because of their lack of satisfaction in reality, the world appears much more replete with erotic possibilities than is the case in fact. The world of romantic fiction, in which everything else is subordinate to the heroine's securing an ideal husband, is not dissimilar.

Idealization also is characteristic of both hysterics and romantic fiction. Hysterics tend regularly to idealize their objects, including the analysts to whom they turn for treatment. This trait takes origin in early childhood, and may be supposed to be the result of a failure to make a relationship of a satisfying kind with their actual parents. As a result of this failure, the child ceases to look for satisfying relations with real people, and uses his imagination to create substitutes for real people in the form of idealized images. One of the principal reasons for the failure of hysterics to make happy relationships is their tendency to project these phantasy images upon real people. Ultimately, the actual person fails to come up to the phantasy, so that the hysteric is perpetually disappointed, and looks elsewhere for her ideal.

In all the examples discussed here, the imagination is used to create substitutes for reality, which may be assumed to have been disappointing. Freud's formulation, taken from a paper written in 1908, is entirely apposite. No doubt this is related to the fact that Freud's early patients were mostly hysterics; for it is still true that it is to hysteria that the original theories of psychoanalysis can be most fruitfully applied. But not all phantasy is hysterical: nor is the imagination only utilized as an escape from real life. In treating art as nothing but day-dream, Freud neglects to distinguish those works in which, as Lionel Trilling points out, 'the illusions of art are made to serve the purpose of a closer and truer relation with reality'.[20] Anyone who has had his perception sharpened, or his awareness intensified by literature, must surely agree with this observation. A great observer like Proust, for example, can make one notice and understand far more of the motives underlying apparently trivial pieces of human behaviour than one could have done without his aid, in very much the same way that Freud himself does. Proust is reputed not to have read Freud, but he would have appreciated 'The Psychopathology of Everyday Life', and Freud's careful analysis of what might have appeared to anyone else to be minuscule irrelevances. It is curious that Freud does not have appeared to realize that phantasy might serve the purpose of enhancing man's grasp of reality; but so it seems, at least to judge by what he writes in his earlier publications. This is one of the reasons for the often reiterated complaint that psycho-analysis is unable to distinguish between bad art and good. An Ian Fleming or a romantic lady novelist are indeed using phantasy to enable us to escape from reality, and we need not necessarily depise their efforts at providing us with what may be a useful safety-valve. In so far as such literary efforts serve a 'therapeutic' or healing func-tion, they may be compared to abreaction: the provision of an opportunity to 'blow off steam'; to rid the psyche of impulses which cannot find expression in ordinary life, as well as compensating for the disappointments of reality. But the great novelists are not con-cerned with escape. George Eliot, Tolstoy, and Proust, to take but three examples, are concerned to depict life as it is lived, and to make some sense out of it. Their imaginations are used, as Freud's was, to penetrate below surface appearances to reach a deeper and richer truth. Their novels are attempts to make some kind of coherent, integral whole out of their own experience and view of life; and, by virtue of their perceptions, our own lives are enriched. The difference between abreaction and integration is one to which I shall return.

REFERENCES

1. FREUD, Sigmund. 'Creative Writers and Day-Dreaming' (London: The Hogarth Press and The Institute of Psycho-Analysis, 1959) Standard Edition, Vol. IX, p. 144.
2. Ibid, p. 144.
3. Ibid, p. 145.
4. Ibid, pp. 146-7.
5. Ibid, p. 150.
6. ROLFE, Fr. (Frederick, Baron Corvo.). *Hadrian VII* (London: Chatto & Windus, 1959).
7. SYMONS, A. J. A. *The Quest for Corvo* (London: Cassell, 1955).
8. PEARSON, John. *The Life of Ian Fleming* (London: Jonathan Cape, 1966).
9. FLEMING, Ian. *Dr No* (London: Jonathan Cape, 1958) p. 201.
10. FREUD, Sigmund. 'The Paths to the Formation of Symptoms', Lecture 23 (London: The Hogarth Press and The Institute of Psycho-Analysis, 1963) Standard Edition, Vol. XVI, p. 376.
11. KINSEY, Pomeroy, Martin & Gebhard, *Sexual Behavior in the Human Female* (London: W. B. Saunders, 1953) p. 682.
12. Ibid, p. 687.
13. Ibid, p. 670.
14. Ibid, pp. 669-70.
15. MANN, Peter H. *The Romantic Novel. A Survey of Reading Habits* (London: Mills & Boon, 1969) p. 22.
16. Ibid, p. 24.
17. DUNBAR, Jean. *Yesterday, Today and Tomorrow* (London: Mills & Boon, 1970) p. 191.
18. KINSEY, Pomeroy, Martin & Gebhard. *Sexual Behavior in the Human Female* (London: W. B. Saunders, 1953) p. 670.
19. DEUTSCH, Hélène; *The Psychology of Women* (London: Research Books, 1947) Vol. 1, p. 94.
20. TRILLING, Lionel. 'Freud and Literature', in *The Liberal Imagination* (London: Secker & Warburg, 1951).

3

The Conscious Motives of the Artist

In the last chapter, I concluded that Freud's view of creative writing as wish-fulfilling day-dream could be fruitfully applied to certain genres of fiction: and some examples were adduced of novels which support this hypothesis. It is clear that Freud's interpretation derives primarily from a consideration of the work produced rather than from an examination of the activity producing it. That is, Freud's principal concern was with the content of the piece of writing he was considering, rather than with the question of why the writer should choose this particular way of expressing his unsatisfied wishes. Life is such that even the most fortunate human being must needs have some desires which remain for ever unfulfilled; and every one of us has had day-dreams on this account. Yet, in spite of the flood of books which is published each year, comparatively few of us turn to literature, or indeed to any other creative activity, as a compensation for our disappointments. A man may be aware of an unfulfilled wish without having any desire to portray it or to communicate it to others.

It can be argued that the very possession of a talent for self-expression in one or other of the creative fields determines whether a man makes use of an art to express his phantasies; and it is true that the discovery of a particular talent encourages its possessor to exercise his skill. There is pleasure to be obtained in manipulating clay or paint, in choosing precisely the right word to express one's meaning, or in the discovery of a new tune. Moreover, creative talent generally makes itself apparent in childhood; and if, as often happens, it is encouraged by the praise of parents, it may take on a momentum of its own, in common with other activities which have won the approval of authority. A child can be trained to accept the idea that painting or composing or writing are valuable activities in themselves, and pursue one or other without ever asking himself why he does so. Mozart, for example, who had already started to compose at the age of four, must have discovered immediately that his efforts delighted his father Leopold. No doubt other forces were at work within him; but the fact that his early efforts at composition won

29

him so much interest and approval was reason enough for him to continue.

However, the very opposite is true of Handel. Although Handel's elderly surgeon father may not have been quite the ogre which tradition paints, there seems no doubt that he did originally oppose his son's passion for music, and that Handel's talent had to persist in the face of considerable discouragement. It is not improbable that Handel's rather marked swings of mood, from exhilaration to depression, were related to this early parental disapproval.

But the possession of even notable talent does not necessarily mean that it will be used in a creative or original way. We must all be acquainted with gifted people who clearly could be creative, but who are not interested in so being. Conan Doyle depicted such an individual in Sherlock Holmes' brother. Mycroft Holmes was acknowledged by the detective to be his intellectual superior, whom he even consulted in one or two particularly taxing cases. But Mycroft recoiled at the idea of actually having to rush about and do things; and many who are highly endowed with ability shrink from the effort, frustration and dedication which inevitably attend the production of anything original. For example, verbal skill of a high order is required by Parliamentary draughtsmen, and by lawyers who specialise in drawing up complicated wills and trusts. The ability to state what one means in so unequivocal a fashion that it cannot be misinterpreted is rarely bestowed. Yet persons with this gift do not necessarily feel any compulsion to make use of it in writing anything original.

It is harder to determine whether unutilized skills exist in other fields. Words are our current method of communication, and everyone is expected to be able to use them to some extent. The same is not true of painting or music. Nevertheless, there are some parallels to be discerned. There certainly exist some people who are musically endowed in the kind of way which would be invaluable in a composer, but who are not impelled to write music. Such people can translate a tune in the head into notes on paper with a facility which is the envy of those who lack this gift. They can often read music fluently, transpose with ease; emend or arrange the compositions of others, and interpret with sensitivity. In other words, they seem to possess the skills which are necessary to musical composition (a combination of gifts which seems rather uncommon), but lack the compulsion of originality. Who, for example, has ever heard of

Erwin Nyiregyhazy? This incredibly gifted musical prodigy was the subject of an intense study by Révész, director of the psychological laboratory at Amsterdam.[1] He started to compose before he was four, had absolute pitch, and a remarkable musical memory. Yet, like many another child prodigy, and in spite of becoming a professional musician, he seems never to have fulfilled his early promise. (Only about 10% of child prodigies become adult virtuosi.) He disappeared from the concert world, and was last heard of in the 1930s playing as a studio pianist in Hollywood. A single example of his pianistic skill has been re-recorded from an Ampico piano roll; his performance of Liszt's Mazeppa G139 no. 4.

Similarly, there are certainly some people who are gifted at drawing, or who have a particularly lively sense of colour, but who are not impelled to use these talents for anything more exciting than a holiday sketchbook or the decoration of a house. No doubt, like the rest of us, these gifted people have their dissatisfactions and their day-dreams. But, in spite of their endowments, they do not express their day-dreams in creative fashion. Freud's formulation, apt as it is for certain genres of creative endeavour, must leave us dissatisfied by its incompleteness: for it does not explain why some people seem compelled to formulate their phantasies, whilst others, equally gifted, and equally given to day-dreams, do not.

Moreover, there are a number of people who exhibit the opposite constellation. Psychiatrists, especially, will recognize that there are some unfortunate individuals who possess originality, but who lack the talent to express their originality in any medium. Schizophrenics, for example, often seem to possess an original vision. Because of their partial withdrawal from the world, and their relative imperviousness to conventional influence, schizophrenics look at the world from an angle so unusual that one longs for them to be able to elaborate their vision into a work of art. But it is seldom that they can do so. Indeed, if they could they would probably not be schizophrenic: partly because, as we shall see, creative work tends to protect the individual against mental breakdown; and partly because the acquisition of the skills required to practise an art, or to transmute an original idea into comprehensible form, demands a 'strong ego', that is, an actively executant aspect of personality which most schizophrenics conspicuously lack. Jung gives a good example when he writes of a locksmith's apprentice who became incurably insane at the age of nineteen:

31

never been blessed with intelligence, but he had, among
ιs, hit upon the magnificent idea that the world was his
ɔok, the pages of which he could turn at will. The proof
e simple; he had only to turn round, and there was a new
pας r him to see.

'This is Schopenhauer's "world as will and idea" in unadorned,
primitive concreteness of vision. A shattering idea indeed, born of
extreme alienation and exclusion from the world, but so naïvely and
simply expressed that at first one can only smile at the grotesqueness
of it. And yet, this primitive way of looking lies at the very heart of
Schopenhauer's brilliant vision of the world. Only a genius or a
madman could so disentangle himself from the bonds of reality as
to see the world as his picture-book.'[2]

There are also persons, who are not at all abnormal in any obvious
sense, who combine originality with inarticulateness. Publishers'
readers are familiar with the individual who submits a manuscript
containing material of originality and worth, but who cannot formulate what he has to say in a form intelligible to the general, or sometimes to any, reader. It may demand hours of patient listening and
editing to help such an individual to express himself in a way which
does justice to his conceptions.

The idea that people who practise the arts do so because they are
endowed with a particular skill and need to exercise it cannot be
maintained. Those who possess such a skill do not necessarily employ
it. Those who lack any such skills may passionately want to create,
and may, at some level, be quite original. In spite of this, they cannot,
unaided, produce anything of value.

As we have seen, Freud said that psychoanalysis could throw no
light upon the technique or the gift of the artist. Yet Freud would
have been the first to agree that artists are, like the rest of us, only
human; and that the same conflicts, and the same disappointments
afflict the artist as plague us all. Although psychoanalysis may not
be able to explain the nature of the artist's gift, it might be expected
to give some reason why the artist is driven to make use of it. As we
have seen, even highly gifted people do not necessarily do so, in
spite of having day-dreams.

According to Freud, the goals at which the artist is aiming, but
which he cannot attain except in phantasy, are honour, power,
riches, fame, and the love of women. But is it true that it is always
because he is disappointed in the pursuit of these goals that the

artist turns to his creative activity? Might it not rather be that, recognizing his gift, he consciously decides to use it to attain his ends? Creative achievement, both in science and in art, is rather highly regarded in Western culture of the twentieth century. Even Philistines, who profess to despise the arts, recognize the value which others bestow upon the artist; whilst those who do take pleasure in litera-ture, art and music (a vastly increased number during the past thirty years) believe the artist to be a very special person possessing *Mana* exceeding that of priests, royalty, or politicians. Some artists attain to honour and fame; and a few to riches. Nor, so far as one can discern, are artists notably less successful than other men in gaining the love of women. It is true that not many attain much power; although both the pianist–composer Paderewski and the novelist Disraeli became prime ministers of their respective countries. If one possessed both the gifts and the inclination, might not a policy of pursuing one or other of the arts be a realistic and direct way of achieving the goals postulated by Freud, rather than a product of disappointment at *not* being able to achieve them? After all, unless possessed of inherited wealth, a man has to pursue some occupation.

Dr Johnson, when congratulated by Hawkins upon being engaged in a work that suited his genius (an annotated edition of Shakespeare), replied: 'I look upon this as I did upon the Dictionary; it is all work, and my inducement to it is not love or desire of fame, but the want of money, which is the only motive to writing that I know of.'[3] Would he have said the same about his own, more original writings? Perhaps he would, but, if so, his psychological perception would have been sadly at fault. Of course, authors are not indifferent to money. Indeed, a perusal of *The Author*, a journal published by the Society of Authors, is disillusioning to those who idealize writers, since the bulk of this publication is devoted to discussing how authors may increase their earnings, demand more from their publishers, ob-tain advantage from subsidiary rights and so on. But, if earning large sums of money is a principal objective, writing is hardly a profession to be advised. One of the reasons that authors are particularly pre-occupied with money is that, for most of them, the financial reward of their work is precarious and meagre. Some years ago a corre-spondence in the London *Times* surprised many people by revealing that even very well-known and highly esteemed novelists were quite unable to make a living from their books, a conclusion later reinforced by Richard Findlater in *The Book Writers*.[4] Many authors only succeed in earning enough to support themselves by engaging in broadcasting, by writing reviews, film scripts, or articles for newspapers. Very few indeed make enough money from royalties alone to support even a modest standard of living.

Until very recently, at least in Britain, it was impossible for a composer to make a living out of his works. In a recent broadcast Imogen Holst was asked why her father, the composer Gustav Holst, went on teaching until the end of his days. She pointed out that he enjoyed teaching; and then went on to say that he was bound to engage in some occupation other than composition simply for financial reasons. If the composer of *The Planets*, *Egdon Heath* and *The Hymn of Jesus*—to mention only three of his best-known works—was unable to make a living from composition, what hope had contemporaries of less merit and less fame? Today, as Miss Holst pointed out, the position is somewhat easier, because of the large appetite for new music of the broadcasting companies. Moreover, the skilful technician can engage in the highly profitable occupation of writing music for the cinema; though at what cost to his creativity is hard to determine. Some very good music has been written for film by Sir William Walton, Malcolm Arnold and others; but the limitations imposed by having to tie the music strictly to the action means that the composer cannot choose for himself a vital dimension of his composition, its length. Most composers, therefore, rate film music as 'incidental' music, and separate it sharply from original compositions which truly reflect their own creative personality.

In the visual arts, a few young painters and sculptors gain an early notoriety, and may thereby gain wealth too. But they are a tiny proportion of the hordes of intelligent and gifted youngsters who yearly emerge from art schools, and who will be forced to use their talents in industrial design and 'commercial' art. It is a sad comment on our culture that there is a negative correlation between the higher forms of creative production and financial reward, whereas the lower and more ephemeral forms are much more lavishly rewarded. Journalism, advertising, 'popular' music, and cartoon are all far better paid than are the writing of novels, the composition of symphonies, or the painting of pictures. Dr Johnson's thesis can hardly be maintained. There are easier ways of making money for able people than the practice of the arts; and although an artist may indeed be driven to create by want of money, he is unlikely to have adopted this way

34

of life as a way of making money in the first instance, or very mis-
guidedly if he did so.

Riches and power are so unlikely to come the way of the artist
that we may dismiss the idea that his primary motive in practising
his art is the acquisition of either. What about the other goals which
Freud adduces as the product of 'instinctual needs which are too
clamorous'? Although artists, as suggested above, do not seem less
successful than other men in gaining the love of women, there does
not seem to be much evidence that they are more so. It is true that
there is a particular type of woman who regards herself as a 'femme
inspiratrice', and who therefore attaches herself to creative men in
the belief that she is especially qualified to nurture his genius. Lou
Andreas Salome, the mistress of Rilke, the expositor of Nietzsche,
the confidante of Freud, is one example of the type. Alma Mahler
is another. She was first married to the composer, Gustav Mahler.
After his death she became the mistress of the painter Kokoschka.
For a short while she was married to the architect Walter Gropius;
and then became the wife of the writer Franz Werfel. No doubt, in
order to win the favours of such women, a man must needs be creative; but it is hard to imagine any man deliberately setting out upon
an artistic path in order to do this. It is often supposed that artists
are more promiscuous than most men, and therefore possibly more
successful than most at gaining feminine sexual compliance, if not
'the love of women'; but the evidence is not conclusive. In a study of
painters ranging from antiquity to the French Revolution, the art
historians Rudolf and Margot Wittkower write: 'The subject to
which this chapter is devoted—the love-affairs of artists—has produced singularly conflicting opinions among scholars. There are
those who find that artists show a marked leaning towards celibacy,
while others maintain that they are predominantly of an amorous
or even promiscuous bent. Nineteenth-century biographers often
describe the artists of the past as simple and staunch family men.
Tales to the contrary were taken either as exceptions or as malicious
inventions. Modern writers, by contrast, are inclined to discover a
tendency towards homosexuality in artists, past and present.

'The crux of the matter is that each view can be supported, quoting
chapter and verse. Any number of celibate artists can be easily
matched by an equal number of happily married ones, and it would
not be difficult to find a Don Juan for every misogynist.'[5]

We have seen that the type of writer exemplified by Ian Fleming can indeed be a Don Juan both in fact and phantasy; and that both his erotic behaviour and his creative invention may be, in part, as Freud suggests, the product of sexual dissatisfaction. But it is impossible to maintain that all artists are similarly motivated. I have already quoted the view of Eissler in his book on Leonardo, to the effect that works of genius can only be produced at the price of sacrificing sexual happiness. 'Only the blockage of a permanent object attachment can produce that intense hunger for objects that results in the substitute formation of the perfect work of art.' It is true that Leonardo himself was ascetically inclined, disapproved of what he called 'lascivious pleasures', and tried to suppress his own sensuality as far as possible. But Raphael, generally accounted a genius, albeit of a very different kind, had many love affairs; whilst Rubens and Bernini seem to have been both happily married and model husbands. Unless Dr Eissler regards Leonardo, Michelangelo and a few others as the only artists capable of producing 'the perfect work of art', the thesis that art invariably takes origin from the lack of a satisfactory love relationship, at least in the here-and-now, as postulated by Eissler, cannot be supported. The phrase 'at least in the here-and-now' is added because, it may be recalled from Chapter 1, it is not disputed that the artist may, in some instances, be driven to create because of childhood disappointments and dissatisfactions; amongst which the failure or absence of love relationships with parents are of great importance. Eissler might probably argue that a person so deprived would not be capable of 'a permanent object attachment'; but this, although true of some people, is certainly not true of all. What is being disputed here is, first, the notion that a permanent object attachment, however satisfying, can in fact wholly compensate for an unhappy childhood; which is another way of saying that it is unlikely that the whole of a person's 'pregenital' sexuality can be included within an adult, 'genital' relationship. Second, Eissler's view that works of art are substitutes for loved people in any simple and direct way is also denied. The lives of creative people do not support this view, and nor does Freud himself.

In a passage from one of his early papers, Freud writes: 'The relationship between the amount of sublimation possible and the amount of sexual activity necessary naturally varies very much from person to person and even from one calling to another. An abstinent artist is hardly conceivable; but an abstinent young savant is certainly no rarity. The latter can, by his self-restraint, liberate forces for studies; while the former probably finds his artistic achievements powerfully stimulated by his sexual experience. In general, I have not gained the impression that sexual abstinence helps to bring about energetic and self-reliant men of action or original thinkers or bold emancipators and reformers. Far more often it goes to produce well-behaved weaklings who later become lost in the great mass of people that tends to follow, unwillingly, the leads given by strong individuals.'[6] Once again, Freud's ambivalence when he comes to discuss artists is evident, if one compares this statement with the others of his which have already been quoted. But this is to divert attention from the main theme of this chapter.

What I have been discussing is whether the practice of one or other of the arts might be an effective way of fulfilling the artist's desire for power, wealth or love, rather than a turning to phantasy as a substitute. I have concluded that wealth is more easily attained in other ways; that power very seldom comes the way of the artist; and that artists are probably neither more nor less successful than other men in attaining love. But what about honour and fame? Are some artists spurred on by the hope of public recognition; and is the practice of the arts likely to lead to this direct?

Here one must be cautious. Although it is not probable that the pursuit of honour and fame is a prime motive for the artist's activity, it is quite possible that it is a secondary motive. Success, in many professions like medicine or the law, may lead to honour and to a certain degree of fame; but the latter will be generally limited to a small professional circle. How many names of doctors or lawyers are known even to the educated public? But a successful writer may find that his name becomes a household word; quite a number of painters are known to a large public; a few composers attain equal fame, although public recognition of musicians is more often bestowed upon executants. Success in the arts does lead, in quite a few cases, to fame and sometimes to honour. Does the artist have a special need for such recognition; and is it this motive which drives him?

Fr Rolfe, the rejected aspirant to the priesthood, expressed his desire to honour and fame quite naïvely in his fictional phantasy of becoming Pope. Did he also have a phantasy of being a great writer? It is almost certain that he did, and although no amount of recognition could have brought balm to that tortured soul, it is ironic that his merits as a writer should only have attracted much attention posthumously. Very few men are indifferent to fame, and the artist who pursues his solitary calling unrecognized and unrewarded is a rare phenomenon indeed. Yet a few examples do exist. One is the Greek composer Nikos Skalkottas, whose works are still infrequently performed, but which are gradually gaining increasing renown. Skalkottas was born in 1904. Although he became a virtuoso violinist, he abandoned this career, and became a pupil of Schoenberg, with whom he studied from 1927 to 1931. At this point in his life, some profound psychological change overtook him, which led to his almost total withdrawal from society. J. G. Papaioannou,[7] from whose article on Skalkottas this information is taken, attributes this change to 'material difficulties of life'; but it seems unlikely that such difficulties could account for Skalkottas adopting a way of life which excluded any discussion of music with friends, which cut him off so entirely that he never heard any major work of music composed after 1933, and which led to his living and composing 'in a completely secluded world of his own'. It seems much more probable that he had a schizophrenic illness.

However this may be, he composed so compulsively and continuously that, on his death in 1949, he left behind an oeuvre which exceeds in quantity the combined output of Schoenberg, Berg and Webern. It would not be difficult to exceed the total output of the last-named composer alone, but Schoenberg was prolific, and Berg no sluggard. At any rate, Skalkottas left behind some twelve major symphonic works, fourteen concertos, and over fifty works of chamber music, apart from a good deal else. Up to his death hardly any of this enormous production was either published or performed. Yet, according to informed opinion, much of Skalkottas' music is both original and of high quality. It must be extremely uncommon for any creative artist to produce so much in such total isolation that even intimate friends know nothing of it, without apparently seeking any public recognition of his talent. Although creation is a solitary business, it is also a form of communication in most instances, although, as will be seen, there are examples of scientists who kept their new conceptions very dark. Most artists are delighted to attain fame, and some are undoubtedly corrupted by it.

At this time, fame is more easily manufactured and more ephemeral than at any previous time in history. Television, radio, and modern advertising techniques have made it possible for persons to attain fame who would never have done so in any other generation. The 'television personality', who possesses no skill other than a quick wit and a certain ease of manner in public, is a modern phenomenon which has never existed before. A man can now be famous merely because he is widely recognized and for no other reason. The laborious practice of an art is so much more difficult a way of gaining fame than becoming a television personality that one might assume that those who have a particular desire for fame would inevitably aim at the latter 'profession' rather than the former. But this is not the case, in spite of the fact that artists very often seem to desire fame rather more intensely than the majority of mankind. As will appear, the desire for fame and honour is part, but only part, of the artist's motivation. It is bound up with the whole of his personality and artistic activity; so that it cannot be satisfied on its own, as it were, as in the case of a television personality or a model. Fame is a spur for many artists; but fame as a result of success in the practice of their art, not fame for its own sake as an isolated phenomenon.

REFERENCES

1. REVESZ, G. *The Psychology of a Musical Prodigy* (London: Kegan Paul, Trench, Trubner, 1925).
2. JUNG, C. G. *The Relations between the Ego and the Unconscious* (London: Routledge & Kegan Paul, 1953) Collected Works, Vol. 7, p. 141.
3. BOSWELL, James. *Life of Johnson*, ed. Birkbeck Hill (Oxford: Clarendon Press, 1887) Vol. 1, p. 318, n. 5.
4. FINDLATER, Richard. *The Book Writers* (London: The Society of Authors, 1966).
5. WITTKOWER, Rudolf and Margot. *Born under Saturn* (London: Weidenfeld & Nicolson, 1963) p. 150.
6. FREUD, Sigmund. ' "Civilized" Sexual Morality and Modern Nervous Illness' (London: The Hogarth Press and The Institute of Psycho-Analysis, 1959) Standard Edition, Vol. IX, p. 197.
7. PAPAIOANNOU, J. G. 'Nikos Skalkottas', in *European Music in the Twentieth Century*, ed. Howard Hartog (Harmondsworth: Pelican Books, 1961) pp. 336-45.

4

Creativity as Defence

In the last chapter I affirmed that the creative person could not simply be regarded as a disappointed man who turned to phantasy because he was unsuccessful in satisfying his desires in reality. It also appeared improbable that a man would necessarily turn to creative activity because he happened to possess a particular skill. Moreover, although it was admitted that, in exceptional cases, becoming a writer, composer, or painter might lead to fame, to sexual conquests, to the acquisition of wealth, and even occasionally to honour and power, it was thought likely that these conventional prizes, listed by Freud, could be attained by other means which were less laborious.

At this point a critic might interrupt, and point out that not all creative persons find their task laborious. Indeed, the type of fiction discussed in Chapter 2 is a case in point. Ian Fleming, beginning his first book at the age of forty-three, in response to his fiancée's instigation, completed it in under ten weeks. To produce 62,000 words in so short a time is a remarkable achievement. But romantic novelists are sometimes even more prolific, producing many books in the course of a year without apparent strain. In *The Author* of Summer 1967 Winston Graham tells the story of a lady novelist who, one year, gave birth to a son.

'When I went to see her the following Christmas, I said: "How many books have you written this year, May?" She replied apologetically: "Well, only six. But then of course I did have Robert." '[1]

There are also instances of fiction of considerably higher quality being produced at breakneck speed. Robert Louis Stevenson wrote *Treasure Island* at the rate of a chapter a day for sixteen chapters. At this point he reached a block; but, after a very short interval, resumed again at the same pace. Rider Haggard completed *She* in just over six weeks, writing at 'white heat'. It is possible to argue that, in some instances of work produced in a very short time, the idea has been incubating for a much longer preceding period. What has been mulled over for years may appear as a finished product within the brief interval of a few weeks or months. But this is certainly not true of all examples. It seems likely that a good deal of literary work which is produced at high speed belongs to the category of phantasy and romance. It is the story which counts, not the characters or the author's reflections upon life. This is obviously true of 'romantic fiction' of the feminine kind; and also of the James Bond novels. *She* is superior to both; and *Treasure Island* in a different class altogether: but, although both are splendid stories which continue to bring excitement and entertainment to generation after generation, one would hardly turn to either to enrich one's understanding of life or one's grasp of human character. Both still belong to the category of escapist literature.

However, undoubted masterpieces can be produced very quickly. Rossini wrote that he completed *Il Barbiere di Siviglia* within thirteen days. It has been pointed out that a skilled copyist would require as long even to copy the six hundred pages of the score. Mozart composed his three last, and greatest, symphonies, K.543, K.550 and K.551, within a period of about six weeks during the summer of 1788. Schubert wrote his last three, and greatest, piano sonatas in the month of September 1828, only a few weeks before his death on 19th November. The miraculous String Quintet in C major (D.956) was completed in the same month; as was the song cycle known as 'Schwanengesang' (D.957). That death itself was a spur to this burst of creative activity is improbable, in view of Schubert's attitude of acceptance and resignation. Alfred Einstein suggests that he may even have welcomed death as a friend in the manner foreshadowed in the 'Death and the Maiden' verses.

> Gieb deine Hand du schon und zart Gebild,
> Bin Freund, und komme nicht zu strafen.
> Sei guthen Muths ich bin nicht wild,
> Sollst sanft in meinen Armen schlafen.

> Give me they hand, thou fair and gentle creature,
> I am a friend and come not to punish thee.
> Be of good cheer! I am not fierce.
> Thou shalt sleep peacefully in my arms.

'Schubert varied and transfigured this picture of death as the gentle friend of youth in his D minor Quartet (D.810).' And of one of Schubert's songs, 'An die Nachtigall', Einstein writes that it 'has always struck me as a confession of love for the inevitability of death and farewell'.[2]

These wonderful works of two great composers are amongst the treasures of mankind, enriching and deepening our experience. Yet none of them can have been the product of prolonged meditation or careful rewriting. It is arguable that, if Schubert had not been impatient, he might have had second thoughts about the last movement of the String Quintet; but the same is not true of the piano sonatas. Mozart, unlike Schubert, still had three years of life left to him; but it is unlikely that any amount of revision would have improved the G minor Symphony or the 'Jupiter'; and, indeed, although there are some alterations in the score of the latter, Mozart was remarkable in that he made few drafts and comparatively few corrections. It is true that the six quartets dedicated to Haydn show a good many alterations. As he said himself in his dedicatory letter to Haydn: 'Here they are then, O great Man and my dearest Friend, these six children of mine. They are, it is true, the fruit of long and laborious endeavour . . .'[3] This, however, does not alter the fact that, as a general rule, Mozart was able to think in complete wholes to an astonishing degree. 'From the sketch material still in existence, from the condition of the fragments, and from the autographs themselves we can draw definite conclusions about Mozart's creative process. To invent musical ideas he did not need any stimulation; they came to his mind "ready-made" and in polished form. In contrast to Beethoven, who made numerous attempts at shaping his musical ideas until he found the definitive formulation of a theme, Mozart's first inspiration has the stamp of finality. Any Mozart theme has completeness and unity; as a phenomenon it is a Gestalt.'[4]

The miracle of Mozart, however, is generally accepted as unique. It is at least as common for creative work to be accompanied by torment and distress. The accounts furnished by writers and composers themselves are full of complaints about the difficulties they experience in getting started, the periods of frustration and dissatisfaction through which they pass, the false starts, alterations and revisions which have to be undertaken before the work comes 'right'. This is especially true of the initial stages of a new conception. Some creative people appear to embark upon a new project before it has completely matured in their mind; and thus make several starts and many alterations which might have proved unnecessary had they not resorted to precipitate action. As early as 1926, Graham Wallas[5] pointed out that the solution of creative problems begins with a stage of 'Preparation', in which the subject is investigated and studied from a number of different angles. This is generally followed by a period of 'Incubation', in which conscious thought on the problem needs to be abandoned. Nevertheless, during this period, important unconscious or preconscious processes take place in the mind; some kind of preliminary 'scanning' and rearrangement, which is absolutely necessary if a new and satisfying pattern is to emerge. Many creative people, being, as we shall see, active executants, as well as passively open to their own and other people's new ideas, find this waiting period of incubation extremely tiresome. Those, especially, who have been brought up to think that idleness is a sin, and constant activity a virtue, find it hard to believe that there are times when more is accomplished by passivity than by activity. Bertrand Russell furnishes an example of what is meant with his habitual lucidity.

'Very gradually I have discovered ways of writing with a minimum of worry and anxiety. When I was young each fresh piece of serious work used to seem to me for a time—perhaps a long time—to be beyond my powers. I would fret myself into a nervous state from fear that it was never going to come right. I would make one unsatisfying attempt after another, and in the end have to discard them all. At last I found that such fumbling attempts were a waste of time. It appeared that after first contemplating a book on some subject, and after giving serious preliminary attention to it, I needed a period of subconscious incubation which could not be hurried and was if anything impeded by deliberate thinking. Sometimes I would find, after a time, that I had made a mistake, and that I could not write the book I had had in mind. But often I was more fortunate. Having, by a time of very intense concentration, planted the problem in my sub-consciousness, it would germinate underground until, suddenly, the solution emerged with blinding clarity, so that it only remained to write down what had appeared as if in a revelation.'[6]

Creative speed, therefore, divides itself into two. In the cases of both Mozart and Schubert, the period of incubation must have been unusually short, as well as the time taken actually to commit a new work to paper. In other examples, the period of incubation may be very long, whilst the time taken to formulate the new conception may be brief indeed. Darwin's revolutionary idea of natural selection was incubating for at least twenty years before *On the Origin of Species by means of Natural Selection* was published, but he did not take long to write the book. There were also, of course, social reasons for delaying, since his idea overturned conventional religious beliefs. Sometimes both incubation and execution are prolonged. Brahms did not complete his first symphony until he was in his forty-third year. Yet he had made sketches for it, which he showed to Clara Schumann, as long as twenty years before this.

That creative endeavour is often tormenting is easy to illustrate. Beethoven's sketchbooks show how very often he was compelled to revise and rewrite his music. Thackeray described himself as 'sitting for hours before my paper, not doing my book, but incapable of doing anything else'.[7] Chopin is described by Georges Sand as 'shutting himself up in his room for whole days, weeping, walking, breaking his pens, repeating and altering a bar a hundred times, spending six weeks on a single page'.[8] It is remarkable that Chopin produced as much music as he did in his short life, if this was his habitual mode of composition.

Although, therefore, not all creative production of high quality is the product of tormented laboriousness, enough is so to make one wonder why it is that human beings persist in enduring such frustration and misery in bringing their new conceptions to birth. For very often, and especially when the creative person is young and inexperienced, the effort required is considerable, and the reward likely to be meagre. One possible explanation is that, to use a psychoanalytic terminology, creative activity is employed as a *defence*. According to psychoanalytic theory, the human ego is vulnerable to anxiety against which, since anxiety is unpleasant, it attempts to defend itself. Anxiety may take its origin from the external world in the shape of any of the ordinary dangers or mischances which we all encounter. Alternatively, it may arise from within the mind itself, either as a threat from a bad conscience (super-ego), or else from the instinctive reservoir of the id as instinct demanding satisfaction. Besieged, therefore, from three sources, the ego adopts a number of different techniques for meeting and dealing with the anxieties by which it is threatened. These techniques are the various 'defences'.

Anna Freud, in her foreword to the 1966 edition of her book *The Ego and the Mechanisms of Defence*, writes that the book 'deals exclusively with one particular problem, i.e. with the ways and means by which the ego wards off unpleasure and anxiety, and exercises control over impulsive behaviour, affects, and instinctive urges'.[9] In

44

all, she lists and discusses at length some ten defences, including repression, reaction-formation, projection, introjection, and sublimation, and others which will be less familiar to those who are not psychoanalysts. In considering creative activity, sublimation is, of course, the defence which first springs to mind; and sublimation was considered at some length in the first chapter of this book. In common with the other defences I have mentioned, sublimation can be regarded as a way of dealing with instinctive urges, especially pregenital, infantile urges, by redirecting them into socially acceptable channels. As Anna Freud states, and I have already noted, sublimation is in a slightly different category from the other defensive manoeuvres of the ego, since it is employed as much by the 'normal' as by the neurotic, and indeed is an inescapable requirement of civilization. In this context, however, we are more concerned with Anna Freud's first definition of defence than with her second. That is, we are not considering creativity as a way of exercising control over, or redirecting instinctual urges, but rather as a possible 'means by which the ego wards off unpleasure and anxiety'.

Of course, many activities which are not directly 'creative' can be used in this way. In psychiatric practice, it is common to meet individuals who engage in all kinds of pursuits, not for the sake of the activity itself, but because performing them prevents the experience of mental distress. Thus, a man may take his car out on a motorway, not because he wants to get anywhere, but because he wants to get away from himself, a manoeuvre facilitated by fast driving, since this requires a high degree of concentration on the external world. A housewife may busy herself with unnecessary polishing and cleaning because, if she is idle for a moment, she is apt to feel guilty or useless. I contend not only that creative activity can be used in this manner, but that, in more than one respect, it is particularly apt for defensive purposes.

What are the states of 'unpleasure and anxiety' against which creative production may be used as a defence? W. R. D. Fairbairn, an unorthodox and original psychoanalyst, wrote a paper entitled 'A Revised Psychopathology of the Psychoses and Psychoneuroses'[10] which is highly relevant. In his view, there exist two rather fundamental states of mental distress against which the sufferer defends himself, the depressive state and the schizoid state. The emotion characteristic of the former is a feeling of hopelessness and misery. The emotion pertaining to the latter is one of futility and lack of meaning. Although the difference between the one state and the other may not seem very precise when designated in these terms, there is in fact a strong case for making a distinction between them. Not only is schizoid apathy different in quality from depression, as those rather rare people who have experienced both will confirm; but the two states of mind tend to occur in persons of very different temperament and character structure. In Kleinian terminology, the people who are threatened by a sense of futility and meaninglessness are those who have not progressed beyond the very early stage of emotional development called by Melanie Klein the 'paranoid-schizoid' position. Broadly speaking, these are introverted or frankly schizoid characters. The people who suffer from misery and hopelessness have, again according to Melanie Klein, progressed a little further in their emotional development, but are also arrested at an early stage; that of the so-called 'depressive position'. These people are much more extraverted. Both these early stages would come under the heading of 'oral phases' in Freudian terminology; the former being concerned with supposed primitive emotions accompanying the act of sucking and incorporation; whereas the latter is concerned with biting as well as sucking or, in other words, with the discovery and disposal of aggressive feelings towards the very person who is also providing food and love. In theory, therefore, both the schizoid and the depressive states take origin from deprivations and misadventures afflicting the infant during the first year of its existence.

Psychoanalysis, being a discipline which explains mental phenomena in terms of historical reconstruction, has a vested interest in equating 'deep' with 'early'. To psychoanalysts, therefore, it appears obvious that the profound states of alienation and misery, designated as the schizoid and depressive states, must originate in earliest infancy. Those who are not psychoanalysts would not necessarily agree upon causes and origins; but most psychiatrists would concur in acknowledging that the schizoid and the depressive temperaments can be differentiated, and that states of mental distress in the two types of personality are also different in quality. However melancholy a depressive may be, the observer generally feels that there is some possibility of emotional contact. More especially, he may be able to sense the repressed rage which hides behind the face of misery. The schizoid person, on the other hand, appears withdrawn and inaccessible. His remoteness from human contact makes his state of mind less humanly comprehensible, since his feelings are not communicated.

If such a person becomes psychotic (schizophrenic), this lack of connection with the external world and other people becomes even more obvious; with the result that the sufferer's behaviour and utterances appear inconsequential and unpredictable.

In Fairbairn's view, the emotional difficulties which, in the course of the child's development, have given rise to his later proclivity to relapse into schizoid or depressive states, underlie all the common forms of neurosis. In fact, he regards hysterical, phobic, obsessional and paranoid symptoms as themselves defences against schizoid apathy or depression. In other words, if, during the course of analysis, the patient's neurotic symptoms are abolished, he will come face to face with his real and most basic emotional problems, which are invariably concerned with, or explicable in terms of, his earliest relation with the mother, who is, after all, by far the most important person in the child's universe; and the person with whom it is most necessary that he should interact in a fruitful way if his later emotional adjustment is to prove successful. There is now good reason to suppose that this hypothesis is objectively true, as well as pragmatically useful in the practice of analysis, since it has been shown that the young of other primates, if separated from the mother at an early enough age for long enough, and not allowed to mix with their peers, suffer irreversible damage which precludes them from mating or making normal social relationships.

To avoid relapsing into either a depressive or a schizoid state is clearly of paramount importance; and any means of doing so, however laborious, must needs be a welcome relief to the sufferer. We are seeking to discover why it is that some people engage in creative work when it is not obvious that this will bring any immediate reward, and when, to them, such work is both difficult and demanding. If it can be shown that such work serves the same defensive function as do neurotic symptoms (in Fairbairn's scheme of pyschopathology), we might be justified in concluding that we had discerned at least part of the answer.

It is certainly possible to demonstrate not only that some creative people are of predominantly schizoid or depressive temperaments, but also that they use their creative capacities in a 'defensive' way. This is particularly obvious in the case of persons of depressive temperament; but it can also be shown that schizoid people use their capabilities in the same fashion. Moreover, consideration of these problems makes it increasingly obvious that certain types of creative

47

thought are only possible for certain types of temperament; and this is particularly the case when we consider the schizoid creator.

In addition, the hypothesis that creative activity is sometimes used as a defence provides an explanation as to why it is that creative people often attach such enormous importance to their work that it would be appropriate to describe it as an addiction. Such individuals pursue their creative endeavour so relentlessly that they are never able to take a holiday from their work, and feel miserable or ill if they cannot engage in it. Just as a diabetic deprived of insulin will become ill, so a creative person deprived of his work may become mentally disturbed. This hypothesis may also serve to explain why the rare type of artist, like Nikos Skalkottas, to whom I referred in the last chapter, may persist with his work even when it brings no recognition or acknowledgment. If creative work protects a man against mental illness, it is small wonder that he pursues it with avidity; and even if the state of mind he is seeking to avoid is no more than a mild state of depression or apathy, this still constitutes a cogent reason for engaging in creative work even when it brings no obvious external benefit in its train.

The fact that creative, or any other activity, can be used as a defence does not mean that it is always thus employed. Nor is it claimed that this hypothesis reveals the motivating force driving every creative artist or scientist. But that some are thus driven is clear; and the next chapters will be devoted to a description of the schizoid and depressive temperaments and to giving some examples of how these temperamental endowments are related to creativity.

REFERENCES

1. *The Author* (London: The Society of Authors) Vol. 78, no. 2.
2. EINSTEIN, Alfred. *Schubert*, trans. David Ascoli (London: Cassell, 1951) pp. 359-60.
3. KING, A. Hyatt. *Mozart's Chamber Music* (London: BBC, 1968) p. 18.
4. HERTZMANN, Erich. 'Mozart's Creative Process', in *The Creative World of Mozart*, ed. Paul Henry Lang (London: Oldbourne Press, 1964) p. 28.
5. WALLAS, Graham. *The Art of Thought* (London: Jonathan Cape, 1926).
6. RUSSELL, Bertrand. 'How I Write', in *Portraits from Memory and Other Essays* (London: Allen and Unwin, 1965) p. 195.

7. HARDING, Rosamond E. M. *An Anatomy of Inspiration* (Cambridge: W. Heffer, 1940) p. 15.

8. Ibid, p. 18.

9. FREUD, Anna. *The Ego and the Mechanisms of Defence* (London: The Hogarth Press and The Institute of Psycho-Analysis, 1968) p.v.

10. FAIRBAIRN, W. R. D. *Psycho-Analytic Studies of the Personality* (London: Tavistock Publications, 1952) p. 28.

5

Creativity and the Schizoid Character

The type of person whom psychiatrists designate 'schizoid' is characterized by detachment and emotional isolation. Often, but not invariably, an individual with this character structure gives an impression of coldness combined with an apparent air of superiority which is not endearing. There is a lack of ordinary human contact; a feeling that such a man is unconcerned with, if not superior to, the ordinary, mundane preoccupations of average people; that he is 'out of touch' with, or 'on a different wave length' from, the people with whom he mingles but does not mix. Very often, the schizoid person is accused of keeping other people 'at arm's length' and of avoiding intimacy; an accusation which is in fact justified, since this is just what such a person feels compelled to do. Sometimes such an individual is said to be 'wearing a mask'; an observation which is also accurate, since schizoid individuals habitually play roles which, intellectually, they believe to be appropriate, but which do not reflect what they are actually feeling. Thus, a schizoid person may decide that it is morally right to be generous, or tactful, or considerate, and behave appropriately in accordance with this decision. Because, however, his behaviour originates from an intellectual decision rather than expressing his true feelings, it is likely that all that will be conveyed to the recipient of his attentions is an impression of exaggeratedly good manners. Such a man lacks the personal touch: the feeling, if not of intimacy, then at least of some shared common ground upon which one person meets another as a human being. There is in fact a divorce between thinking and feeling; an embryo form of the 'incongruity of affect' seen in schizophrenia which is familiar to psychiatrists. It is this incongruity which accounts for the unpredictability of the patient's behaviour and responses in that condition, since, to the observer, there appears to be a complete lack of correspondence between what the patient says and the emotion he displays.

As I said, it is likely that schizoid disorders of personality take origin from a disturbance in the infant's earliest relation with the mother. Whether this is so or not, there can be no doubt that the schizoid person carries with him into adult life attitudes and emotional responses which mature persons have long since outgrown, but which are not surprising if considered as pertaining to an infantile stage of development. The more fundamentally insecure a person is, the more he is likely to fail to grow beyond his earliest emotional attitudes, or to regress into a state where such attitudes become apparent when things go badly with him.

The human baby is born into the world in a state of helplessness which makes him vulnerable, both physically and mentally. If his basic needs are adequately met, he acquires confidence and a sense of security. This is what Erik Erikson has appropriately named a 'sense of basic trust'.[1] If, however, his needs are not met, or he is suddenly deprived by, for example, the mother's death or disappearance, he is likely to develop a basic *mistrust* of people which makes it appear dangerous for him to become emotionally involved. In other words, both loving and being loved seem fraught with risk and anxiety; with the result that, in adult life, such a person tends to avoid emotional involvement. Since, however, it is emotional involvement which gives meaning to life, there is a constant risk that life itself will appear meaningless, and the individual will suffer from that schizoid sense of futility which I mentioned in the last chapter. One result of this is that schizoid people have a particularly marked tendency to seek for meaning and significance in things rather than in people; a fact which is highly relevant to creativity. It is, of course, because emotional involvement with people appears dangerous that the schizoid person remains detached and isolated.

A second characteristic of schizoid people is paradoxical. It consists of a sense of extreme weakness and vulnerability vis-à-vis others, combined with its exact opposite, a sense of superiority and potential, if not actual, omnipotence. This curious combination of opposites seems to originate from the infant's perception that, on the one hand, he is a helpless creature, entirely at the mercy of adults; on the other, since there is no clear differentiation of the self from other objects, the whole world seems comprised by the self. Moreover, if the infant is fortunate enough to have his needs satisfied, at any rate for a time, without much delay, his omnipotent phantasy is reinforced by reality. If a child has only to yell for someone to come running to minister to him, it must be easy for him to maintain the illusion that he is the centre of the universe. We all accept that

51

C

children are both self-centred and comparatively incompetent at the same time, and take time to discover that they cannot expect that others will always do everything for them, and also that they have the capacity to do things for themselves. The combination of omnipotence and helplessness is simply an exaggeration of childish tendencies with which everyone is familiar; an extrapolation backwards into infancy of childish selfishness and dependency. It is clear from the utterances of children, as soon as they begin to speak, that they both resent their actual position of weakness, and also entertain phantasies of being immensely powerful. One has only to consider the games which they play with adults to realise that one of a child's main ambitions is to be 'big and strong like Father'. These phantasies of power are an important part of growing up, for the developing child reaches out, as it were, to the power which he feels himself to lack, and which he envies adults for possessing. As the normal child grows up, first within his own family, and secondly, and more importantly, within his own age group, his interaction with others gives him a lively sense, *in reality*, of his actual position in the human hierarchy. At home, his parents may still tower above him; but his brothers and sisters, some younger, some older, provide him with a varying picture of human power and responsibility; and the children of his own age with whom he interacts in street, playground and school, demonstrate that, although there may be many who are more capable than himself, there are also some who are less so.

Schizoid people, on the other hand, very often fail to develop any realistic sense of their position in the human hierarchy, because at a very early stage, they ceased to interact genuinely with their peers. Thus they often continue to feel themselves to be unrealistically weak and incompetent on the one hand, and to have equally unrealistic phantasies of power on the other. Moreover, the less satisfaction a person gains by interacting with people and things in the external world, the more will he be preoccupied with his own inner world of phantasy. This is a notable characteristic of schizoid people, who are, as I have said, essentially introverted; preoccupied with inner, rather than with outer, reality.

As an example of how feelings of inferiority and omnipotence can co-exist it is pertinent to recall the case of a man whose main complaint was of phobic anxieties. He was paralysed by fear of situations in which anyone could exercise power over him, and would rather have died than had to submit himself to an operation. For him,

anyone who had the slightest authority over him was a potential tor-
turer, a castrator in the old-fashioned Freudian sense. He was unable
to tolerate any portrayal of violence on stage or screen without
making sure that an escape route was easily available to him; for
he took such portrayals subjectively, imagining himself invariably
in the place of the victim. No more vivid example of a persistent
sense of being in the weak and inferior position vis-à-vis other
people could be imagined. And yet this same man felt himself to be
omnipotent, or at least did so throughout his boyhood and adolescence. For, unlike many schizoid people, he was in fact physically
courageous; and thus won all the fights at school in which he engaged.
In addition, he was gifted with a powerful intelligence of which he
made good use from an early age, so that he outstripped his contemporaries academically, and came first in most subjects. At heart he
was isolated and uncertain of himself, especially in any situation or
relationship involving emotion, for he did not believe himself to be
lovable, only powerful. So long as he remained successful, his self-
esteem could stay intact; for an inner conviction that one is a cut
above everyone else is a good substitute for feeling oneself to be
lovable so long as it lasts.

This particular individual suffered, as I have said, from fears of
violence at the hands of anyone who might have power over him.
Other schizoid individuals lay more emphasis upon the arbitrariness
and unpredictability of those whose power they fear. A small child
is, in reality, at the mercy of whoever is in charge of him. If his needs
are met in a comparatively rational way, he will grow up to think
of the world as equally comparatively predictable. Thus, if he is fed
when he is hungry, allowed to sleep when he is tired, played with
when he is lively, and cleaned when he is wet and dirty, there will
appear to be a firm connection between what goes on in the external
world and what he himself is feeling. But suppose that none of this
happens. Suppose that he is fed only to suit his mother's convenience,
irrespective of whether he is hungry or not; that he is kept awake
when he is tired, and put down to sleep when he wants to play; that
he is changed at irregular intervals, whether or not he needs to be. It is
easy to see that, to such a child, the world will appear incomprehensible and unpredictable. Because what actually happens is utterly unrelated to the child's feelings, the world will appear to him to be
ruled by capricious giants. These authorities have no understanding
of his needs, and do not therefore relate what they do to what the

child is feeling. It is easy to see that such a dislocation between the inner and outer worlds of the child must lead to an intensification of his preoccupation with his own phantasy, and a sense of despair that he will never be able to wrest satisfaction from the external world nor understand what appears entirely arbitrary.

With merciless accuracy, Kafka describes exactly such a world in his novels. In *The Trial*, for example, he describes how Joseph K. is arrested and accused of a crime which is never even disclosed to him: and then brought before a court whose workings are entirely mysterious.

'In many ways the functionaries (of the Court) were like children. Often they could be so deeply offended by the merest trifle—unfortunately, K.'s behaviour could not be classed as a trifle—that they would stop speaking even to old friends, give them the cold shoulder, and work against them in all imaginable ways. But then, suddenly, in the most surprising fashion and without any particular reason, they would be moved to laughter by some small jest which you only dared to make because you felt you had nothing to lose, and then they were your friends again. It was both easy and difficult to handle them, you could hardly lay down any fixed principles for dealing with them.'[2] This is the world of an unhappy, alienated child brought forward into adult life. It is difficult for the adult who has had a relatively normal, healthy upbringing to imagine a world in which his own feelings and what goes on in the external world are completely unrelated. But suppose he was transported to a foreign country in which the language and customs of the people were entirely unknown; in which nodding signified 'no' and shaking the head 'yes'; in which shouting and stamping were signs of approval; and quietly smiling speech indicated the utmost disgust; in which eating was so private a matter that two people were never seen to do it together, whilst sexual intercourse was entirely promiscuous and completely public.

We know, from the researches of Gregory Bateson and others, that at least some people who become schizophrenic in later life have suffered from what he so aptly named 'double-bind' situations. These are usually created by the parent saying one thing whilst meaning another. 'You are a good boy' or 'I love you' can be said in such a tone that the message conveyed is exactly the opposite. This creates a dislocation between feeling and its expression which is extremely confusing to a small child, who 'understands' people much more through their actions and tones of voice than through their words. Or a child can be put in a situation where anything he does is wrong—told to go out and play, for example, but to be careful not to get dirty: injunctions which, in many situations, are incompatible with each other and thus contradictory. In another passage, Kafka describes how a manufacturer comes into the bank in which K. works as Assessor to consult him, and then passes on to confer with his superior the Assistant Manager. 'The manufacturer lamented that his proposals were being cold-shouldered by the Assessor, indicating K., who under the Assistant Manager's eye had once more bent over the papers. Then as the two of them leaned against his desk, and the manufacturer set himself to win the new-comer's approval for his scheme, it seemed to K. as though two giants of enormous size were bargaining above his head for himself.'[3]

According to his biographer, Max Brod, Kafka, throughout his life, continued to attribute to his father almost magical powers, and longed for an acknowledgment and recognition from him which he never felt able to obtain. At the age of 36 he wrote a long 'Letter to my Father' in which he attempts to delineate the relationship. It is clear that the overpowering sense of irrational guilt from which Kafka suffered, and which is made so obvious in *The Trial*, took origin from being always made to feel inadequate and in the wrong in comparison with his father. The 'Letter to my Father' is intended to redress the balance; but it does not do so, because Kafka realizes that it is his own weakness, as much as any tactless, overweening behaviour on his father's part, which has accounted for his defeat. At the end of the letter, the father is supposed to be answering the son's accusations. 'I admit we fight each other, but there are two kinds of fight. There is the chivalrous fight, where two independent opponents test their strength against each other, each stands on his own, loses for himself, wins for himself, and there is the fight of the vermin, which not only bite but at the same time suck the blood on which they live. They are really the professional soldier, and that is what you are. You cannot stand up to life, but in order to set your-self up in it comfortably, free from care, and without self-reproach, you prove that I robbed you of your capacity to stand up to life, and shoved it in my pocket.'[4]

In another passage, Kafka writes of his failure to face marriage—he broke off his engagement—and makes a comparison between himself and his father in which he has nothing and the father has everything. 'The chief obstacle to my marriage is the conviction, which I can no longer eradicate, that to keep a family, particularly to be the head of one, what is necessary is just what I recognize you have—just everything together, good and bad just as it is organically united in you, viz strength and contempt for others, health and a certain excess, eloquence and standoffishness, self-confidence and dissatisfaction with everybody else, superiority to the world and tyranny, knowledge of the world and distrust of most people in it, and then advantages with no disadvantages attached, such as industry, endurance, presence of mind, fearlessness. Of all these qualities I had comparatively almost nothing.'[5]

The feeling of the child's powerlessness compared with the parent persisted and impaired his whole adaptation.

The same feeling is evident in Kafka's religious attitude. His emphasis is on the powerlessness and insufficiency of man, and the enormous difficulty man has in discovering his true path to salvation. There is an Absolute, 'but it is incommensurable with the life of man . . . The eternal misunderstandings between God and man induces Kafka to represent this disproportion again and again in the picture of two worlds which can never understand one another . . . Since the book of Job in the Bible, God has never been so savagely wrought with as in Kafka's *The Trial*, and *The Castle*, or in his *In the Penal Colony*, in which justice is presented in the image of a machine thought out with refined cruelty, an inhuman, almost devilish machine. Just the same in the book of Job, God does what seems absurd and unjust to man. But it is *only* to man that this seems so, and the final conclusion arrived at in Job as in Kafka is that the yardstick by which man works is not that by which measurements are taken in the world of the Absolute.'[6] As we shall see, Einstein's concept of relativity rests upon a similar premise.

Kafka also wrote about the bringing up of children, and, quoting Swift, 'parents are the least of all others to be trusted with the education of their children', goes on to point out how the parents' subjectivity and emotional investment in their children interferes with the true appreciation of the children as separate individuals. 'Even the greatest love of parents is, in the educational sense, more selfish than the faintest love on the part of the salaried educator. It cannot be otherwise . . . Those are the two methods of education of parents, both born of selfishness—tyranny and slavery of every shade, whereby the tyranny can express itself very tenderly—"You must

56

believe me, because I am your mother"—and the slavery very proudly—"You are my son, therefore shall I make you my saviour" —but they are two frightful means of education, two anti-educational means, calculated to tread the child back into the ground from which it came . . .'[7] The reason why an immediate fair adjustment is absolutely impossible—and only a fair adjustment is a real adjustment, only such an adjustment has any permanence—within this family animal is the inequality of birth of its parts, that is the immense superiority in power for many years of the father and mother over against the children.'[8] The source of the schizoid individual's persistent sense of inner weakness and inadequacy is amply confirmed in this passage, whether or not it is justified by his parents' actual behaviour.

In the last chapter, I suggested that creative activity was a peculiarly apt way for the schizoid individual to express himself. Having just had a glimpse of the inner world of such an individual, it is possible to understand why this should be so. First, since most creative activity is solitary, choosing such an occupation means that the schizoid person can avoid the problems of direct relationships with others. If he writes, paints or composes, he is, of course, communicating. But it is a communication entirely on his own terms. The whole situation is within his own control. He cannot be betrayed into confidences which he might later regret. He can express whatever he does want to reveal with such exactitude that there is less chance of being misunderstood than might obtain with more casual and spontaneous exchanges. He can choose (or so he often believes) how much of himself to reveal and how much to keep secret. Above all, he runs little risk of putting himself in the power of another person. As we have seen, the tragedy of the schizoid person is that he fears love almost as much as he fears hate; for any close involvement carries with it the risk of being overborne or 'swallowed' by the other party. Some form of interaction with other people is felt to be necessary, as it is to all of us, but this interaction is better undertaken at a safe remove. To show oneself only through the medium of a book, a picture, or a string quartet, is to protect oneself whilst at the same time enjoying the gratification of self-revelation. Fairbairn is entirely right when he states that 'exhibitionistic trends always play a prominent part in the schizoid mentality';[9] and this is so as a compensation. It springs from the fact that such a person is actually more hidden and inaccessible than the average. It is also relevant here to quote

57

Winnicott's remark on his paper 'On Communication'. 'In the artist of all kinds I think one can detect an inherent dilemma, which belongs to the co-existence of two trends, the urgent need to communicate and the still more urgent need not to be found.'[10]

Second, creative activity enables the schizoid person to retain at least part of his phantasy of omnipotence. Indirect communication by way of a work of art makes it possible for the artist to keep hold of a sense of superiority. Since the ordinary person cannot emulate him, he can enjoy the satisfaction of being 'different', and a cut above the average. Moreover, what can be more omnipotent than creating one's own world? A great novelist, for example, creates characters and situations which, if good enough, become imperishable. The world of Dickens will survive long after most of us have been entirely forgotten. Such an achievement appeals to and feeds the omnipotent phantasies which we have all had as infants, and which, in schizoid characters, are particularly persistent. Very often this omnipotent act of creation must act as a compensation for its opposite: the sense of being powerless in a Kafkaesque world of giants.

Third, creative activity, for the schizoid person, reflects his own scheme of values in which, as we have seen, the characteristic feature is that a greater importance is attributed to inner reality than to the external world. Originally, we suppose, this emphasis sprang from the child's experience of a lack of correspondence between outer and inner reality. What more fruitful way of redressing the balance than by portraying one's inner world in a work of art and then persuading other people to accept it, if not as real, at least as highly significant? Part of the satisfaction which a creative person obtains from his achievement may be the feeling that, at last, some part of his inner life is being accepted which has never been accorded recognition before. Moreover, since art became an individual matter rather than a task for anonymous craftsmen, creative work is generally recognized as being especially apt for expressing the personal style of an individual (which is of course closely related to his inner world). The value we place upon authenticity is often exaggerated; yet there is a sense in which it is justified. However good a painting or a piece of music may be, taken quite apart from its creator, the fact that it is or is not another expression of the personality of a particular artist is important. For it either is or is not an addition to our knowledge of that artist; a further revelation of that mysterious, indefinable and fascinating thing—his personality.

Fourth, certain kinds of creativity are peculiarly apt for overcoming the sense of arbitrary unpredictability detected in Kafka. If the world seems nonsensical, one has no power over it, and no way of predicting what will happen. Bertrand Russell, a solitary child who later had considerable difficulty with personal relationships, reports in his Autobiography: 'At the age of eleven, I began Euclid, with my brother as my tutor. This was one of the great events of my life, as dazzling as first love. I had not imagined that there was anything so delicious in the world.'[11] Since Bertrand Russell writes of his childhood that 'the grown-ups with whom I came in contact had a remarkable incapacity for understanding the intensity of childish emotions',[12] it seems likely that Euclid possessed so strong an appeal for him because geometry represented sense and order as opposed to chaos. How wonderful to be one's own Euclid, and impose one's own order upon a world which has hitherto seemed unpredictable. As we shall see in the next chapter, it is at least arguable that some of the greatest achievements in scientific thought rest upon a basis of finding an unpredictable, arbitrary world intolerable.

Fifth, creative activity can undoubtedly act as a defence against the threat which overhangs the schizoid person of finding the world meaningless. As we have seen, the 'schizoid state,' postulated by Fairbairn as being one basic state of mind against which many neurotic symptoms are defences, is characterized by a sense of meaninglessness and futility. For most people, interaction with others ('object-relations') provides most of what they require in order to find meaning and significance in life. For the schizoid person, however, this is not the case. Creative activity is again peculiarly apt as an alternative. For both the ability to create, and the productions which result from such ability, are generally regarded as possessing value by our society, even when conventional success is not in question. Just as we do not query the fact that personal relationships are important, so we also assume that creativity has significance. There can be no doubt that many artists, and many scientists too, disappointed in personal relations, find in their work a meaning and a value which more ordinary people only find in human relationships. Moreover, such work is more to be relied upon than people who, especially in the eyes of a schizoid person, often appear capricious and untrustworthy, and indeed sometimes are so in reality.

REFERENCES

1. ERIKSON, Eric H. *Identity* (London: Faber and Faber, 1968) p. 96.
2. KAFKA, Franz. *The Trial*, trans. Willa and Edwin Muir (London: Secker & Warburg, 1956), p. 136.
3. Ibid, p. 146.
4. BROD, Max. *Franz Kafka: A Biography* (London: Secker & Warburg, 1948) p. 18.
5. Ibid, pp. 19-20.
6. Ibid, pp. 137-80.
7. Ibid, pp. 168-70.
8. Ibid, p. 168.
9. FAIRBAIRN, W. R. D. 'Schizoid Factors in the Personality', in *Psycho-Analytic Studies of the Personality* (London: Tavistock Publications, 1952) p. 16.
10. WINNICOTT, D. W. 'Communicating and Not Communicating Leading to a Study of Certain Opposites', in *The Maturational Processes and the Facilitating Environment* (London: The Hogarth Press and The Institute of Psycho-Analysis, 1965) p. 185.
11. RUSSELL, Bertrand. *The Autobiography of Bertrand Russell* (London: Allen and Unwin, 1967) Vol. 1, p. 36.
12. Ibid, p. 23.

6

New Models of the Universe

To label as schizoid a man so universally admired as Albert Einstein is to court attack from the psychologically naïve. Yet Einstein provides the supreme example of how schizoid detachment can be put to creative use. As we said earlier, men of schizoid personality often put others off by their coldness, and show a somewhat unpleasing face to the world. This was not true of Einstein, who impressed everyone who met him by his gentleness and wisdom. He was, indeed, something of a saint: a man who seemed to others to possess simple goodness, and what some called spiritual grandeur. Unlike Newton, his only peer in the field of scientific generalization, he lacked the paranoid component so often found as part of the schizoid constitution; unless his extreme intolerance of authority is rated as belonging to this category. In all other respects he fits exactly the picture outlined in the last chapter; and it will be argued that his particular type of creativity was not only inseparable from his character structure, but also fulfilled for him all five of the functions listed at the end of that chapter.

His son, Albert Einstein, Jr, writes that Einstein was 'a very well-behaved child. He was shy, lonely and withdrawn from the world even then. He was even considered backward by his teachers. He told me that his teachers reported to his father that he was mentally slow, unsociable and adrift forever in his foolish dreams.'[1] Very early indeed, Einstein set himself the task of establishing himself as an entirely separate entity, influenced as little as possible by other people. In school, he did not revolt, he simply ignored authority. His first attempt to assert his individuality is interesting. His parents, although Jewish, were largely indifferent to religion. Einstein, whilst still a schoolboy, deliberately emphasized his Jewish origin and went through a period of religious fervour which he later described as his 'first attempt to liberate myself from purely personal links'.[2]

Personal links are, for most ordinary people, the basis of their security in the world. If these links are suddenly severed, as happens under Communist régimes when the secret police seize a man and deliberately isolate him completely from his friends and relatives, the average victim becomes mentally disturbed, often within a few weeks, and may go through a psychotic episode. A certain degree of dependence upon other human beings—'mature dependence' as Fairbairn called it—is an important component of the 'normal' man's sense of security and reality. But schizoid people treat personal links as threatening. For them, other people are either unpredictable or else potentially engulfing. Their consequent alienation from others has the positive effect of rendering them less susceptible to the ill-effects of solitary confinement. If personal links have not meant much, deprivation of those links will not mean much either, and so schizoid characters stand prison and resist brainwashing better than most of us. We do not know what infantile or other emotional experiences may have determined Einstein's avowed ambition to free himself from all personal ties; but this aim remained with him all his life, as did his dislike of authority and his resentment of everything which interfered with the freedom of the individual. This included even his own sense impressions, which he regarded as unreliable. As he wrote: 'Perception of this world by thought, leaving out everything subjective, became partly consciously, partly unconsciously, my supreme aim.'[3] Einstein agreed with the finding of psychoanalysis that our perception of the external world is primarily dependent upon our physical (tactile) experience. Common speech still equates 'tangible' with 'real'. 'I believe that the first step in the setting of a "real external world" is the formation of the concept of bodily objects of various kinds. Out of the multitude of our sense experiences we take, mentally and arbitrarily, certain repeatedly occurring complexes of sense impressions (partly in conjunction with sense impressions which are interpreted as signs for sense experiences of others), and we attribute to them a meaning—the meaning of the bodily object. Considered logically this concept is not identical with the totality of the sense impressions referred to; but is an arbitrary creation of the human (or animal) mind. On the other hand, the concept owes its meaning and its justification exclusively to the totality of the sense impressions which we associate with it.

'The second step is to be found in the fact that, in our thinking (which determines our expectation), we attribute to this concept of the bodily object a significance, which is to a high degree independent of the sense impression which originally gives rise to it. This is what we mean when we attribute to the bodily object "a real existence".

The justification of such a setting rests exclusively on the fact that, by means of such concepts and mental relations between them, we are able to orient ourselves in the labyrinth of sense impressions. These notions and relations, although free statements of our thoughts, appear to us as stronger and more unalterable than the individual sense experience itself, the character of which as anything other than the result of an illusion or hallucination is never completely guaranteed.'[4]

In other words, the evidence of the senses is not to be trusted; (and it must be remembered that the baby's earliest experience of personal relationships is through the sensation of touch). Only the relation between concepts within the mind itself can be trusted, not the relation between the self and the external world, or the self and other people.

This is the 'omnipotence of thought' carried to an extreme. In potential madmen, such a way of looking at the world can easily turn into a delusional system. The paranoid psychotic who builds such a system on the basis of a mistaken perception of the attitude of other people towards him often impresses the observer with his unshakeable logic. If his premise is accepted, that he is persecuted and plotted against, all else follows perfectly rationally. It is his initial concepts which are at fault, *not the relation between them.*

Although Einstein's professed endeavour was to separate his thinking as much as possible from the concrete unreliability of sense impressions, yet he retained sufficient contact with reality for his thought to be scientifically viable. His was not a system of pure ratiocination, unconnected with the external world, in spite of his apparent efforts to make it so. Einstein's laws proved to be an advance on previous scientific thought because the effects predicted by them turned out to be better in accord with observation. In other words, where his theories touched the external world they worked. Had they not done so, they could have been dismissed as being as equally 'delusional' as the phlogiston theory, which postulated that, when matter was burnt, a purely hypothetical substance called 'phlogiston' was given off, a substance later proved to have no existence. It is, of course, this capacity for extreme abstraction combined with a retention of contact with reality which makes creative achievements of this order so remarkable. It is one striking example of the combination of opposites which I shall later argue is characteristic of creative people.

The relation between what is tangible and what is commonly regarded as real is worth a further glance. One characteristic held in common by most schizoid people is a relative detachment from the body. Einstein, who was militantly unconventional in appearance, clearly based none of his self-esteem upon his physical appearance, although physically very powerful. Although twice married, and reported, at any rate in middle life, to enjoy 'the good things in life', the body clearly did not rate high on his list of priorities, for the body is perhaps the area of our experience in which subjectivity rears its ugly head most easily. As Proust put it: 'Indeed it is the possession of a body that is the great danger to the mind, to our human and thinking life . . .'[5] In the first chapter of *The ABC of Relativity* Bertrand Russell points out most cogently that 'it is touch that gives us our sense of "reality". Some things cannot be touched: rainbows, reflections in looking-glasses, and so on. These things puzzle children, whose metaphysical speculations are arrested by the information that what is in the looking-glass is not "real". Macbeth's dagger was unreal because it was not "sensible to feeling as to sight". Not only our geometry and physics, but our whole conception of what exists outside us, is based upon the sense of touch.' But Einstein discovered that 'much of what we learned from the sense of touch was unscientific prejudice, which must be rejected if we are to have a true picture of the world'.[6]

Schizoid people are notoriously 'out of touch' with their own bodies, and very often out of touch with those of others as well. The phenomenon of the person who can only have sexual intercourse with the aid of a phantasy is a schizoid phenomenon. So is the unawareness of physical discomfort, hunger or even pain which is characteristic of the stereotype of the unworldly scholar eccentric. The evidence now is, partly from psychoanalysis, and partly from experimental studies with subhuman primates, that the infant's experience of touch with the mother's body is enormously important for its whole future social and sexual adjustment—its adjustment to reality, in fact. Schizoid people, theoretically because of some very early maternal lack or mismanagement, 'lose touch' and come to regard close involvement (being closely 'in touch') with another person as potentially dangerous, as we saw in the last chapter. Perhaps the detachment required to construct a view of the universe based on the kind of observer Einstein had in mind in which touch cannot operate or be imagined to operate, is only possible for a person who has been compelled, from an early age, to create substitutes for touch in coming to terms with, and building up, his infant picture of the world.

At the age of twelve, Einstein finally freed himself from conventional religious belief; although he retained a firm belief in some rather undefined 'cosmic religion' which was entirely suprapersonal. The God who, in his famous phrase, 'does not play at dice', was not a deity concerned with men, but rather a personification of order. Einstein firmly believed that there was a greater reality outside the merely personal, and that this reality was harmonious and governed by laws which could, at any rate in part, be discovered. It is typical of such a character that, for him, 'God' should not be a person. It is also characteristic that, like Bertrand Russell, and at the same age of twelve, Einstein should have found that Euclid transported him. 'Man was capable, through the force of thought alone, of achieving the degree of stability and purity which the Greeks, before anybody else, demonstrated to us in geometry.'[7] Although Einstein was a saintly character, generous, kind, and with a lively social conscience, he was not much involved with individual human beings. His passion was for causes, not for people; and, indeed, his judgement of individuals to whose appeals for charity he responded seems to have been undiscriminating.

As with Bertrand Russell, love for humanity seems largely to have replaced love for individuals. Perhaps this is why his first marriage went wrong. As his perceptive biographer observes: 'His social conscience seems almost detached from its object: the man.' She goes on: 'He has never really needed human contacts, but has deliberately freed himself more and more from all emotional dependence in order to become entirely self-sufficient. Real intimacy and the unconditional sharing of thoughts and feelings with another person, so that they become almost another self, is an experience he has hardly ever had: he fears it because it threatens the complete inner freedom which is essential to him.'[8]

For Einstein, creativity was partly motivated by a desire to escape from ordinary life, in order to find a harmony and peace which everyday existence could not provide. 'Man moves the centre of gravity of his sentimental life and looks for the calm and balance that he cannot find in the too narrow circle of his personal life.'[9] His biographer also describes how, in the course of ordinary social interchange, he would 'fall silent and stop listening to you. He would rise to his feet without a word, or remain sitting motionless. The effect would be the same. He would be unreachable . . . One never got rid of the feeling that his presence among us was only on temporary loan.'[10]

The most remarkable thing about Einstein's achievement is that his discoveries were made almost entirely by thought alone, unsupported at first by much experiment, or indeed by much mathematics. The paper on the special theory of relativity, published in 1905, contains no references, very little mathematics, and quotes no authority. Indeed, his actual knowledge of mathematics was, at the time, sketchy compared with that of other leading physicists. 'It was like him to begin his work—and to achieve more than most mathematical physicists in a lifetime—with the aid of nothing but his own, pure unaided thought. No one else would have started with that suspicion of mathematical techniques. At twenty-three he was already the man whom the world later wished, and failed, to understand. He had absolute confidence. He had absolute faith in his own insight. He was set on submerging his personality, for good and all, in the marvels of the natural world.'[11] This is not to say that he was entirely indifferent to conventional success. He was far from shunning publicity; and in fact achieved world-wide recognition early in life, in spite of the fact that very few people were qualified to grasp his new conceptions.

As is generally appreciated, Einstein upset conventional ideas of space and time. Until he advanced the special theory of relativity, it was generally assumed that time was an absolute; that is, that two events either took place simultaneously, or that one preceded the other. Relativity theory showed that this was not so, and that the same event might appear to one observer to precede another event, to another observer to be simultaneous with it, and to yet another to take place after it. Relativity is so called because it shows that many more things only appeared to be what they seemed from the point of view of a particular observer and were not absolute. To a scientist, this is obviously intolerable, since science wishes to describe and understand phenomena as they are *absolutely*, uncontaminated by the prejudices of any particular observer. As Bertrand Russell points out, it is unfortunate that the theory of relativity has been thus named. For, instead of proving that everything in the physical world is relative, as people who do not understand the theory assume, relativity 'is wholly concerned to exclude what is relative, and arrive at a statement of physical laws that shall in no way depend upon the circumstances of the observer'. Einstein demonstrated that the circumstance of the observer had more effect upon what he observed than was previously supposed. 'But he also showed how to discount this effect completely ... This was the source of almost everything that is surprising in his theory.'[12]

Einstein really did provide a new model of the universe; and, in order to create this, he had to detach himself from the conventional point of view to an extent which is only possible for one who, early in life, made 'leaving out everything subjective' his supreme aim. Such detachment can only be achieved by the person with a predominantly schizoid psychopathology. In terms of science, Einstein was right to protect himself from being too much influenced or too much emotionally involved with other people. The imaginative feat required to conceive of how the universe would appear to an observer travelling at near the speed of light (for it is to such observers that relativity applies; Newton is mostly good enough for human speeds on earth) could only be achieved by a person who was singularly uninfluenced by conventional teaching; who had in fact protected himself against conventional teaching; who was intolerant of authority; and who, to use C. P. Snow's final word about him, was 'unbudgeable'. Einstein's world view depended on being able to free himself from the subjective prejudice implicit in being a dweller upon earth; and upon having sufficient imagination to put himself in the position of an observer travelling independently in space at a very high speed. He was both supremely confident and supremely unconfident at the same time: convinced that he could find the answers and was right; yet so suspicious of influence that he had to keep his distance from people. Einstein is a perfect example of the truth of Gibbon's remark that 'Conversation enriches the understanding, but solitude is the school of genius.'[13]

One other feature of Einstein's personality is worth mentioning; his passion for music. Until old age, he was an enthusiastic violinist. From the account given by the pianist Manfred Clynes, who visited Einstein within a few years of his death, his favourite composer was Mozart. He also said to Clynes that it was as important for him to improvise on the piano as it was for him to work on his physics. 'It is a way for me to be independent of people,' he said. 'And this is highly necesssary in the kind of society in which we live.'[14] Music, being the most abstract of the arts, and the least obviously connected directly with human experience, is often the passion of schizoid people, who delight in discovering that there is a way of experiencing and expressing emotion which is impersonal. We can see, therefore, that Einstein provides a striking example of a person whose creativity served all the functions postulated at the end of Chapter 5. Through his work, he was able to communicate and express himself without coming into close contact with others. His avowed aim was to conquer the world through thought alone, an 'omnipotent' phantasy which proved, in reality, to be a supremely successful tool for the further apprehension of the structure of the universe. His insistence upon the importance of his own inner world of creative thought has already been demonstrated. As a good scientist, he of course insisted that his ideas should be confirmed by experiment; but there is no doubt the ideas came first and the experiments afterwards. As he wrote himself: 'A theory can be proved by experiment, but no path leads from experiment to the birth of a theory.'[15] That in some sense his inner world was originally unpredictable or chaotic is attested by his determination to substitute abstract thought for the evidence of his senses, and by his delight at discovering the ordered world of geometry. We do not know whether he ever found the world meaningless or futile; but he certainly went through a mental upheaval at the age of sixteen which was severe enough to enable him to obtain a certificate from the school doctor stating that he had a nervous breakdown and must take six months off school. It seems highly probable that part of the motivation of his intense desire to create originated from his lack of close contacts with other people, and the consequent threat of finding the world devoid of meaning. In 1936 he wrote 'I live in that solitude which is painful in youth, but delicious in the years of maturity',[16] a sentence which demonstrates both his early distress and his isolation, and also his capacity for creatively coming to terms with it.

Einstein provides an example of a man whose detachment from human beings resulted in an universal benevolence remarkably free from hostility or touchiness. He could be tactless. There are stories of his having prolonged conversations with persons to whom he had been introduced, and subsequently utterly failing to recognize them. But the main outline is of a saintly character, able to play with children, kindly, and benign, so long as people fulfilled his one essential condition—to leave him alone when he wanted to be so.

Our next example, though very different in some ways, illustrates with equal cogency the main thesis of this chapter. Isaac Newton, the only other genius of comparable stature in the same scientific field, shared with Einstein a number of schizoid traits of personality. In addition, however, he was far more suspicious of, and hostile to, other human beings; characteristics which may justifiably be related to a basic mistrust engendered by the circumstances of his early childhood.

Newton was born, prematurely, on Christmas Day 1642. His father had died three months before his birth, so that, during this very early period of his existence, the puny infant had his mother's undivided attention. This idyll was rudely shattered, however, by his mother's remarriage and removal to another house just after the boy's third birthday. Newton was left in the care of his maternal grandmother; and, although his mother's new home was near enough for him to have been able to see her frequently, we know from his own account that he passionately resented what he felt as a betrayal. In a confessional list of sins, recorded when he was twenty, he blames himself for having harboured the wish to burn their house over his mother and stepfather. When Newton was eleven, his stepfather died; with the result that his mother returned to him, together with two stepsisters and a stepbrother. Newton remained devoted to his mother, and nursed her personally in her last illness. Indeed, it was probably his tie to her which prevented him ever marrying. There is some evidence to suggest that his sexual orientation was primarily towards his own sex: but, according to witnesses in whom he confided in old age, he lived and died a virgin. That the tie to his mother remained in spite of her 'betrayal' is not surprising in the light of what we understand of childhood phantasy. One characteristic feature of such phantasy is to make a sharp division between 'good' and 'bad' of such a kind that the mother or her substitute may appear at one time as an idealized goddess, and at another as an evil witch. In the ordinary course of development, these two extreme images become fused, so that the child becomes aware that one and the same person can be both loving and neglectful or punitive at times, as all real human beings are bound to be. But this fusion depends upon a continuity of relationship; opportunities repeated over and over again to discover that love can continue and persist in spite of apparent interruptions. Where the relation between mother and child is seriously interrupted, as happened with Isaac Newton, the old, primitive images persist, with the result that other human beings are either idealized as wholly good and unequivocally devoted to the subject, or else seen as wholly bad and intent on doing him an injury. Newton's idealized image of the mother he remembered in infancy remained: but so did the memory of her desertion, with the result that he became secretive, touchy, and fearful that his discoveries would be stolen from him by others.

Newton, like Einstein, was unorthodox in his religious beliefs. In an age when belief in the Trinity was obligatory, Newton remained a secret Unitarian. Throughout his life, he was deeply preoccupied with religious speculation, and seems, like many a prophet, to have been convinced that he had a direct personal relationship with a God who inspired him. Such a conviction is not infrequent in schizoid characters of religious bent, who are apt to substitute a relation with God for the human contacts which they find so difficult. Newton left behind him an immense mass of theological manuscripts: millions of words devoted to chronology, church history, doctrine and prophecy. As one biographer writes of him: 'To force everything in the heavens and on earth into one rigid, tight frame from which the most minuscule detail would not be allowed to escape free and random was an underlying need of this anxiety-ridden man.'[17] His religious unorthodoxy and desire for complete independence may also be assumed to have influenced his decision not to enter the Church as a means of retaining his Fellowship at Trinity; a step which was normally demanded. At Newton's request, Charles II provided by letters patent that the holder of the Lucasian professorship, to which Newton had succeeded in 1669, need not take holy orders.

Newton also shared with Einstein a distrust of the physical senses; and an indifference to things of the body. In a note-book he wrote: 'The nature of things is more securely and naturally deduced from their operãcons one upon another ȳ (than) upon o(u)r senses.'[18] His neglect of his physical person was notorious. He slept little, often forgot to eat, and sometimes to dress himself, and never took exercise. As a boy he had spent little time playing with his fellows, preferring to exercise his ingenuity in making mechanical models. As a man, he remained an isolate. During the thirty-one years of his residence in Cambridge, he was a recluse; the very archetype of the absent-minded, solitary scholar. His reluctance to become involved with other human beings was far more extreme than that of Einstein. Newton's fear of the influence of others upon his work was exceptionally marked; so much so that he sometimes failed to make due acknowledgment to his predecessors, as if he felt that his own revelation must be uniquely personal and uncontaminated. Brodetsky writes: 'He was always somewhat unwilling to face publicity and criticisim, and had on more than one occasion declined to have his name associated with published accounts of some of his work. He did not value public esteem as desirable in itself, and feared that publicity would lead to his being harassed by personal relationships—whereas he wished to be free of such entanglements . . . Apparently Newton hardly ever published a discovery without being urged to do so by others: Even when he had arrived at the solution of the greatest problem that astronomy has ever had to face he said nothing about it to anybody.'[19]

As a boy, Newton, again like Einstein, did not seem to his teachers to be anything remarkable. The dreamy boy grew up into a youth with a rigid, Puritanical conscience; a punishing super-ego which would not let him rest, and which forced him to record his sins in obsessive detail. As we shall see when discussing the influence of the depressive temperament upon creative persons, this type of conscience may drive a man to create as a means of self-justification. In early youth, Newton was anxious, insecure, hypochondriacal and self-disparing. Indeed, depressive traits are more in evidence than paranoid tendencies. It was only in middle life that he ceased self-denigration and began to accuse others of the faults of which he had previously found himself guilty.

Newton's quarrels with other scientists were famous, and need not detain us here. His disputes with Hooke, with Flamsteed and with Leibniz are amply documented. But there was a period in his life at which his suspicion and hostility to others overstepped the bounds of sanity. The details of this illness remain obscure, but in 1693 Newton became sufficiently disturbed in mind for rumours of his insanity to gain widespread acceptance. In September of that year he wrote to Pepys, Locke and other friends accusing them of being atheists or Catholics, and of trying to embroil him with women. Various factors may have contributed to this 'paranoid episode', as we should now label it. Insomnia and physical ill-health due to Newton's neglect of himself certainly played a part. So, probably, did disappointments in his alchemical experiments, and a failure to obtain various positions of eminence to which it had been suggested that he might be appointed. Professor Manuel believes that Newton became infatuated with a young man named Fatio de Duillier, and that it may have been the partial recognition of his own homosexual predilections which temporarily shattered his mental stability. Be this as it may, there seems little doubt from Newton's own correspondence that the crisis was largely over by the end of 1693. In 1696 he was appointed Warden of the Mint; then Master of the Mint; and President of the Royal Society in 1703. He became a powerful public figure and was knighted. One of his tasks as Warden of the Mint was to stamp out forgery; and he appears to have pursued and prosecuted coiners and counterfeiters with a fierce relish characteristic of paranoid men who attain power.

Newton's discoveries, like Einstein's, depended upon an extreme scepticism of authority combined with a powerful drive to make a new synthesis which would make sense out of the universe. In Newton's case, the disruption of conventional ideas about the universe had been partially carried out by Kepler, on the one hand, and by Galileo on the other. But their points of view appeared incompatible; and it was only because Newton realized this, and was able to discard parts of both their theories that he was able to make a new synthesis in which the laws of motion applied equally as well to bodies in the heavens as they did to bodies upon earth. Both Newton and Einstein, it must be assumed, had suffered the kind of anxiety so well described by Kafka, and were left, therefore, with an intense need to create an all-embracing, explanatory scheme which would alleviate the discomfort of living in an arbitrary or contradictory world. Intolerance of discrepancies, the realization that something does not fit, as a motive for creation, will be further discussed in a chapter on the obsessional personality. In considering the achievements of Newton and Einstein we are looking at phenomena which cannot be explained as motivated merely by a desire for order, important though this is. Both syntheses depend upon a power of abstraction only found in those in whom there is an almost complete divorce between thinking and feeling; an alienation from human emotion. The new synthesis pursued with such intensity is as much an attempt to heal a split in the self as it is to comprehend the universe.

In his seminal book, *The Flight from Woman*,[20] Karl Stern examines the alienation from the feminine, instinctual and physical which is characteristic of certain philosophers. Descartes, for example, shared with both Newton and Einstein a distrust of the 'evidence of the senses'. In fact, he refers to the body as possibly illusory, and to sensations as deceptive. From this root arose Descartes' philosophy, which was based on doubting everything which could be doubted. His famous dictum, 'I think, therefore I am', represented the first principle of his philosophy; a datum which he could not doubt, and which therefore became the foundation upon which his thought could rest. It is significant that this first principle is a purely mental phenomenon and also highly subjective. As Bertrand Russell points out: ' "I think, therefore I am" makes mind more certain than matter, and my mind (for me) more certain than the minds of others.'[21] Cartesian dualism, the almost complete divorce of mind and matter which is the most notable feature of Descartes' philosophy, seems to have originated from the deprivations of his own early childhood; for Descartes' mother died when he was just over one year old. Although Descartes had one affair with a servant girl by whom he had an illegitimate daughter, he never married; and by far the majority of his relationships with women were intellectual and platonic. Indeed, one of his bluestockings was the death of poor Descartes. Queen Christina of Sweden, who attached him to her court, made the philosopher rise at five every morning to give her lessons. Descartes, who was always delicate, caught cold as a result, became quickly very ill, and died in February 1650. Descartes showed a restlessness which is rather typical of the maternally deprived. During his twenty-year sojourn in Holland, he moved house no less than twenty-three times.

As Karl Stern points out, there are many other examples of a similar kind. Schopenhauer, the son of an intellectually pretentious woman with no heart, shows quite clearly in his philosophical writings his hatred of women, his disgust with the physical, and his wish for a world of pure abstraction and reflection, uncontaminated by Nature. Sartre, the very paradigm of the alienated man, writes of Nature with nausea, and of love as being unrealizable. It is not difficult to find many other examples. There can be no doubt that what psychiatrists call 'schizoid psychopathology' has played an important part in many philosophies, and especially in world-views which depend upon an unusual capacity for abstraction. Whether it is right to use the word 'psychopathology' in this connection is a question to which we shall return. It will be suggested that a good deal which psychoanalysts, especially, label 'pathological' may be implicit in the human condition, and a necessary part of our specifically human adaptation.

REFERENCES

1. GOERTZEL V. and M. G. *Cradles of Eminence* (London: Constable, 1964) p. 248.
2. VALLENTIN, Antonia. *Einstein* (London: Weidenfeld & Nicolson, 1965) p. 9.
3. Ibid, p. 9.
4. EINSTEIN, Albert. *Out of my Later Years* (London: Thames and Hudson, 1950) pp. 60-61.
5. PROUST, Marcel. *Time Regained*, Vol. XII of *Remembrance of Things Past*, trans. Andreas Mayor (London: Chatto & Windus, 1970) p. 456.
6. RUSSELL, Bertrand. *The ABC of Relativity* (London: Allen and Unwin, 1958) p. 10.
7. VALLENTIN, Antonia. *Einstein* (London: Weidenfeld & Nicolson, 1954) p. 11.
8. Ibid, pp. 83-84.
9. Ibid, p. 109.
10. Ibid, p. 27.
11. SNOW, C. P. *Variety of Men* (London: Macmillan, 1967) p. 73.
12. RUSSELL, Bertrand. *The ABC of Relativity* (London: Allen and Unwin, 1958) p. 16.
13. GIBBON, Edward. *The Decline and Fall of the Roman Empire*, ed. J. B. Bury (London: Methuen, 1898) Vol. V, p. 337.
14. MICHELMORE, Peter. *Einstein. Profile of the Man* (London: Frederick Muller, 1963) p. 225.
15. VALLENTIN, Antonia. *Einstein* (London: Weidenfeld & Nicolson, 1954) p. 105.
16. EINSTEIN, Albert. *Out of My Later Years* (London: Thames and Hudson, 1950) p. 5.
17. MANUEL, Frank E. *A Portrait of Isaac Newton* (London: Oxford University Press, 1969) p. 380.
18. Ibid, p. 75.
19. BRODETSKY, S. *Sir Isaac Newton* (London: Methuen, 1927) pp. 69 and 89.
20. STERN, Karl. *The Flight from Woman* (London: Allen and Unwin, 1965).
21. RUSSELL, Bertrand. *History of Western Philosophy* (London: Allen and Unwin, 1955) p. 586.

7

Creativity and the
Manic-Depressive Temperament

In the last chapter, I showed that certain types of creative activity were closely associated with, and dependent upon, the presence of schizoid traits of personality. In this chapter, the relation between creative endeavour and the so-called manic-depressive temperament will be explored.

As we have seen, the schizoid person is concerned to withdraw as much as possible from other people, because he fears their destructive influence upon himself. Only by isolating himself can he preserve himself and the illusion of omnipotence. This may lead him to construct a new world order, as did both Newton and Einstein; a world which he has himself created, into which, if possible, no disturbing or alien factors are allowed to enter. This world is essentially solipsistic. It is one man's conception, or a direct revelation to one man from God. It is not even necessarily a communication. What matters is the discovery of the pattern. As we saw in the case of Newton, priority of discovery was important; but communicating discovery was not. Self-esteem is not primarily dependent upon the opinion of others, therefore; but upon the creation of an internally self-consistent system in which the creator plays the part of God. If the creator is sufficiently out of touch with reality, his system may be dismissed as delusion. If, on the other hand, like Newton and Einstein, his conceptions accord with a reality 'out there' which can be tested, the new scheme may vastly increase comprehension.

The person of manic-depressive temperament is very different from the schizoid individuals we have so far examined. His principal concern is also to protect himself from the danger of loss of self-esteem; but, unlike the schizoid person, his self-esteem is much more directly dependent upon a 'good' relation with others. Like the schizoid person, he fears other people in some ways; but it is not so much the fear of attack or being overwhelmed, as the fear of withdrawal of love and approval. Now, if a man fears the withdrawal of love, it follows that he must have experienced it. The schizoid person has little conception of the supporting function of love, because he seems never fully to have trusted it. His self-esteem depends primarily upon power, rather than upon being approved of. But the manic-depressive, or cyclothymic person, has progressed further in emotional development than this. Having experienced love, he has been able to give up his solipsistic world, and relinquish his illusion of omnipotence. But the price of this renunciation is dependency. If self-esteem depends on receiving love from others, the recipient is at once put in the position of having to maintain a good relation with the source of supply. This means, for the small child, that he must learn to accommodate himself to the wishes of his parents; fit in with their demands; and in general to be 'good', or he will find that they are no longer 'good' to him. It seems quite likely that this early step in emotional development is related to the point at which the infant becomes aware of his mother as a recognizable whole person, rather than merely an instrument which either fulfils or denies his desires. If one lives in the arbitrary, unpredictable world of a Kafka, it is impossible to know what will please the high-and-mighty, who are good to one or bad to one quite irrespective of how one behaves. But directly a more personal relationship has become established, the arbitrariness largely disappears, and the source of love is seen as a person who can be influenced to give or withhold love by means of one's own behaviour. In Kleinian terminology, the change from the paranoid-schizoid position to the depressive position is perhaps best seen in this change in relation to persons in the external world. In the case of 'normal' persons, it is to be assumed that they receive enough supplies of love from those who care for them for self-esteem to become built-in (the introjection of a good object). Alternatively, one could say that normal people become conditioned by receiving enough love as small children to expect that others will give them approval, and thus proceed through life with confidence. People who remain in the depressive position have no such built-in confidence. They remain as vulnerable to outside opinion as a baby is vulnerable to the withdrawal of the breast. Indeed, for such people, the good opinion of others is as vital to their well-being as milk is to the infant. Rejection and disapproval are a matter of life and death; for unless supplies of approval are forthcoming from outside, they relapse into a state of depression in which self-esteem sinks so low, and rage becomes so uncontrollable, that suicide becomes a real possibility.

Since Freud investigated melancholia, it has been generally recognized that depressives have a particular difficulty in handling their aggressive impulses. Instead of being able to express aggression against others who frustrate or deprive them, they turn their aggression inwards against themselves in self-reproach, punish themselves for the hostility they feel, and tend to kill themselves instead of those whom they believe will not love them.

This masochistic way of behaving is often reflected in a predominantly submissive adaptation to others—a continuation into adult life of 'good' behaviour designed to placate and to ingratiate. The potential depressive learns to identify himself with others very early, in order not to offend those upon whose approval he relies. In doing so, he suppresses his own individuality; the inevitable price of over-adapting to the supposed requirements of others. The opposite of this depressive adaptation is manic behaviour, in which the wishes and needs of others are disregarded, conscience is overthrown, and ingratiation supplanted by ruthless self-seeking. That these two opposite ways of behaving can alternate in the same person will surprise no one who has read what has already been said about omnipotence and helplessness in earlier chapters.

How can creative activity serve to alleviate the emotional problems of one whose psychopathology is predominantly depressive? First, since the artist is often highly regarded, it is obvious that the recurrent production of creative work, if at all successful, brings recurrent injections of self-esteem. A depressive, convinced that he is unloved by those close to him, may seek to win a more general recognition of his merits by acquiring public acclaim; and producing creative work is one way of doing this. (There are, of course, others. Many extremely successful people, be they leaders, millionaires, television personalities or stage performers, are spurred to achievement by depressive psychopathology.)[1] Normal people are dependent for a sense of their own value upon love which they receive from their families and friends. Depressives, having no such source of self-esteem, are driven to seek it elsewhere.

One feature of this type of psychopathology is that the effect of the injection does not last. Success does bring self-esteem, reassurance, and even elation to the depressive; but the improvement is generally short-lived. In the end, no amount of external success compensates for what has not been incorporated in early childhood; the irrational sense of his own value which the loved and wanted child assimilates automatically as part of his birthright.

Michelangelo received more acclaim, and attained a more lofty position than any artist before him. Yet this universally recognized genius, who could afford to be haughty with popes, remained, as his sonnets demonstrate, forever the prey of depression and self-denigration. Raphael, who portrayed him in the *School of Athens*, was surely right to show him lost in solitary contemplation in the traditional pose of Melancholy.

> He who from nothing made all things ordained
> That time in two parts should be severed; one
> He handed over to the mighty sun,
> The other with the nearer moon remained.
>
> From this event, fortune and fate sprang forth,
> Mischance or happiness to each man fell.
> To me was sent the dark time, I know well,
> For it has always been with me since birth.
>
> And like all things which make a counterfeit
> Of their own nature, so I make my fate
> More black by feelings full of pain and grief.
>
> Oh then it is a comfort to find one,
> Like you, whose fate is always in the sun,
> And share some part of what is your whole life.[2]

It is surely significant also that Michelangelo, in his huge fresco of *The Last Judgement*, paints his own portrait upon the empty skin of a flayed martyr. Indeed, emptiness is a characteristic plaint of depressives. However much is poured in from outside, it is never enough to fill the aching void.

Great artists who are predominantly of depressive temperament may, like Michelangelo, produce masterpieces over which they have had to labour for years. The less gifted, or the more deprived, may not be able to tolerate long intervals between obtaining the supplies of self-esteem which they need. Some writers, for example, are so driven to produce short works in rapid succession that they never do themselves justice. The immediate rewards of journalism are seductive in this respect. Seeing oneself in print every week, or even every day, is immensely reassuring to some characters. But this need for quick recognition carries the disadvantage that it may preclude the production of more serious, lengthy work. Many journalists cannot face the long period without reward demanded by writing a novel. They 'want it now'; and having found a way of getting it, cannot give up this source of immediate satisfaction.

In addition to gaining self-esteem by producing work which wins him recognition, the depressive can allow to emerge in his work the aggressive feelings which he finds such difficulty in expressing in real, day-to-day encounters with other people. Getting one's own back on parents is, of course, a favourite pastime amongst novelists. Perhaps the most vindictive example is Samuel Butler's *The Way of All Flesh*. But a creative work provides a more subtle vehicle for the expression of aggression than by simply acting as a means of abreacting hostility. Any work which becomes public property is a kind of self-assertion. Most people do not expect that their opinions, tastes or ideas of beauty, will become known beyond the confines of their own immediate circle. The depressive person is less than normally assertive within his own group, on account of his need to ingratiate, and his capacity for identification. If a man habitually says 'Yes' in order to please others, he is in danger of disappearing as a separate entity. The maintenance of individuality requires at least a minimum of self-assertion. But the practice of an art gives a man an opportunity to express himself without any immediate need to fit in with the opinions of others. In fact, the work may be a much more valid piece of self-expression than what is revealed in action or conversation in 'real' life.

When this is so, the work, rather than the person, becomes the focus of self-esteem. Many people of this temperament, during the course of childhood and adolescence, give up hope of being loved for themselves, especially since they habitually conceal their real natures. But the hope raises itself again when they start to create; and so they become intensely sensitive about what they produce, more sensitive than they are about their own defended personalities in ordinary social life. To mind more about one's book or painting than one does about oneself will seem strange to those who are sure enough of themselves to *be* themselves in social relations. But if a book or a painting contains more of the real person than is ever shown in ordinary life, it is not surprising that the producer of it is hypersensitive. A good example is Virginia Woolf, who went through agonies every time she produced a new book, and was desperately vulnerable to what the critics said about it, in spite of the fact that most of them were her intellectual inferiors. Her depressive temperament manifested itself in recurrent attacks of depression and finally in her suicide.

This substitution of the work for the self can be of almost any degree. In special instances, where an artist completely identifies himself with a particular production, it may result in the work never reaching completion. As we shall see when discussing creative block, a work may become 'overdetermined': that is, it may come to be so much a matter of life and death to the creator that he dare not complete it. If the whole of one's self-esteem comes to be bound up in the production of a particular work, it is too dangerous to risk its exposure, and it may, therefore, be put off and put off by means of one excuse after another. More commonly, it becomes impossible to proceed at all, although the reason for the block is generally unconscious. The torments which people suffer, and the compulsive way in which they force themselves to engage in a task which brings no pleasure, but only pain, is often highly distressing.

As I have indicated, depressives bear within them more than the usual share of resentment against parents who, whether in fact or phantasy, may be supposed to have deprived them of the love they needed in infancy. But this hostility has become deeply repressed and, with it, much of the normal 'aggression' which is required in order to maintain the individual as a separate entity, and enable him to stand up to others. It is an unfortunate feature of the human condition that the individual who has, because of its intensity, to defend himself against any possible emergence of his hostility, is also obliged to deprive himself of a normal degree of self-satisfaction. Defences are usually overdone; as can be seen so clearly in the masochistic, submissive adaptation above. Manic-depressives never 'get it right' in their human relations; since they tend either to be overbearing and too assertive, or else submissive and ingratiating.

In certain instances, this repression of aggression may be lifted in producing creative work, which allows the expression of rebellion and hostility without subjecting the artist to the disadvantages of actual confrontation with another person. This is one way round a dilemma characteristic of the depressive; which is that he cannot easily stand up to other people without fearing that the destructive power of his own hostility will annihilate them. Some depressives alternate between being more than usually aggressive towards others, and being more than usually sympathetic. Winston Churchill, for example, was ruthlessly aggressive towards enemies, and often labelled a war-monger. Yet, when enemies were defeated, he was exceptionally magnanimous both privately and publicly. The fear of having been too destructive is compensated for by understanding and generosity.

Rebellion against the past, and therefore against parents and all they have stood for, is another way in which creativity can subserve the expression of aggressive impulses. Revolutionary genius is not the only form of genius; but it is certainly a very important one. Bernard Berenson once defined genius as 'the capacity for productive reaction against one's training';[3] a remark which may not apply to all creative geniuses, but which certainly applies to some. A great innovator, like Beethoven, has to make a break with the past before he can create his own, individual work; and this is in essence an 'aggressive' move, a criticism of what has gone before as insufficient, if not actually irrelevant and false. Stravinsky's remarks about earlier composers whom he despised are as waspish as they are amusing, but he sometimes fails to do justice to those he attacks. It may be necessary for rebellion against the past to be overdone if the way to new conceptions is to be opened; but no one familiar with the utterances of creative artists about either their immediate predecessors or their contemporaries will take such remarks as an expression of balanced judgment. Very often, of course, a revolution in style is greeted with as much 'aggression' as went into creating it. The Impressionists, when their works were first exhibited, outraged and horrified the critics, because, in their eyes, these painters were casting aside all the principles and conventions which had hitherto governed painting.

Which comes first, the destruction of the old, or the creation of the new? Obviously, to the observer, discarding the past must precede the innovation. But, within the mind of the artist, the order might be reversed. Does a new idea ever occur to a person who has not already abandoned or broken with the past? Many people will probably take the latter view; but, in the case of people with a predominantly depressive psychopathology, it is likely that destruction precedes, rather than follows, the development of the new approach.

Melanie Klein's reconstruction of the inner world of the infant is open to many objections, in that it is impossible to prove what she alleges. But her ideas have proved valuable guides in helping us to understand the psychology of both depression and paranoia. Melanie

ein maintains that the infant suffers intense anxiety over the dis-
very that he himself might lose or destroy the person on whom he
depends because of his destructive feelings towards her. The stage is
thus set for the development of guilt. Once the capacity for guilt is
established, the possibility of making reparation also occurs. There
is more than a little truth in the idea that part of the compulsion to
create may be motivated by the idea of making restitution for what
has been destroyed. As Adrian Stokes puts it: 'I believe that in the
creation of art there exists a preliminary element of acting out of
aggression . . . followed by restitution.'⁴ Whereas the schizoid person
is trying to make sense out of an arbitrary and unpredictable universe,
the depressive is trying to replace a world which he feels he has himself destroyed.

What makes a person rebel to the extent that he feels he may have
seriously injured or actually destroyed those against whom he is
rebelling? The person of depressive temperament behaves as if he
were insatiable; as if he had never had enough. It is reasonable to
assume that this is in fact the case. Of course, all mothers are almost
bound to be frustrating at times, and therefore to provoke anger
from their children as well as love. In the case of 'normal' people, the
love so much outweighs the frustration that episodes of the latter,
and therefore of the hate to which it gives rise, can be surmounted
in the surety that love outweighs hate, and that loss of a loving relation is only temporary. The depressive has no such assurance.
When things go wrong between him and the persons with whom he
is emotionally involved it seems as if nothing can restore the balance.
A quarrel is devastating; because there is no firm base to which to
return, no surety of an underlying positive relation. This is why the
depressive's anger is seen by him as so destructive. He must repress
it; for, if he does not, he is in danger of destroying his relation with
his loved person for ever.

It therefore becomes particularly important for persons of depressive temperament to make reparation after any disagreement
with those they love, however trivial. Many such people give lavish
presents after a quarrel; are extravagantly eager to 'make it up'; and
feel very ill at ease until they are quite certain that the loved person
has forgiven them. The reassurance which people of this kind so
constantly seek is really reassurance that the other person can tolerate
the hostility which they are generally able to control, but which is
always in danger of breaking out.

If we can see this process, which must be familiar to many people, in terms of actual day-to-day relationships, we can better understand it as a purely *internal* process in the case of people who make reparation through creativity. A man who destroys the world which has been passed on to him by his mentors, who, by his very innovations, implies that his teachers are either wrong or insufficient, can assuage the sense of guilt which he feels at his rebellion by producing creative work which is acclaimed and recognized as valuable, if not by his teachers themselves, at least by those contemporaries who have insight enough to recognize him. For a man who rebels in this way is destroying, not so much anyone in the outer world as objects in the inner world which, as a small child, he made part of himself or introjected. He is rebelling against the standards he was taught, the beliefs in which he was reared, and the criteria by which he was brought up to live. This leaves a gulf, a void which has to be filled.

Implied in the work of every artist is his own individual point of view. As Somerset Maugham writes: 'The fact remains that to describe a novelist as a mere story-teller is to dismiss him with contumely. I venture to suggest that there is no such creature. By the incidents he chooses to relate, the characters he selects and his attitude towards them, the author offers you a criticism of life. It may not be a very original one, or very profound, but it is there; and consequently, though he may not know it, he is in his own modest way a moralist.'[5]

Reparation is one way of dealing with depression; the so-called 'manic defence' is another. When a man becomes manic, he reverses and denies his depression. Characteristically, he becomes overactive, as a contrast to the inhibition of activity in depression. Instead of being sensitive to the needs and wishes of others, he becomes inconsiderate, irritable, demanding; often riding roughshod over other people or attacking them without consideration. Instead of being depressed, he alleges that he feels splendid, and triumphantly proclaims his ability to overcome every obstacle. Instead of professing poverty or lack of ability, he omnipotently claims both wealth and complete self-confidence.

It is fairly easy to detect the presence of the depression such a person is attempting to deny. The whole attitude of omnipotence is overdone. The expansive gestures are hollow; the wealth has no secure base; the claimed skills no proof in reality. And yet the manic defence can work for a while; so long as the person does not become exhausted. Moreover, what is produced, in the case of a creative person, is not

D

necessarily inferior to the work achieved in more sober moments.

The composer Robert Schumann is a good example. Although some biographers have erroneously labelled him schizophrenic, there can be no real doubt that his mental disorder was manic-depressive, as Eliot Slater and Alfred Meyer have demonstrated. Schumann had mood-swings of considerable amplitude throughout his life. Careful examination of the relation between these changes of mood and the compositions which Schumann produced reveals that his creativity was associated with periods in which he was excited and happy, whereas the coming of a depressive episode tended to stop production. 'If one examines a chart of Schumann's production against the years, the inhibitory effect of his depressive phases and the excitatory effect of the elevated phases are made strikingly obvious. 1840 and 1849 were his peak years, and in both of them he was in a consistently elevated mood throughout the year. In most of the other years he had some weeks or months of depression, not enough to distinguish one year from another on the chart; but the year 1844 was remarkable for low spirits practically throughout the entire year. It was also noteworthy that, regardless of quality, his production was consistently high in the four years 1850-3. Despite the onset of symptoms of an organic type (it is likely that Schumann developed GPI in addition to his manic-depressive disorder) he was unusually free from depressive and hypochondriacal moods during these years, apart from a phase of depression in April and May 1852.'[6] In 1854 Schumann threw himself into the Rhine, was rescued, but spent the remaining two years of his life in hospital. Of course, if a person becomes so manic that he is obviously mentally ill, he is unlikely to produce very much good work, since he is usually too restless to settle to it, and also is only too likely to mistake phantasy for reality in believing that the ideas which teem through his over-active brain are as much proof of his powers as if they had been more carefully worked out and committed to paper. But at least some great creators appear to have produced masterpieces when running as hard as they could from their underlying depressions, and being very overactive and grandiose in the process.

It is likely that Balzac was of manic-depressive constitution. His physique was that generally associated with this temperament; pyknic, that is to say, with short legs, a prematurely protuberant belly, a plump, rather flabby face, and a habit of talking both a great deal and very loudly. Nor is it only his genetic constitution which supports the supposition that he had more than his share of psycho-pathology. As was customary in those days (he was born on 20th May 1799) he was put out to nurse. But his wet-nurse resided some way away, and his mother seldom visited him. 'Honoré never forgave his mother for letting him be thus separated from her: "Who can say how much physical or moral harm was done me by my mother's coldness? Was I no more than a child of marital duty, my birth a matter of chance . . .? Put out to nurse in the country, neglected by my family for three years, when I was brought home I counted for so little that people were sorry for me . . ." Later he was to say, "I never had a mother".'[7] One biographer, André Maurois, refers to this statement as 'a cruel exaggeration, written in a moment of anger'. However, he percipiently goes on: 'But a child's feelings are none the less acute for being in part unwarranted. There are bastards of the imagination, born in wedlock, who nevertheless feel themselves to be rejected by their parents, without knowing why. These more than others long for worldly triumphs, to compensate for their deep-rooted sense of loss.'[8] At the age of eight he was sent to the Oratorian College at Vendôme where he remained for the next six years, without once visiting his own home. According to his own account, his mother only visited him twice during this period, although the school was but thirty-five miles distant.[9] This is good evidence of actual, real neglect on the part of Balzac's mother, as is the parsimony which gave him so little pocket-money that he could not share in the games and pastimes of his companions.

Whatever the original cause may have been, Balzac remained, throughout his life, insatiable; hungry both for love and for fame, as if there was a void inside him which no amount of supplies from out-side could ever fill. Whilst still a schoolboy, he would say 'I shall be famous'; and, very early in life, he developed the idea that the will had a limitless power if only a man could learn to concentrate and train it enough. He believed, at any rate in youth, that the world was a jungle, and that success came to the man who, like his famous criminal character, Vautrin, used men and women as pawns and pursued his own ends by means of ruthless calculation. In 1820, he was writing to a friend: 'Before long I shall possess the secret of that mysterious power. I shall compel all men to obey me and all women to love me.' If anyone finds it hard to believe in the psychoanalytic concept of omnipotence which we have already discussed, let him turn to the life and opinions of Balzac. 'My only and immense desires, to be famous and to be loved!' he proclaimed. He achieved both; but it did not prevent him killing himself by creative work; for fame and love were not enough to fill the aching void within which was the fruit of his mother's rejection and coldness to him.

There is also evidence of his mood swings. 'Honoré either thinks himself everything or nothing,' wrote his mother, and his sister Laure wrote back to her: 'Where will you find anyone who equals him in kindness? Honoré is changeable in his moods, it is true, sometimes sad, sometimes gay, but what does that matter? Everyone has their weaknesses.'[10]

In his own correspondence, Balzac refers to himself as 'being born to unhappiness' and, in spite of his grandiose phantasies, as being 'a mediocrity, possessed only of a spirit without fire or ferment . . . a dwarf cannot lift the club of Hercules.' At twenty-five he was found by a friend looking over the parapet of a bridge into the Seine and admitted to him that he was contemplating suicide.

The contrast between his imagined ruthlessness, his belief in the use of the will to outwit and exploit others, and his actual kindness and generosity, is typical. As we have seen, the person of depressive temperament is often unusually kind and generous, and also perceptive of the needs of others. That this partly springs from an over-anxiety to please, a need to ingratiate and a drive to make restitution, need not detract from the very positive virtues of such behaviour. But Balzac showed the other side of these virtues in his writings, in which it sometimes seems that the ruthless pursuit of power and money is the only thing which matters, and that love and the more tender emotions are either non-existent, or serve as stepping stones to the attainment of fame. That Balzac's ambition was pathological hardly needs underlining. In his study was a statuette of Napoleon with a piece of paper attached to the scabbard of the figure's sword. 'What he did not achieve by the sword I shall achieve by the pen. *Honoré de Balzac.*'

Everything that Balzac did was larger than life; a typical 'manic' characteristic. His spending was prodigious, so much so that he was constantly in debt. Some of those who have written about him attribute his gross overwork to the need to pay off his debts, and Somerset Maugham, drawing heavily on André Billy's biography, goes so far as to say that: 'It was only under the pressure of debt that he could bring himself to write. Then he would work till he was pale and worn out, and in these circumstances he wrote some of his best novels; but when by some miracle he was not in harrowing straits, when the brokers left him in peace, when editors and publishers were not bringing actions, his invention seemed to fail him and he could not bring himself to put pen to paper.'[11]

It may be that he used debt as a device to force himself to write. Debt can be used like an editor's deadline, as an outside authority which spurs the flagging will into action. But Balzac was always convinced that he could earn a fortune from his writings (and in fact did so, though he never caught up with his expenditure). It seems even more likely that his grandiose, manic imagination constantly mistook the promise of the future for the reality of the present; that he was always certain that his next book would pay for the gross extravagances which he could not wait to indulge himself in, and which again were attempts to compensate himself for what had been missing in his early childhood.

It is interesting that he got his own back on his mother by extracting from her a very large sum to save him from bankruptcy after the failure of his printing and publishing business. This business, incidentally, was financed by his mistress, Madame de Berny, who was forty-five to Balzac's twenty-two; and who clearly represented to him the mother he had never felt himself to have, as well as a lover. (She was actually older than his mother.) Her Christian name, Laure, was that of his mother and also of his favourite sister. Somerset Maugham harshly condemns Balzac for saying that his mother had ruined him: 'That was a shocking thing to say; for, it was he who had ruined her.'[12] But, however much one may condemn him for sponging on his mother, and depriving her of a large portion of her fortune, there seems little doubt that she was in fact both cold and neglectful, and that, however unjustified his condemnation of her may have been on financial grounds, it was correct in terms of feeling and emotion.

The alternation so characteristic of the manic-depressive temperament shows itself in other ways than fluctuation of mood. Balzac alternated orgies of work with orgies of pleasure; and both were so extreme as to be pathological. When working his programme was: dinner at 6 pm, bed till 1 am, work till 8 am, rest till 9.30, then a cup of coffee, and work again till 4 pm. From 4 till dinner at 6 he might receive visitors, or go out of doors, or have a bath. Then the cycle would start again; and he could keep this up for weeks. Whilst working, he ate and drank little; but these frugal periods alternated with gargantuan feasts in which he would empty four bottles of

87

Vouvray without apparent effect, and gorge himself to repletion on oysters and cutlets.

It was typical of manic expansiveness that Balzac should have appropriated the arms of a family which was not his, and added the particule 'de' to his name so that people should suppose him to be of noble birth. In addition, he overdressed and furnished his house with a lavishness which he could not afford. (Manic patients habitually overspend.) He also talked too much; and, although he was very entertaining, was only at his best when he was holding the floor. In spite of his gross overwork, he was almost always late in fulfilling his contracts.This was partly because he corrected and recorrected his proofs so often that they were almost impossible to decipher. The novel *Pierrette* had twenty-nine proofs.

It is also characteristic that he should invent extravagant tales about even his most mundane possessions. A ring given him in Vienna was stolen from the Grand Mogul. His coffee must needs be especially blended. His tea was supposed to come from a supply presented by the Emperor of China to the Emperor of Russia; the plants having been tended by mandarins, and the leaves plucked before dawn by maidens, 'who bore it with song to the Emperor's feet'.[13] His walking-sticks were encrusted with jewels. When he died, at the age of fifty-one, he owed 83,502 francs, although his assets amounted to twice that amount.

Balzac illustrates rather well that a manic defence can in fact work for a long period to protect a person against the depression which underlies it. Balzac's extravagance, flashiness, snobbery, and his habit of holding the floor were all efforts to bolster his self-esteem. His immense body of work, never finished, was a grandiose conception. Other writers have contented themselves with writing about a small section of society, and have often failed if they moved outside this. Balzac took the whole of society, indeed the whole human condition, for his theme. *La Comédie humaine* is what it says it is. Balzac had an astonishing technical knowledge based upon detailed observation. When he describes how a lawyer lived, or a moneylender operated, or a journalist obtained work, one may be sure that he knew what he was writing about. He had an extraordinary passion for facts. Balzac's imagination was one of the most remarkable that there has ever been; but it was an imagination which took flight from a solid basis of fact. His characters are intensifications and exaggerations of reality. They may be oversimplified. Ruling passions are seldom quite as imperious as Balzac painted them. But his characters convince because they are based on observation. The fact that they are larger than life is a manic exaggeration. Baudelaire wrote: 'From the peak of the aristocracy to the lowest level of the plebs, all the actors in the Comédie are more furious in living, more vigorous and cunning in conflict, more long-suffering in misfortune, more greedy in pleasure, more angelic in devotion, than the comedy of the real world shows them to be.'[14] This is true; but Balzac's exaggerations are based upon the reality of the external world. If we contrast his imagination with that of an introverted, schizoid writer like Kafka, we at once see how realistic he is in comparison. This is especially so when he comes to write about money, a subject too often avoided by so-called 'realistic' novelists.

When discussing Newton and Einstein we described the new world order which each created as essentially solipsistic. The remarkable thing about each system was how far it actually did correspond to the realities of the external world and could be shown to do so by experiment. But the theory came first; the proof afterwards, as Einstein revealed himself when he made the remark, already quoted, that 'theory can be proved by experiment; but no path leads from experiment to the birth of a theory'.

Balzac, the extravert, propounds precisely the opposite theory. When it first occurred to him to bring all his novels within a single, grand design, he described in a letter how he would start with *Etudes de Moeurs*, 'a complete picture of society'. This would be followed by *Etudes philosophiques*, 'the why of sentiments, the what of life'. In the former there would be individuals treated as types; in the latter, types depicted as individuals. Then comes the *Etudes analytiques*, in which principles are described, as opposed to effects and causes. 'But having composed the poem, the exposition of an entire system, I shall propound its scientific theory in an 'Essai sur les forces humaines.'

In other words, Balzac is also a system-maker, like the scientists. But he proceeds from without inwards, unlike the great physical theorists. First, he describes the facts; then their apparent causes; and only then attempts to construct a theory. It is the exact opposite to the way of thinking of an introverted theorist, although, of course, the latter's achievement also depends on knowing many facts.

Balzac killed himself by his manic overactivity. In 1848, the year of revolutions, he certainly had a recurrence of depression, complicated by his increasing cardiac failure. Characteristically, this followed upon a longish period when he had not been working as hard as usual. The remarkable thing about his activity is how effectively it did protect him. In fact it is not uncommon, in ordinary life rather than in psychiatric practice, to encounter individuals of similar temperament and behaviour. The inability to stop working, to enjoy holidays, to allow time for relaxation or personal relationships, is often found amongst intensely ambitious men. In psychiatric practice, it is more often found amongst politicians and financiers than amongst artists. Millionaires are often of this character structure. Politicians often arrange life so that they are busily engaged all the time they are awake. When Parliament is sitting, they need never come home at night. When it is not, there is the constituency, the books and papers to be read, the committees to attend, the associations and societies demanding speeches. Political life is an ideal one for men who need to be ceaselessly occupied, who are driven to seek power by an inner insecurity, and who substitute extraverted activity for the self-knowledge which comes from cultivating personal relationships. There are many who go straight from work to sleep, with little or no interval between the two, in which self-doubt might assail, or depression cloud, the prospect before them. Defences of a manic, hyperactive kind are many and various; but, as this chapter has demonstrated, the reason why some of the creative use their gift in this way is that creative production can be a particularly effective method of protecting the self from the threat of an underlying depression.

REFERENCES

1. See STORR, Anthony. 'The Man', in *Churchill: Four Faces and the Man* (London: Allen Lane The Penguin Press, 1969).
2. MICHELANGELO. *The Sonnets of Michelangelo*, No. XLI, trans. Elizabeth Jennings (London: The Folio Society 1961) p. 67.
3. BERENSON, Bernard. *The Italian Painters of the Renaissance* (London: Phaidon Press, 1959) p. 201.
4. STOKES, Adrian. *The Invitation in Art* (London: Tavistock Publications, 1965) p. 23.
5. MAUGHAM, Somerset. *Ten Novels and their Authors* (London: Heinemann, 1954) p. 17.
6. SLATER, Eliot and Meyer, Alfred. 'Contributions to a Pathography of the Musicians: Robert Schumann', *Confinia Psychiatrica 2*, 65-94 (1959).

7. MAUROIS, André. *Prometheus: The Life of Balzac*, trans. Norman Denny (London: Bodley Head, 1965) pp. 24, 28.

8. Ibid, p. 28.

9. HUNT, Herbert J. *Honoré de Balzac* (University of London, Athlone Press, 1957).

10. MAUROIS, André. *Prometheus: The Life of Balzac*, trans. Norman Denny (London: Bodley Head) 1965, pp. 93, 95.

11. MAUGHAM, Somerset. *Ten Novels and their Authors* (London: Heinemann, 1954) p. 111.

12. Ibid, p. 111.

13. HUNT, Herbert J. *Honoré de Balzac* (University of London, Athlone Press, 1957) pp. 128-9.

14. Quoted in MAUROIS, André. *Prometheus: The Life of Balzac*, trans. Norman Denny (London: Bodley Head, 1965) p. 420.

8

Creativity and the Obsessional Character

The relation between creativity and the obsessional character is of considerable interest, since many of the world's great creators have exhibited obsessional symptoms and traits of character. Dickens, Swift, Dr Johnson, Ibsen, Stravinsky, Rossini and Beethoven are amongst this distinguished company. And yet, in many ways, the obsessional personality so familiar to us from description in psychiatric and pyschoanalytic textbooks might be supposed to be the very opposite of creative in personality and temperament. For we rightly associate creativity with spontaneity, freedom, and an absence of fixed preconception; whereas the obsessional is controlled, inhibited, and rigid in his ideas. The exploration of this apparent contradiction is, I believe, valuable in throwing light upon the creative process.

Perhaps the most striking feature of the obsessional temperament is the compulsive need to control both the self and the environment. Disorder and spontaneity must be avoided so far as is possible, since both appear threatening and unpredictable. One feature of this need to control is the extreme tidiness so characteristic of obsessionals. If there is a place for everything and everything is in its place, then order and control have been achieved. Since dirt is commonly regarded as disorder, as something alien which has intruded itself into a system, rather than being a natural part of it, an excessive concern with cleanliness is a frequent concomitant of obsessionality. Rooms must be free of dust; clothes both neat and free from stain; the body itself free of both grime and odour. The obsessional's habitual disgust with bodily functions, especially with those of excretion, entirely bears out Freud's contention that the origin of obsessionality is connected with the training of the child to order and control its excretory processes. A perusal of *Gulliver's Travels* will rapidly disclose Swift's preoccupation with both urination and defaecation, and his disgust with the body. On Gulliver's return from his voyage to the Houyhnhnms, he cannot even bear his wife to kiss him.

'As soon as I entered the House, my Wife took me in her Arms, and kissed me; at which, having not been used to the Touch of that odious Animal for so many Years. I fell in a swoon for almost an Hour. At the Time I am writing, it is five Years since my last Return to England; during the first Year I could not endure my Wife or Children in my Presence, the very Smell of them was intolerable; much less could I suffer them to eat in the same Room. To this Hour they dare not presume to touch my Bread, or drink out of the same Cup; neither was I ever able to let one of them take me by the hand.'[1]

Disgust with the products of excretion commonly extends itself to include other bodily functions; so that sweat, sputum, nasal and aural secretions, and also semen, all become included under the one heading. Anxiety which was originally focused upon controlling the elimination of urine and faeces attaches itself to anything which comes out of the body. The form of impotence known as *ejaculatio retardans*, in which orgasm is either long delayed, or else never occurs at all, is generally a disorder to be found in obsessionals who want to control their sexuality, just as they want to control everything else, and who dare not 'let go' even when such abandonment of control is appropriate. Constipation, is of course, common; and the advertisements for laxatives which lay stress on the virtues of 'inner cleanliness' are aimed at obsessionals.

The tight control which has become habitual often makes it difficult for obsessionals to dive, to turn head over heels, or to vault a gymnasium horse; all activities which necessitate letting go at a critical moment.

Even if one does not accept the Freudian equation of money with faeces, it is easy to understand that obsessionals are likely to be parsimonious and miserly. Free spending is a form of letting go. It also involves a disregard for the future which is alien to the obsessional, who is concerned to make the future as controlled and predictable as possible. Obsessionals plan, insure, and look ahead in order that they may not suffer the anxiety of the unexpected. In very many ways, they live in the future to the detriment of their experience of the present. If one is constantly preoccupied with what *may* happen, it is difficult or impossible to be fully engaged in savouring and appreciating what is happening in the here and now. Obsessionals may, for this reason, entirely fail to be carried away by emotion in theatre or concert hall; they are too preoccupied with planning how to get home or with being on time for their train.

A meticulous concern with exactness is another obsessional characteristic. In some walks of life this kind of precision is obligatory, and those who possess it naturally are at an advantage. Bank clerks, who used to spend much of their time adding columns of figures and making sure that their books balanced, are often of obsessional temperament; and so are those who, like lexicographers and parlimentary draughtsmen, are chiefly concerned with absolute precision in the meaning of words and sentences. For the writer, this is a double-edged characteristic. Precision in the use of words is of course valuable; but it can be carried to the point of absurdity. Dorothy Parker, the American short-story writer, said in an interview: 'It takes me six months to do a story. I think it out and then write it sentence by sentence—no first draft. I can't write five words but that I change seven.'[2] Jean Cocteau wrote of himself: 'My worst defect comes to me from childhood, like nearly all that I have. For I remain the victim of those obsessive rhythms which make some children idiots ... arranging their plates in a special way at table, or stepping over certain grooves in the pavement. In the midst of my work these symptoms grip me, forcing me to resist that which is pushing me along, involving me in some strange crippled style of writing, hindering me from saying what I would.'[3] The reluctance of some obsessional writers to 'let go' and take the risk of letting their ideas and feelings pour out of them often manifests itself in a kind of obsessive seeking for absolute correctness, to the detriment of their productivity.

At what point does a concern with precision becomes pathological? It is often difficult to say: just as it is sometimes difficult to distinguish between a reasonable precaution and an obsessional ritual. One important distinction is that between a compulsion which the individual resents or feels to be absurd, and a meticulous bit of behaviour in which he engages voluntarily. To have to check the front-door or the gas-taps, when one *knows* that they are safe, is pathological. To feel oneself compelled to go over and over a composition even though one knows it is unlikely to be improved by so doing is also abnormal. But deliberately to try to improve that with which one is dissatisfied, or to check what one is not sure of, should not be regarded as obsessive behaviour. In other words, a compulsion to check and re-check only becomes a pathological symptom when the individual *knows* that such re-checking is unnecessary, but feels compelled to carry out this activity *against* his conscious intention. In such cases, the re-checking activity has turned into a ritual which signifies something other than a need to make sure.

A woman who felt compelled to arrange and rearrange her hair before she could go out to such an extent that it might take hours before she could make herself venture forth was really demonstrating a feeling of her own unacceptability. It is rational to be neat and tidy. It is normal to take trouble about one's appearance, in order to make oneself attractive and acceptable to others. But there must come a point at which preoccupation with appearance becomes abnormal, although it is hard to say exactly where this point may be. In Victorian times it was not abnormal for a young woman in high society to start dressing for a dinner party at 4.30 in the afternoon. But in these days, when clothes are simpler, and the social climate less hierarchical, such lengthy preparation would generally be a sign of obsessional psychopathology.

Another woman used, from time to time, to become obsessed with the length of her skirt. This not only had to be exactly even all the way round; but also exactly the 'right' length. If it was too short, people would notice and think that she was indecent, or a bit of a whore. If it was too long, they would consider her frumpish and old-fashioned. The result of this preoccupation was that she wasted hours of time altering the length of her skirts, or a great deal of money in constantly taking them back for alteration to the dressmaker. They could, of course, never be exactly the 'right' length since what was felt to be wrong could not be put right by a merely external activity. When what may start as a rational concern becomes an obsessional ritual, a shift in meaning has taken place, so that an external activity comes to represent an inner psychological process. This woman found herself unable to come to terms with what she found unacceptable in herself. Although very largely unaware of it, she was seething with resentment. Ostensibly 'Christian' and unselfish, she was actually 'selfish' in that her household was often incommoded by her symptoms. At some level, she knew that she was not as 'nice' as she appeared. She therefore had to take especial plans to keep up her appearance of 'niceness', or else other people might detect what she was really like. Her rituals were a way of trying to pretend to herself and others that she was as 'nice' as she appeared.

If a child has been made to feel guilty enough in early childhood about the natural dirtiness, untidiness, and carelessness of appearance characteristic of his age, he will tend to carry into adult life an excessive concern with all these externals. He will also take with him a load of resentment. It probably requires an authoritarian or morally disapproving background to make a child feel sufficiently guilty to develop severe obsessional symptoms in adult life, although many children exhibit some as a passing phase. More especially, a good many children are brought up in such a way that they never feel loved in the irrational way that we all demand; to be loved irrespective of how we behave; 'for ourselves' alone. Sensitive children may quickly learn that love is conditional on good behaviour; and that if they are dirty, untidy, careless or uncontrolled in any way, love will be withdrawn from them. Moreover, parents with such standards are often excessively concerned with what the neighbours think; so that the child comes to believe that good manners are more important than spontaneous feeling, and tidiness and cleanliness more essential than being able to let go and enjoy oneself.

Obsessional rituals of the kind described are pathological and often disabling. The compulsive hand-washer, the obsessional cleaner and tidier, the checker of gas-taps, the cook who has to sieve everything in case there is broken glass in it, the woman who has to have a bath every time she has defaecated, are all wasting time, and displacing what should be a concern with their inner life on to externals of little importance. They are either using their rituals to ward off sexual and aggressive impulses which would come to the surface if they were given any opportunity to do so; or they are defending themselves against a depressive or schizoid state; or, like the woman described above, they are trying to ward off paranoid ideas that other people would attack and denigrate them. The obsessional behaviour is, in these instances, essentially defensive. It is a symbolic attempt to purge the mind of unacceptable emotions and impulses. It fails, because one cannot ultimately expel parts of one's own nature. In the end, one has to assimilate, or continue to be neurotic. We have to accept that both we and Celia shit; that we are selfish, grasping and often hostile: that we have sexual desires which are not 'nice'; that we are envious and competitive.

But what is surprising is that the same kind of obsessive activity which we have just labelled pathological can also serve a positive function. Many small children go through a period of obsessionality without turning into obsessional neurotics in later life. Such children often demand ritual observances from their parents at bed-time, in order to ward off the dangers of the dark. They demand that the process of saying good-night should be exactly repeated in the same order; or that the bedclothes should be arranged in a particular way;

or that the toy animals should be mustered in a rank order. These precautions no doubt serve the function of exemplifying symbolic control over impulses which, in the dark, are apt to come into the child's consciousness in a way which they do not during the busy extraversion of the day. The fact is, however, that these precautions often work; and the child who might lie awake fearfully if the rites were not performed goes cheerfully to sleep because of them.

Moreover, the rituals which children themselves carry out, rather than asking their parents to perform, can also be seen as having a positive function. The 'lines and squares' ritual on city pavements; the ritual counting of steps; the balancing between left and right, so that equality is maintained, may seem as futile as the compulsions we have earlier described in adults. But these transient rituals of childhood may in fact be the beginning of autonomy, and signify a break away from dependence upon the parents. For directly a child begins to perform his *own* rituals, he is asserting his ability to protect himself against the dangers of both outer and inner worlds, rather than demanding that his parents shall do it for him. The rituals are serving the function of easing the transition from the complete dependency of earliest childhood to the partial independence of the latency period; and all such transitions, like those of adolescence, for example, are marked by an increase in symbolic, ritualized behaviour which has the purpose of underlining and rendering actual the inner, psychological change. Moreover, a ritual, at first indistinguishable from the kind of compulsion we have been describing, may actually serve a valuable purpose by putting a person in touch with his own inner life, or by inducing in him a state of mind conducive to health and progress. Religion has always made use of ritual for inducing suitable states of mind in the faithful, whether what is desired be penitence, exaltation or simply a state of reverent attention during which the worshipper may receive the Holy Spirit. Freud, in an early paper on 'Obsessive Actions and Religious Practices', compares the ceremonials of religion with the rituals of the neurotic. 'Thus a ceremonial starts as an *action for defence* or *insurance, a protective measure.*

'The sense of guilt of obsessional neurotics finds its counterpart in the protestations of pious people that they know that at heart they are miserable sinners; and the pious observances (such as prayers, invocations, etc,) with which such people preface every daily act, and in especial every unusual undertaking, seem to have the value of defensive or protective measures.'[4]

But is religious ritual no more than a way of warding off repressed instincts of sex and aggression which threaten to raise their ugly heads? Freud recognizes that obsessive acts contain an element of compromise in that they may give indirect or partial expression to the very impulses against which they act as a defence. Thus, a compulsive handwasher whom I knew felt compelled to wash each finger separately by rubbing it up and down inside the closed palm of the other hand. Every time he washed his hands he was making an obscene gesture signifying coitus. The ritual had started originally as an attempt to purge himself of the guilt surrounding masturbation. He was both cleansing himself of sexual guilt, and, indirectly, expressing sexuality at the same time. According to Freud, religions all demand instinctual renunciation but 'the character of compromise which obsessive actions possess in their capacity as neurotic symptoms is the character least easily detected in corresponding religious observances. Yet here, too, one is reminded of this feature of neuroses when one remembers how commonly all the facts which religion forbids—the expressions of the instincts it has suppressed—are committed precisely in the name of, and ostensibly for the sake of, religion.'[5]

Here, although he does not say so, Freud may be thinking of the sadism of the Inquisition, the intolerance and quarrelsomeness of religious fanatics, or even of the curious practices of the early Christians, whose dislike of sex resulted in the most particular regulations on the subject. 'The enumeration of the very whimsical laws, which they most circumstantially imposed on the marriage-bed, would force a smile from the young, and a blush from the fair.'[6] It is fairly obvious that enormously detailed catalogues of forbidden sexual sins are both listing prohibitions and simultaneously revealing a compulsive interest in the subject, thus fulfilling the compromise which Freud postulates.

It is odd, however, that Freud lays so little emphasis upon the fact that ritual may have a positive function.

The technique of psychoanalysis itself displays ritual elements. The quiet room, the patient's position on the couch, and the analyst's seat behind him; the omission of conventional greeting, the fixed length of the session, are all conventions which serve the purpose of better enabling the patient to get in touch with his own inner world.

Indeed, Freud did recognize this, when he refers to 'ceremonial' in his paper of 1913 'On Beginning the Treatment'. 'Before I wind up these remarks on beginning analytic treatment, I must say a word about a certain ceremonial which concerns the position in which the treatment is carried out. I hold to the plan of getting the patient to lie on a sofa while I sit behind him out of his sight.'[7] Yet Freud seems to have continued to regard ritual almost exclusively in terms of defence, and very little in terms of any positive function. This is perhaps because of his ambivalence, already noted in an earlier chapter, towards the value of creative activity. If creativity is invariably regarded as a substitute for more primitive activities, rather than as possessing value in its own right, then it is natural enough to look upon rituals which conduce to the creative performance as defensive rather than constructive. Although, as we have seen in the last two chapters, creative activity can be regarded as a defence against schizoid or depressive states, and is certainly used as such in some instances, it would be facile to regard this as the whole story. It seems more probable that man's creativity is but one example of a whole range of activities which he undertakes because he is so constituted that he cannot achieve complete satisfaction from purely 'instinctive' behaviour. In other words, 'Man shall not live by bread alone';[8] a truth which needs restating in different words, since psychoanalysis constantly implies that happiness is almost exclusively dependent upon sexual fulfilment. This subject will be further discussed in a later chapter.

However this may be, there is no doubt of the positive function of obsessional ritual. A number of artists display ritual behaviour which serves the purpose of inducing the right frame of mind for creative activity; and many cannot start work without some ceremonial. Stravinsky's study in Hollywood, described by Nicolas Nabokov, demonstrated clearly the need for obsessional ritualization characteristic of this composer. 'An extraordinary room, perhaps the best planned and organized work-room I have seen in my life. In a space which is not larger than some twenty-five feet by forty feet stand two pianos (one grand, one upright) and two desks (a small elegant writing desk and a draughtsman's table). In two cupboards with glass shelves are books, scores, and sheet music, arranged in alphabetical order. Between the two pianos, the cupboards, and desks, are scattered a few small tables (one of which is a kind of "smoker's delight": it exhibits all sorts of cigarette boxes, lighters, holders, fluids, flints, and pipe cleaners), five or six comfortable chairs, and the couch Stravinsky used for his afternoon naps.' As Eric Walter White, his biographer, observes: 'For Stravinsky, the act of composition is an ordered rite that demands a work-room equipped with the appropriate instruments and tools.' Ramuz described his manuscripts thus: 'Stravinsky's scores are magnificent. He is above all (in all matters and in every sense of the word) a calligrapher ... His writing desk resembled a surgeon's instrument case. Bottles of different coloured inks in their hierarchy had each a separate part to play in the ordering of his art. Nearby were indiarubbers of various kinds and shapes and all sorts of glittering steel implements: rulers, erasers, pen-knives, and a roulette instrument for drawing staves invented by Stravinsky himself. One was reminded of the definition of St Thomas: beauty is the splendour of order. All the large pages of the score were filled with writing with the help of different coloured inks—blue, green, red, two kinds of black (Ordinary and Chinese), each having its purpose, its meaning, its special use: one for the notes, another the text, a third the translation; one for titles, another for the musical directions; meanwhile the bar lines were ruled, and the mistakes carefully erased.'

As E. W. White observes: 'There is something rather inhuman about these meticulously planned and written pages, in which the composer seems to be emulating the characterless finish of an engraved plate.'[9] Although Mr White would probably not agree, some might think that this inhumanity is reflected in at least some of Stravinsky's compositions, which can reflect the aridity and lack of spontaneity apt to bedevil obsessionals to whom spontaneity of feeling is a problem. Stravinsky's fear of loss of control, which we have already discussed as an obsessional characteristic, is very evident. 'Stravinsky's reaction from *The Rite of Spring* was severe. He seems to have felt he had given free rein to the Dionysian impulse and it was time to pull up before matters got out of control. The first signs of change were his concentration on small scale ensembles instead of the big orchestras demanded by the earlier scores.'[10] For Stravinsky, *The Rite of Spring* was a psychological landmark. 'The powerful originality of *The Rite of Spring* represented an important personal victory gained by Stravinsky over the inhibitions of his miserable childhood. For years he had tried to revolt from the stultifying restrictions of his family life; and now that he had succeeded in doing so in terms of artistic expression, it was particularly appropriate that the image that had precipitated his release should have been that of spring—"the violent Russian spring that seemed to begin in an hour and was like the whole world cracking", and which, by his own admission, was the most wonderful event of every year of his childhood.'[11]

The composer Rossini was famous for the rapidity with which he worked. According to his own account, admittedly written long after the event, he completed *Il Barbiere de Siviglia* in thirteen days.[12] At first sight, it would seem unlikely that this apparently uninhibited bon viveur should display any obsessional traits. Yet, when it came to composition, at any rate during the latter part of his life, the resemblance to the account of Stravinsky given above is very striking. The Roman painter, De Sanctis, gives the following description (quoted in Weinstock's biography of the composer).

'Rossini takes the greatest pains when copying out his writings, never wearying of perfecting them, often going back to read them over and alter notes, which he is in the habit of erasing with a scraper with truly singular patience. One never would say that a man of such fervent imagination could lend himself to such minutiae. Another thing that I observed about him was the regularity of his habits, not to mention the symmetrical order in which he placed the furniture and objects around him. The room that he habitually occupied for many hours a day, both for receiving and for working, was his bedroom. There, the writing table was in the centre, and on it set out in perfect order were the papers, his indispensable scrapers, the pens, the inkstand, and whatever else he needed for his writing. Three or four wigs were placed in a row on the mantel, evenly spaced. On the white walls hung some Japanese miniatures on rice paper, and some Oriental objects had been placed like a trophy on the chest of drawers; the bed, against the wall, always neat; a few simple chairs around the room. It all had the look of neatness and order, which it is a pleasure to see, but which did not give the notion of a room lived in by an artist, whom we more easily imagine inclined to disorder. When, struck by that perfect orderliness, I showed my surprise to the Maestro, he said to me: "Eh, my dear fellow, order is wealth".'[13]

Interestingly enough, there is some evidence that Rossini was of manic-depressive temperament (which, of course, is not incompatible with obsessionality), although the clinical picture is complicated by the chronic urethritis and other physical disabilities from which he suffered. During 1839-43 he experienced many episodes of severe depression, 'moods of black despair, at times so unreasoning as to resemble incipient madness'.[14] Rossini retired from operatic composition in 1829, at the age of thirty-seven, after having completed *William Tell*. It has for long been supposed that this was because he could not face competition with Meyerbeer, whose operas gained more performances than his own; but contemporary evidence does not support this. It seems probable that there were two factors. First, Rossini's eighteenth-century style was being superseded by romanticism, and he found himself out of sympathy with 'the new music'. As he said himself: 'Retiring in time requires genius too.'[15] Second, it seems possible that his ill-health and tendency to depression played a part in his retirement. Certainly his bad health continued for many years, during which he composed very little. It was not until 1857 that he began to compose again. From then until his death in 1868 he produced a variety of compositions, mostly fairly short, which he designated *Péchés de Vieillesse*—sins of old age, and some religious music. It appears that his urge to compose reasserted itself as his spirits improved.

Both Rossini and Stravinsky clearly exhibit the meticulousness and extreme tidiness so characteristic of the obsessional personality; yet both are productive in a way which one might not expect, judging from the inhibitions upon producing anything with which we are familiar in studying obsessional neurotics. It is probable that the extreme orderliness of the desks and tools of the trade is an outward and visible sign of the order which these composers wish to produce in their compositions. Instead of their tidiness being a time-wasting compulsion, it has turned into a 'rite d'entrée'; a ceremonial observance which facilitates, rather than hinders, composition.

In certain instances, even the restrictions and inhibitions which limit the free expression of an obsessional personality in actual living can act as a spur to creative production. Often there is within such an individual a wish to rebel, to free himself from the inhibitions of conscience, and the compulsions of exactitude. The drive towards self-realization may represent a wish to achieve a new autonomy; freedom from the nagging voice of a Puritan super-ego; or even, in some cases, freedom from the restrictions of the hated body itself. These motives appear clearly enough in the work of the playwright, Ibsen. (Freud, incidentally, was particularly interested in Ibsen, and wrote a character analysis of Rebecca in *Rosmersholm*.)[16]

Ibsen possessed nearly all the obsessional traits of character which we have so far mentioned. In early life, he developed a pernickety interest in clothes; invariably took a long time to dress in the morning; and would retreat behind a hedge rather than risk his clothes being dirtied by a passing vehicle. His passion for order and cleanliness was reflected in the rooms in which he worked, where never a speck of dust was allowed to obtrude itself. Although a compulsive rewriter, who destroyed, scribbled over, and corrected his manuscripts again and again, the final copy despatched to his publisher was invariably immaculate. He was intolerant of unpunctuality, and himself over-anxious about time, always arriving far too early at the station in case he missed his train. He was also meticulous about money, recording his exact earnings with scrupulous care, investing prudently, and living economically. In matters of sex he was extremely inhibited; so much so, that his perceptive biographer, Michael Meyer, believes that he was impotent during the latter part of his life. At any rate, he was so shy that he was reluctant to expose his genital organs even to a doctor who wished to examine him; and so physically timorous that any psychoanalyst would conclude that he suffered from an extreme fear of castration. The various infatuations with much younger women which characterized his latter years, and which found echoes in the plays, especially in *The Master Builder*, were idealized rather than consummated; and there is ample evidence to support his distaste for the body, and especially for physical sexuality.

It is entirely reasonable to suggest that Ibsen's preoccupation with personal freedom sprang as much from his need to emancipate himself from the restrictions of his own personality as from the limitations of society. Thus Michael Meyer writes: 'Critics still occasionally write about *A Doll's House* as though it were a play about the hoary problem of women's rights ... *A Doll's House* is no more about women's rights than Shakespeare's *Richard II* is about the divine right of kings, or *Ghosts* about syphilis, or *An Enemy of the People* about public hygiene. Its theme is the need of every individual to find out the kind of person he or she really is and to strive to become that person. Ibsen knew what Freud and Jung were later to assert, that liberation can only come from within ...'[17] In his last play *When We Dead Awaken*, one of the couples ascends to the top of a mountain to be killed by an avalanche; whilst the other descends to safety. What one couple regards as life, the other regards as death. 'As long as people remain imprisoned in flesh, Ibsen seems to say, they are dead; it is only when the body dies that the dead awaken.'[18] In *Brand* Ibsen portrays an individual who sacrifices love to rigid principle; and in *John Gabriel Borkman* a man who married for advancement rather than for love. In *The Master Builder* sexuality is repeatedly symbolized by spires, and Solness' love for the much younger Hilde is a spiritual castle in the air, rather than a real, down-to-earth relationship. We may indeed be grateful for Ibsen's inhibitions, and for his lack of personal fulfilment in marriage. Had his sensuality found full expression, the whole of his later work must have been of a different order.

In connection with Stravinsky and Rossini, it was suggested that their extreme passion for external order acted as a rite d'entrée, an outward and visible ceremonial, which reflected their desire to bring the order of art to bear on their own inner worlds of imagination. Wagner, too, had his rite d'entrée, but it was of a very different kind. 'In the very last years of his life he could not work unless surrounded by soft lines and colours and perfumes. His almost morbid sensitivity multiplied enormously the ordinary pleasant or unpleasant sensations of touch and of sight. When in a difficulty with his composition, he would stroke the folds of a soft curtain or table cover till the right mood came. Not only the fabrics but the lines about him had to be melting, indefinite; he could not endure even books in the room he was working in, or bear to let his eyes follow the garden paths; they suggested the outer world too definitely and prevented concentration.'[19]

Wagner's love of silk and satin was fetishistic in intensity. He spent large sums (generally of other people's money) in providing himself with elaborate satin dressing-gowns, trousers, lace shirts and the like. In fact, he was accused of frank transvestism on the basis of a Viennese dressmaker's bills; although the garments he ordered may have been designed for a mistress rather than for himself. In this interpretation, Ernest Newman is relying on Ashton Ellis, an early biographer, who idolized Wagner. Robert Gutman is not so concerned to protect him. Writing of Wagner in his later years, at the time of the composition of *Parsifal*, he describes him thus: 'The fires no longer flared: sparks were now precious. And the fresh fuels banking the flames had to be ever richer and rarer. His needs for silks, satins, furs and perfumes had reached the fetishistic. A strange compulsion forced him to pull on ludicrous travesty. That his skin was extremely sensitive may explain his silk chokers and underwear but hardly those quilted, shirred, bowed, laced, flowered, fringed, and furred gowns he dragged through his private rooms.'[20]

It is often affirmed that creativity is an expression of the bisexuality which can be discerned within most human beings. Moreover, it is not improbable that transvestism and fetishism sometimes represent a kind of creativity manqué, a ludicrous attempt to express infantile sexual feelings which have not yet become fully sublimated. However this may be, the whole luxurious, elaborate, voluptuous decoration of the room in which Wagner composed was itself a ritual designed to exclude the external world, and enable him to concentrate exclusively upon that inner world of the imagination from which emerged his enormous masterpieces.

Ritualistic activity, therefore, often performs for the artist the very opposite function from that which it exercises for the obsessional neurotic. Instead of preventing awareness of emotion beneath the surface of consciousness, it aims at bringing these to the surface. The obsessional neurotic excludes the inner world; the artist excludes the outer; and both may use the selfsame ritual to accomplish their aim. But whereas the neurotic generally feels compelled to engage in his rituals against his will, the artist willingly performs whatever rite may aid his creative intention.

Although the last statement is largely true, it is also, unfortunately, an oversimplification. For it is possible to look upon the obsessional rituals of the neurotic as embryonic creative activities. Even the housewife, intent upon ridding her kitchen of every speck of dust, is making some effort to impose order upon chaos. As Mary Douglas has pointed out in her interesting study *Purity and Danger*, notions of dirt are relative. 'We can recognize in our own notions of dirt that we are using a kind of omnibus compendium which includes all the rejected elements of ordered systems. It is a relative idea. Shoes are not dirty in themselves, but it is dirty to place them on the dining-table; food is not dirty in itself, but it is dirty to leave cooking utensils in the bedroom, or food bespattered on clothing.' In short, if we disregard the recent discovery that dirt and the transmission of disease by bacteria are connected, dirt may be defined as 'matter out of place'. 'Dirt, then, is never a unique, isolated event. Where there is dirt there is system. Dirt is the by-produce of a systematic ordering and classification of matter, in so far as ordering involves rejecting inappropriate elements. This idea of dirt takes us straight into the field of symbolism and promises a link-up with more

105

obviously symbolic systems of purity.'[21] However, as Freud pointed out, and as we have already seen from the examples given, obsessional rituals are not merely techniques of exclusion and rejection. Very often they contain some element of expressing the very impulses against which they are a defence, which implies a certain attempt at integration; that is, the simultaneous expression of two opposing tendencies. It is true that most neurotic rituals are sterile, and do not achieve their purpose. But this may be because the person who carries them out does so against his will and is generally unconscious of their significance. It would be rash indeed to assert that so widespread and valuable a form of behaviour as ritual is invariably pathological.

In fact it is probable that civilization could never have come about, were it not for another function of ritual; that of providing the means by which instinctual energy can be transformed and transferred from one function to another. Jung gives as an illustration the rite practised by the Wachandi of Australia. 'They dig a hole in the ground, so shaping it and setting it about with bushes that it looks like a woman's genitals. Then they dance round this hole all night, holding their spears in front of them in imitation of an erect penis. As they dance round, they thrust their spears into the hole, shouting: "Pulli nira, pulli nira wataka!" (Not a pit, not a pit, but a cunt!) Obscene dances of this kind are found among other tribes as well.'[22] This rite serves to transmute some of the sexual energy available into cultivation. In the same chapter, Jung notes that: 'the old custom of the "bridal bed" in the field, to make the field fruitful, expresses the analogy in the clearest possible way; as I make this woman fruitful, so I make the earth fruitful. The symbol canalizes the libido into cultivating and fructifying the earth.'[23]

Symbolic, ritualistic activity can be seen as a link between the inner and outer worlds of the subject; a bridge which facilitates the transfer of emotional energy from one world to the other. Moreover, the traffic operates in both directions. Who can doubt that Wagner's stroking of satin is a displacement of a more primitive wish to stroke flesh? This fetishistic ritual can be seen as a halfway house between physical sensuality and its transmutation into music: an incomplete sublimation of the primitive drive into art. But the stroking also has another function. It serves to put Wagner 'in touch with' his inner world of emotion and sensuality. By using this ritual he can withdraw the libido from the external world, and reactivate his inner feelings. Just as a 'neurotic', obsessional ritual both expresses and acts as a defence against aggressive and sexual drives; so the creative ritual also has a double meaning and a double function. 'Neurotic' rituals are only so pejoratively designated because they are sterile and serve no obvious purpose. If they were functional, they would not be called neurotic.

Obsessional characters, in addition to the traits we have discussed, possess a particularly well-developed ability to ritualize and create symbols. This is partly dependent upon their distaste for the physical, and partly upon what Freud referred to as 'precocity of ego-development'. In his paper on 'The Disposition to Obsessional Neurosis', Freud postulates that emotional development and intellectual development may not proceed hand-in-hand. In cases where the latter outstrips the former, an emotional immaturity may persist and co-exist with a striking ability to intellectualize, symbolize and ritualize, all of which latter functions require a developed ego as opposed to a chaotic id. The tendency of obsessionals to discount emotion and to exalt intellect at its expense is one consequence of this type of development, as is the use of 'intellectual' defence mechanisms against the emergence of emotion in psychoanalytical treatment. Freud postulates that obsessionals remain fixated at a pregenital stage of development—the so-called anal–sadistic stage. It is a period at which the child becomes aware, originally through his experience of toilet-training, that he himself has the power to 'let go' or to hold on and retain, and thus to acquiesce in or to defy parental wishes. He thus becomes aware of a certain *autonomy*, as Erikson phrases it, a potential independence from parents, as opposed to the almost complete dependency of its earlier infancy. At this stage, therefore, the child's relation to those he loves is characterized by *ambivalence;* that is, feelings of both love and hate which either alternate or co-exist. Obviously, it is only when a much greater degree of independence has been reached than is possible at this age that the full capacity for love can be attained. One cannot wholeheartedly love those whose authority restricts one's autonomy; and this is an inescapable condition of early childhood.

Obsessionals therefore tend to retain more than the 'normal' share of hate, in addition to the love they feel towards others; and in this respect resemble the manic-depressive characters we earlier examined. They thus have an especial need to sublimate, or erect other defences against, their instinctual drives, since these are easily felt to be dangerously hostile. A good deal of their predilection for ritual and symbol takes origin from this source.

A similar origin may be postulated for the many and various perverse sexual phantasies which so often plague obsessionals. These phantasies, commonly sado-masochistic in nature, often have no direct connection with coitus as such, because they take origin from a pregenital stage, before the idea of coitus could become meaningful or even conceivable. Freud's notion of a premature ego-development is relevant here. He writes: 'I suggest the possibility that a chronological outstripping of libidinal development by ego development should be included in the disposition to obsessional neurosis. A precocity of this kind would necessitate the choice of an object under the influence of the ego-instincts, at a time when the sexual instincts had not yet assumed their final shape, and a fixation at the stage of the pregenital organization would thus be left.'[24] In other words, a precocious child may find that its intellectual development has actually impeded, instead of advanced, its emotional development. Notions which to an ordinary child might remain vague and unformulated may become crystallized and firmly imprinted. If we add to this the distaste for the genitals of both sexes so characteristic of obsessionals, the stage is set for an infantile sexual phantasy to usurp and retain all the emotional investment which, in maturely-developed adults, pertains to the genitals and to coitus.

Such phantasies are often highly ritualized, which is why they are relevant to our present discussion. The very common phantasies of flagellation fall into this category, as may be discerned in any pornographic bookshop. In these phantasies, the act of beating is invested with the excitement and emotion which pertains to the sexual act in those who have reached the genital stage of development. Often, quite elaborate stories are invented in order to provide a setting and an excuse for introducing the act of beating in a 'natural' way. Swinburne's novel *Love's Cross-Currents* is a case in point.[25] The poet's sado-masochistic preoccupations can, of course, easily be descried in his poetry; notably, for example, in *Dolores*.

In a very interesting essay on the Marquis de Sade, Geoffrey Gorer suggests that some instances of sexual perversion may occur in individuals who are creative, but who lack the technical talent to express their creative urge. He points out that the sado-masochistic clients of prostitutes often require the latter to act a quite elaborate part, with costumes, props and the like. In fact, the sexual activity may be 'a special type of theatrical performance, with an audience of one'. Moreover, playwrights, actors and sadists share the same wish; to control the emotions of the audience or the sexual partner; an extension of the control so characteristically desired by obsessional neurotics, although Mr Gorer does not mention this. In the case of de Sade, Mr Gorer suggests that he 'was an active sado-masochist at least in part because, despite his best endeavours, he was incapable of being an adequate tragedian or playwright; and also that this sequence of perverse sexual behaviour as a substitute for creative artistic satisfactions may well have wider application than this single case'.[26] This is an interesting idea; and one which occurred to the present author independently, although reached by a different path of thought. Mr Gorer thinks of perversion as a regressive substitute for creativity. To me it appears more as insufficiently sublimated infantile sexuality; a half-way house, as it were, between primitive impulse and work of art. This possibility will be further explored in a later chapter.

Here it must suffice to say that ritualization and symbolization occur in other sexual perversions, notably in fetishism and trans-vestism. As Freud observed, there is, in such cases, a particular distaste for the female genitals. Elaborate rituals of dressing and cross-crossing are substituted for the sexual act, or engaged in as necessary preliminaries to arouse enough excitement to permit intercourse without distaste. These phantasies are abortive and unsatisfactory attempts to substitute a symbolic activity for the act of sex. As Bernard Meyer noted in his biography, Conrad shows evidence in his novels of a fetishistic interest in shoes, hair and fur; all common fetishes encountered in clinical practice. One would expect that obsessional artists would show an enhanced capacity for symbolization and displacement; and it is therefore not surprising to encounter this particular form of it, for fetishes are symbolic objects which act as substitutes for parts of the body.

Pornography itself is a boring, sterile and repetitive form of literature. Yet it is a remarkable human feat to be able to substitute words as a sexual stimulus in place of touch. Interestingly enough in this context, it has been observed that there is a relation between education and the ability to react to erotic stimuli other than direct contact, the poorly educated responding not at all, the more highly educated responding much more readily. In the Kinsey research on sex offenders the team reports that 'rather large proportions of the men reported little or no arousal from pornography in spite of the fact that almost all had been exposed to it ... The poorly educated are apt to be much more pragmatic and require something more concrete in order to respond. Thus an uneducated male from the lower socio-economic stratum may say "Why get worked up about a picture? You can't do nothing with a picture." '[27] It is of course this same group who show the least interest in cultural pursuits and little capacity to respond to works of art.

We have seen that creative activity may represent an attempt on the part of an obsessional character to transcend the limitations and restrictions of his own personality, or even to escape altogether from the body. Some forms of creativity are clearly related to the obsessional's wish for order. The fact which does not fit into the current scientific hypothesis may give rise to the same irritation as the crooked picture, the dirt in the corner, or the clothes dropped on the floor. It is something outside the ordered scheme, and therefore out of control. Science itself has often been described as an obsessional activity for this reason. For scientific advance depends essentially upon the replacement of hypotheses which have proved inadequate to cover all the facts by new theories which are more all-embracing. Einstein's law of gravitation was preferred to Newton's because it better explained certain discrepancies from Newton's hypothesis; notably an apparent anomaly in the motion of the perihelion of the planet Mercury.

If an obsessional person is able to investigate and create, he may be able to displace a good deal of his internal hostility on to the solution of problems. One such scientist described how technical problems annoyed him so much that he felt compelled to solve them in order to purge himself of rage. 'I'll beat the bastard,' was the phrase he habitually employed. He had no doubt that his hostility, which sprang from a notable degree of neglect in childhood, contributed to his problem-solving capacity. In the same way, a pianist described his piano playing as essentially a way of purging himself of hostility. He 'attacked' the piano and mastered it, and learned to express in his playing the forcefulness of which he had been unable to make use in human relations.

We have seen that ritual is not only a method of defence; but also a means of transmuting instinctive impulses to give them expression in less direct and more acceptable ways. Ritual is thus a convention; a standardized method of control in which impulse and instinct are, as it were, tamed and allowed symbolic or indirect expression. Two obvious examples from ordinary life spring to mind. The so-called 'party' as habitually given in Western society has as its main object the provision of opportunity for the sexes to encounter each other, to acknowledge mutual attraction, and to flirt, without pursuing this sexual encounter to its logical conclusion. There is an opportunity for sexual display (hence the dressing-up so characteristic of party going); an opportunity therefore for the partial expression of the promiscuous urges which all of us possess. Yet the party is itself a ritualized activity with its own social rules, which serve to contain and control the impulses for which it is providing expression.

The other example is the game. This provides opportunity for the expression of competitive, aggressive impulses; but because of the ritual element, the strict 'rules' see to it that these impulses do not get out of hand. A consideration of games, however, leads us on to consider play in general; and this constitutes the subject of the next chapter.

REFERENCES

1. SWIFT, Jonathan. *Gulliver's Travels. A Voyage to the Houyhnhnms* (London: Nonesuch Press, 1963) p. 285.
2. *Writers at Work*. The Paris Review Interviews (London: Secker & Warburg, 1958) Vol. 1, p. 72.
3. COCTEAU, Jean, in *The Faith of an Artist*, ed. John Wilson (London: Allen and Unwin, 1962) p. 83.
4. FREUD, Sigmund. 'Obsessive Actions and Religious Practices' (London: Hogarth Press and Institute of Psycho-Analysis, 1968) Standard Edition, Vol. IX, pp. 123-4.
5. Ibid, p. 126.
6. GIBBON, Edward. *The Decline and Fall of the Roman Empire*, ed. J. B. Bury (London: Methuen, 1897) Vol. II, p. 36.
7. FREUD, Sigmund. 'On Beginning the Treatment' (London: Hogarth Press and Institute of Psycho-Analysis, 1968) Standard Edition, Vol. XII, p. 133.
8. *The Gospel according to St. Matthew*, ch. iv., v. 4.
9. WHITE, Eric Walter. 'Stravinsky', in *European Music in the Twentieth Century*, ed. Howard Hartog (Harmondsworth: Pelican Books, 1961) pp. 56-8.
10. Ibid, pp. 61-2.
11. WHITE, Eric Walter. *Stravinsky, The Composer and his Works* (London: Faber and Faber, 1966) p. 28.

12. WEINSTOCK, Herbert. *Rossini* (London: Oxford University Press, 1968) p. 59.
13. Ibid, pp. 317-8.
14. Ibid, p. 203.
15. Ibid, p. 320.
16. FREUD, Sigmund. 'Those Wrecked by Success' (London: Hogarth Press and Institute of Psycho-Analysis, 1968) Standard Edition, Vol. XIV, pp. 324-31.
17. MEYER, Michael. *Henrik Ibsen* (London: Hart-Davis, 1971) Vol. II, *The Farewell to Poetry*, p. 266.
18. Ibid, Vol. III, *The Top of a Cold Mountain*, p. 308.
19. NEWMAN, Ernest. *Wagner as Man and Artist* (London: Gollancz, 1963) pp. 159, 140.
0. GUTMAN, Robert W. *Richard Wagner* (London: Secker & Warburg, 1968) p. 395.
21. DOUGLAS, Mary. *Purity and Danger* (London: Routledge & Kegan Paul, 1966) pp. 35-6.
22. JUNG, C. G. *Symbols of Transformation* (London: Routledge & Kegan Paul, 1956) Collected Works, Vol. 5, p. 150.
23. Ibid, p. 151.
24. FREUD, Sigmund. 'The Disposition to Obsessional Neurosis' (London: Hogarth Press and Institute of Psycho-Analysis, 1968) Standard Edition, Vol. XII, p. 325.
25. SWINBURNE, Algernon Charles. *Love's Cross-Currents* (New York: New American Library, 1964).
26. GORER, Geoffrey. *The Danger of Equality and Other Essays* (London: The Cresset Press, 1966) pp. 215-16.
27. GEBHARD, Paul H. et. al. *Sex Offenders* (London: Heinemann, 1965) pp. 670-1.

9

Creativity and Play

The perceptive reader who has reached this point will have noticed that our discussion of the motives of creativity is showing a progressive shift from being principally concerned with 'psychopathology' to laying greater emphasis upon 'normality'. We have seen that creativity can provide expression for the wish-fulfilling phantasies of the dissatisfied; that it can act as a defence against schizoid and depressive states; that it can reflect a compulsive need to order and control. But, although it is legitimate to label such characters as Fr Rolfe, Isaac Newton, and Schumann as 'pathological' in the clinical, psychiatric sense, such diagnoses look dubious when we come to consider people who appear as well-adjusted to life as Einstein and Stravinsky. To be unusual is not the same as to be unhappy or abnormal. Psychoanalysis has often been accused of failing to distinguish between art and a neurotic symptom. It also frequently fails to discern the difference between a neurotic symptom or pathological defence and a psychological technique of a positive kind which serves the individual well in the task of relating his own subjective world to the world outside himself in which we all engage, and which constitutes the process of living. The ritual is a case in point. It would obviously be absurd to call play pathological; yet Freud comes very close to it when he dismisses it as phantasy.

In Chapter 2, Freud's comparison of the writer's activity with that of the child at play was quoted. 'The creative writer does the same as the child at play. He creates a world of phantasy which he takes very seriously—that is, which he invests with large amounts of emotion—while separating it sharply from reality.'[1] Freud goes on to write: 'As people grow up they cease to play, and they seem to give up the yield of pleasure which they gain from playing.'[2] But since no one ever really gives up something from which he has obtained pleasure, this abandonment of play is more apparent than real. Instead of playing, so Freud alleges, adults construct phantasies. In this view, both play and phantasy are negatively labelled as mere evasions of real life.

113

Freud was an austere character who, in spite of his appreciation of Jewish humour, professed an essentially serious view of life. People in fact play considerably more than he admitted. Although adults, both human and animal, tend to play less than they did when they were juveniles, they continue to spend at least some proportion of their time in play, and to derive considerable pleasure from so doing. Indeed, Freud himself continued to play chess in coffee-houses until he was forty-five, although Ernest Jones tells us he gave it up altogether after 1901.[3] But play of some kind, whether it be in the form of sport, games of skill, or hobbies, is surely an important part of human existence, which cannot simply be dismissed as an escape from reality. Perhaps both art and play have a function which eluded Freud, at least at this fairly early stage of his theorizing. That this was so is not really surprising. One of Freud's most notable characteristics as a thinker was his invariable practice of reducing everything to the lowest common denominator. He took an almost masochistic delight in interpreting the whole of human endeavour in terms of Eros and Thanatos; that is, as derived from sex and aggression. Even the Jewish humour of which he was so fond is reductive; for it generally depends upon the deflation of pretension and the detection of self-interest behind sentiment. Neither play nor creativity can easily be derived from, or reduced to, simple, instinctive drives; and it is for this reason that Freud's view, illuminating though it is in many respects, ultimately fails to satisfy us.

Indeed, if a work of art could be regarded as being derived in a simple or direct way from the sexual or self-preservative drives, this enquiry into creativity would soon be rendered superfluous. For one of the theses of this book is that art serves a valuable function in the human scheme of things; and one which cannot be understood if art is regarded merely as a substitute for something more primitive. Indeed, if we were to accept Freud's original thesis, we should be compelled to dismiss art as biologically non-adaptive; an activity which actually militated *against* survival. For anything which encourages man to avoid reality rather than to participate in it, accept it, or master it, must surely serve him ill when it comes to the crunch of actuality. The man who has spent his life day-dreaming is less likely to be effective than the man of action who has become accustomed to dealing with real problems in real life. If all art fell into the category of wish-fulfilment, and was no more important than the type of productions discussed in Chapter 2, there would be a good deal

114

to be said for discouraging it. Romantic novels may possibly
force a sentimentally distorted attitude to life, and therefore interfe.
with a realistic adaptation. But art is much more than wish-fulfilment.
Freud's original explanation is unsatisfying, particularly when we
come to consider those works of art which enhance and deepen our
appreciation of reality rather than providing us with an escape from
it. The same is true of play, which is why we are here considering it.

It would be clearly wrong to consider art and play as identical
activities, but it is true that they possess a number of features in
common. Indeed, it can be argued either that art is a derivative of
play, or else that both activities take origin from a single source.
This is Freud's view, already quoted above. Although both art and
play are considered by Freud as an escape from reality, it must be
added that he does recognize the importance with which the child
invests his playing. 'The opposite of play is not what is serious but
what is real.'[4]

Play and art are alike in that both activities appear, superficially
at any rate, to lack the compulsion associated with biological necessity. We seem not to have to play in order to survive; nor are we
obviously compelled to paint pictures, compose music, or sculpt
statues. Although one can imagine that a man might be forced by
another to create something, it is generally true that art is a voluntary
activity, and that creativity flourishes best in the absence of compulsion. The same is true of play. For, although one might compel a
child to play a game against his will (a notorious bêtise of English
schools), the game will straightaway lose one of the characteristics
that makes it play. As Huizinga wrote: 'Play to order is no longer
play: it could at best be but a forcible imitation of it. By this quality
of freedom alone, play marks itself off from the course of the natural
process. It is something added thereto and spread out over it like a
flowering, an ornament, a garment.'[5]

If it is accepted that both play and art are essentially voluntary,
it follows that both are generally disinterested activities. Although
games can be turned into ways of making a living by those who are
particularly skilful players, they do not originate in this way. Although
creative production may turn out to be financially rewarding, men
do not primarily engage in it for the sake of financial gain, as we saw
in Chapter 3. Both games and works of art stand somewhat outside
the ordinary course of life, and do not appear to be associated with

the immediate satisfaction of wants and appetites. The idea that a novelist, for example, could sit down and write a popular romance for cash with her tongue in her cheek is almost certainly false.

To be at all convincing, the story must be a genuine representation of the author's own inner world of phantasy. If it is not so, it does not persuade the reader. Moreover, the considerable effort of writing a novel can hardly be sustained on a basis of calculated pretence. Of course it is true that not all a creative person's productions reflect the highest level of which he is capable. Composers write incidental music as well as symphonies; and the novelist Graham Greene makes a specific distinction between what he calls 'entertainments' and his other, more serious, novels. But these lighter productions are as genuine a representation of the emotions and mentality of their creator as are their more profound creations. Schubert's dance music and 'café' music is as authentic, though not as profound, as the A minor Quartet (D.804) or the B minor Symphony (D.759); and both take origin from something which was actually taking place within Schubert himself, rather than being constructed as an exercise. Although the need for money may be a powerful stimulus to composition, it remains a secondary, rather than a primary, motive force; a catalyst, rather than one of the elements of the creative process.

Although both art and play have a necessary element of spontaneity, both are also concerned with order and with form. Organized games have rules to which the players must adhere, and a game is spoiled if the rules are broken. In this way a game is a microcosm, set apart from ordinary life, and much better ordered than our habitual, chaotic existence. The game displays a formalized pattern in which each player knows his task and how he should behave. For the duration of the game, the participants have the delight of knowing exactly what is expected of them. As we saw in Chapter 8, ritual is reassuring, and this is one reason why men cling to it.

Works of art are similarly concerned with order. Although the great creators are often distinguished by their propensity to break rules, there are always rules for them to break. A work of art without any order or arrangement is inconceivable. Leonardo advised painters to look at damp-stained walls and unevenly coloured stones in order to stimulate their imagination; but he was well aware that it was what the artist made of the images he thus discovered which really mattered. Gombrich makes this point with his usual clarity in *Art and Illusion*. In Leonardo's *Treatise on Painting*, so Gombrich tells

116

us, there is 'a fascinating echo of conversation he must have had with Botticelli on the need of the artist to be universal and to know the structure of all things he may have to include in a painting. "Our Botticelli" had maintained that such study was unnecessary "because by merely throwing a sponge full of paint at the wall it leaves a blot where one sees a fine landscape". It is true, says Leonardo, that in such a blot you may see "whatever you desire to seek in it. But though they give you inventions, they do not teach you to finish any detail . . . And that painter," Leonardo concludes, "made the most wretched landscapes." '6

Even infant play shows the beginnings of a kind of order, for it is generally much concerned with repetition. One of the first things a baby enjoys is repetitive play with objects. The ball which disappears and returns over and over again will soon evoke gurgles of delight, because the baby knows what is going to happen. A minute degree of order has been introduced into his world, and he recognizes this with pleasure. In the same way, the return of a theme in a piece of music may give us intense delight; of course, it is not until we know the themes well enough to recognize them that we can experience this, especially if the return is delayed. One device which composers use is to state a theme unequivocally and then repeat it so that it is well established in the mind of the listener. Then, instead of re-peating it again at a point where this might be expected, the composer proceeds to prevaricate, and heighten the tension of expectation by altering the original rhythm, harmony or tempo in such a way that the pattern seems almost shattered. When the original theme finally does return, our relief at order being restored is all the greater. A convincing example of what is meant can be found in Leonard Meyer's analysis of the fifth movement of Beethoven's C sharp minor quartet, Op. 131. Anyone who knows this movement will recognize how the listener's expectations are denied fulfilment and progressively post-poned by the fragmentation of the rhythmic and melodic pattern. 'But at the very moment when rhythm, harmony, texture, and even melody in the sense of pattern seem all but destroyed, the little figure which opens the movement and the first phrase raises our hopes and redirects our expectations of completion and return. Now we are certain as to what is coming.'7

The games we play with babies have a good deal in common with this. Once the pattern of hiding a ball and then revealing it is estab-lished, the adult plays variations, postponing the ball's appearance, and increasing tension so that, when at last it is discovered, relief and pleasure are doubled.

The way in which form and order manifest themselves in works of art vary with the art concerned. In the visual arts, the order imposed is spatial. The picture is contained and limited within a frame, and the order within the picture is a matter of the spatial relations of the visual masses which make up the picture combined with gradations of colour and tone. In music, the structure principally depends upon the dimension of time. Music is distinguished from mere noise by the fact that the sounds of which it is composed persist for long enough for the ear to register them as the separate entities we call notes. The duration of these notes, and their combination into themes, set up patterns of tension and resolution. It is the interrelation of these patterns within a framework of defined duration which constitutes music.

In games, both space and time play their part in giving structure to the whole. As Huizinga points out, 'Play is distinct from ordinary life both as to locality and duration ... it contains its own course and meaning ...' He makes the point that games often take place in special spaces marked off for the purpose; in 'the arena, the card-table, the magic circle'. 'The profound affinity between play and order is perhaps the reason why play, as we noted in passing, seems to lie to such a large extent in the field of aesthetics. Play has a tendency to be beautiful.'[8]

As we have noted, Freud came to believe that all the phenomena of life were derived from the interaction of two groups of instincts: 'the erotic instincts, which seek to combine more and more living substance into ever greater unities, and the death instincts, which oppose this effort and lead what is living back into an inorganic state. From the concurrent and opposing action of these two proceed the phenomena of life which are brought to an end by death.'[9] Biologists (and many psychoanalysts also) do not accept Freud's concept of a death instinct; but, like Freud, they are concerned with trying to understand behaviour, and to interpret it in terms of primitive drives. Behaviour which, like art or play, seems to be an 'extra' and cannot easily be interpreted in terms either of self-preservation or the preservation of the species, is apt to appear mysterious to them.

One theory of play which has been advanced by biologists is that it is a way of discharging superfluous energy. The life of the body proceeds in alternating cycles of activity and rest; and, if an animal is full of energy, it may be presumed that play serves to discharge this energy, and that the mild fatigue which follows play may be physiologically beneficial. The objections to this theory are twofold. First, animals may start playing again when they are already panting and exhausted, and are clearly *not* suffering from an excess of undischarged energy. Second, if energy has to be discharged, why should it not be used in something more obviously and immediately useful than play? The kitten does not have to play. It might be trying to catch a mouse.

Because play involves movement, it also involves exploration. The playing animal is thus provided with a constant stream of information about the various features of the environment with which its play brings it into contact. But, as Caroline Loizos points out in her article on the subject, it is not necessary for an animal to play in order to learn about the environment. Why not simply explore it without playing? Not all animals play. Mrs Loizos tells us that rats do not appear to do so. But rats are indefatigable explorers. As she writes: 'Of course it is inevitable that during play an animal will be gaining additional knowledge about what or who it is playing with but if this is the major function of play one must wonder why the animal does not use a more economical way of getting hold of this information.'[10]

Another theory is that play is simply practice. The more an animal exercises its skills in play, the more likely it is that, when it has to perform the same movements in a situation important for survival, like catching prey, it will perform them efficiently. But there is no obvious reason why practice should be playful. Serious practice would do just as well, if not better. 'Quite simply, it is not necessary to play in order to practise: there is no reason why the animal should not just practise.'[11] Moreover, this theory does not really explain adult play. As we stated earlier, adults, both animal and human, continue to play, and play must therefore have a function other than practice.

In observing animals we may feel fairly certain that we can distinguish 'playful' activity from 'serious' activity. Yet, in what does this difference consist? One characteristic of play movements as opposed to serious movements is that the former are exaggerated and uneconomical. The motor patterns employed in play are those which the animal might use in serious contexts; but they are employed

119

in the wrong order, or incompletely performed, or repeated over and over, or exaggerated so that they are inefficient. This is also the character of much human play; for instance, in mock fights as opposed to real fights. As Caroline Loizos affirms, there is a fundamental similarity to the observer between human and animal play. 'This similarity lies in the exaggerated and uneconomical quality of the motor patterns involved. Regardless of its motivation or its end-product, this is what all playful activity has in common; and it is possible that it is all that it has in common, since causation and function could vary from species to species.'[12]

Desmond Morris possesses the rare distinction of being both a zoologist and an artist. His book *The Biology of Art*, is a comprehensive review of what is known about the primitive beginnings of art as demonstrated by the various species of ape which have been induced to paint pictures. He has no hesitation in putting art and play into the same category. 'The answer to why apes, both young and adult, can become engrossed in picture-making to the point where, as we have seen, they may prefer it to being fed and will exhibit temper tantrums if they are stopped is a difficult one to find. It has something to do with the great development in apes, especially chimpanzees, of what I have called "Self-Rewarding Activities". These are actions which, unlike most patterns of animal behaviour, are performed for their own sake rather than to attain some basic biological goal. They are "activities for activities' sake", so to speak. They normally occur in animals which have all their survival problems under control and have surplus nervous energy which requires an outlet. This usually only occurs in young animals whose needs are being looked after by their parents, or in captive or domestic animals whose needs are attended to by their human owners. Actions which are usually referred to as play, curiosity, self-expression, investigation, and so forth, come into this category of self-rewarding activities.'[13]

Huizinga, writing specifically of human play, defines it as 'an activity which proceeds within certain limits of time and space, in a visible order, according to rules freely accepted, and outside the sphere of necessity or material utility. The play-mood is one of rapture and enthusiasm and is sacred or festive in accordance with the occasion. A feeling of exaltation and tension accompanies the action, mirth and relaxation follow.'[14] He has no doubt that, whatever may be said of the plastic arts, play and poetry, and more especially play and music, are intimately connected. 'Poiesis, in fact, is a play-function. It proceeds within the play-ground of the mind, in a world of its own which the mind creates for it.'[15]

Huizinga, being neither a biologist nor a psychoanalyst, is not disconcerted by being unable to relate play and art to basic biological drives. For him, play is a thing on its own, and its most characteristic feature 'the fun of playing, resists all analysis, all logical explanation . . .'[16] The very existence of play continually confirms the supralogical nature of the human situation. Animals play, so they must be more than merely mechanical things. We play and know that we play, so we must be more than merely rational beings, for play is irrational.'[17]

Huizinga and Desmond Morris agree, therefore, in conceiving of play as an 'extra'; something engaged in for its own sake, or for 'fun'. But it is odd to find a biologist apparently content with such an interpretation. For Desmond Morris' explanation of both play and art as 'self-rewarding activities' is not really an explanation at all, but a description. If this description is accepted, we have to discard the fundamental biological principle that the behaviour of an animal is either directly adaptive or else derived from behaviour which is so. The Darwinian principle of natural selection demands that an animal's behaviour should ultimately be related to bettering its own chance of survival, or else to improving the chances of survival of the species. It is true that nature sometimes leads animals into blind alleys. As Lorenz points out, the overdevelopment of the wing feathers of the male argus pheasant is one example. These are used during courtship to attract the female. The cock with the largest wing feathers may indeed be more successful in attracting a female and thus reproducing himself, but selection has so increased the size of the feathers that it is almost impossible for the bird to fly. In this instance, the interest of self-preservation and reproduction are at odds with one another, since the most attractive cock is the one least able to elude an enemy.[18] Neither art nor play appear to be blind alleys of this kind, since they carry no obvious disadvantage for the individual or the species.

But do they carry an advantage? Is play, or the art which each author links with play, quite so superfluous an activity as both Huizinga and Morris imply? It is true that Huizinga derives culture from play, and is thus convinced of its importance. But could it be that there is more to play and art than this in terms of adaptation and survival? One feature shared by art and play is that either can be used to allay boredom. Curiously enough, Desmond Morris omits to mention this function in *The Biology of Art*, from which the passage about the painting of apes was taken. But he enlarges upon it at some length in *The Human Zoo* and, to my mind, thereby renders his category of 'self-rewarding activities' superfluous. For he points out that man and other primates belong to a category of animal which requires constant stimulation if the nervous system is to function at its most efficient. If there are no stimuli impinging upon the organism from the immediate environment, then the animal seeks them out or invents them. Not all animals are like this. Dr Morris divides the specialists from the opportunists. Those species who depend for survival upon one rather specialized technique relax when that technique is able to find realization. 'Eagles, for instance, will thrive in a small empty cage for over forty years without so much as biting their claws providing, of course, they can sink them daily in a freshly-killed rabbit.'[19] Opportunists, on the other hand, survive by not being specialists. Their nervous system has to be on the alert constantly, so that they do not miss any new opportunity. Because of this, they need constant external stimulation, become easily bored, and tolerate the inactivity of captivity extremely badly.

Hence the distressingly restless, repetitious behaviour of some caged animals, who constantly pace up and down and may even become self-destructive in their search for stimulation.

Man is the supreme example of the opportunist animal. At least some of the 'extra' activities in which he indulges (extra in the sense of not being immediately concerned with reproduction or survival) are adaptive in that they provide an additional input of stimulation to the nervous system, thus keeping him alert and preventing boredom. The crossword puzzle keeps us awake on a railway journey; and both games-playing and art can be used in the same way to provide new and exciting stimuli which alert and interest us. However much we might like to emulate cats, who seem able to sleep contentedly for the greater part of the twenty-four hours, it is impossible for us to do so. Some of the 'divine discontent' which leads to both games-playing and to art is due to man's restless hunger for new inputs to keep his brain functioning at optimal capacity. Desmond Morris has no doubt that this is the explanation of man's creativity. 'In the human zoo this creativity principle is carried to impressive extremes. I have already pointed out that disillusionment can set in when the survival-substitute activities of the Stimulus Struggle begin to seem pointless, often because the activities chosen are rather limited in their scope. In avoiding these limitations, men have sought for more and more complex forms of expression, forms which are so absorbing that they carry the individual on to such high planes of experience that the rewards are endless. Here we move from the realms of occupation trivia to the exciting worlds of the fine arts, philosophy and the pure sciences. These have the great value that they not only effectively combat under-stimulation, but also at the same time make maximum use of man's most spectacular physical property—his gigantic brain.'[20] All this is, no doubt, true, so far as it goes. But it does not go nearly far enough.

In primates, at any rate, two more elements enter into play which are both highly relevant to our theme, and may also be considered adaptive in the biological sense. One is that play is primarily a social activity, which brings young animals together, and which may be essential to their achieving mature social and sexual development. The other element is that of ritual. Play, even amongst animals, is ritualized. In play, motor patterns which are used 'seriously' in other contexts where they would be biologically useful, are used in incomplete, exaggerated, or 'pretend' forms. Flight and fight patterns, for example, are constantly employed in this way. Play uses motor patterns which are phylogenetically earlier than play itself. Both aggressive and sexual behaviour patterns are obviously more essential than play for survival; but play makes use of these patterns in a setting in which survival is not for the moment an urgent issue.

This transfer of motor patterns of behaviour from one setting to another is not confined to play. Thus sexual motor patterns are used in non-sexual situations to signify both dominance and submission. Presentation, the female motor pattern in which an animal invites the male to coitus, is characterized by approaching the male, turning the hind quarters in his direction and looking backwards over the shoulder towards him. But presentation is used by both sexes to disarm aggression and indicate submission to a more dominant animal. In the same way, male patterns of genital display are often used as threats or warnings. Chimpanzees show a particular expression so often during play that this expression has come to be known as the 'play-face'. This play-face may also, like presentation, be used to disarm aggression in a more dominant male so that the latter can be approached by a less dominant male without fear of provoking attack.[21]

It is clear that play and ritualized behaviour share many features in common. At a higher level of play than that which we have been discussing, ritual in the form of rules, stereotyped patterns of behaviour and special limitations of time and space are absolutely characteristic. One has only to think of a game of tennis, with its prescribed setting, its formalities of behaviour, rules of procedure, conventions of dress and so on, to see that such a game is a highly ritualized performance. Now, in animals, ritualized behaviour is clearly adaptive. In many species of animal, for example the social insects, there is little conflict between the interests of the group as a whole and the interests of the individual. But primates, man included, are programmed in such a way that the interests of the community and the interests of the group are often at odds with one another. Competition for food, and for mates, is intense, and has to be regulated by 'rules' which prevent aggression getting out of hand. If there were no such rules, the most dominant individual would become a dictator, with the result that, although his individual desires might obtain immediate gratification, his rivals would all be killed and the group disintegrate or disappear. One way of preventing this happening is by the adoption of the convention of territory, so that animals compete for a parcel of land rather than for food direct. Territory has the effect of spreading the group out over the available terrain so that each individual has an area in which it can obtain food and raise a family without threat of interference. Another adaptive device common to many species of primates is the formation of a dominance hierarchy in which peace and order is ensured within the group by an oligarchy of the most powerful males. These have the first right to food and to females; but intervene to stop fights within the group, thus ensuring its coherence and survival. It is only in groups of primates which are confined in zoos, and in which there is a gross imbalance between the proportion of males to females, that bloody fights to the death occur.

The fights which occur between the males of many species of animals, especially in the breeding season, are highly ritualized, with the result that, although dominance is clearly established, the loser of the pair is not destroyed. The adaptive nature of the rituals by which contests are thus made into tournaments rather than lethal battles is not in doubt. The species is much more likely to survive if losers are not destroyed.

Ritual, therefore, serves the purpose of taming or modifying

124

primitive impulses, especially aggressive impulses, in such a way that these impulses can continue to find an outlet and to be expressed, but do not in fact harm other individuals in the group. This ensures that the impulse itself is not repressed or impaired so that, when it comes to a dangerous situation in reality, the individual can make use of aggressive or flight patterns to overcome danger or to escape from it. But, within the group, although competition occurs, it must be competition 'according to the rules', that is, ritualized competition or competition in play.

It seems highly likely that one biological function of play is to teach young animals how to ritualize their primitive impulses of aggression in such a way that they can fit into a social group, whilst at the same time preserving their capabilities for serious fight in reality should the occasion call for it. It is also likely that this ritualization of aggression in play is essential if the young primate is going to be able to learn mating behaviour. In order to mate satisfactorily, it is necessary to learn to ritualize or suppress hostile patterns of behaviour; and animals which have had little opportunity to play cannot do this. If it can be shown, as I think it can, that the apparently superfluous, 'extra' activity of play in fact fulfils an essential function, it will not be difficult to extend this notion to art, which, as we have seen, shares many characteristics with play. So far as I know, the idea that art is biologically adaptive, or at any rate derived from activities which were originally adaptive, has not been advanced before, at least in the terms which I shall employ; and it may therefore appear strange to those unused to thinking in these terms. But the adaptive function of play is much more obvious; and the next chapter is therefore devoted to a further exploration of this subject.

REFERENCES

1. FREUD, Sigmund. 'Creative Writers and Day-Dreaming' (London: The Hogarth Press and The Institute of Psycho-Analysis, 1959) Standard Edition, Vol. IX, p. 144.
2. Ibid, p. 145.
3. JONES, Ernest. *Sigmund Freud* (London: Hogarth Press, 1955) Vol. 11, p. 428.
4. FREUD, Sigmund. 'Creative Writers and Day-Dreaming' (London: The Hogarth Press and The Institute of Psycho-Analysis, 1959) Standard Edition, Vol. IX, p. 144.

5. HUIZINGA, Johan. *Homo Ludens* (London: Temple Smith, 1971) p. 26.
6. GOMBRICH, E. H. *Art and Illusion* (London: Phaidon Press, 1962) p. 189.
7. MEYER, Leonard. *Emotion and Meaning in Music* (Chicago: University of Chicago Press, 1956) p. 155.
8. HUIZINGA, Johan. *Homo Ludens* (London: Temple Smith, 1971) pp. 28-9.
9. FREUD, Sigmund. 'Anxiety and Instinctual Life', Lecture XXXII in *New Introductory Lectures on Psycho-Analysis* (London: The Hogarth Press and The Institute of Psycho-Analysis, 1964) Standard Edition, Vol. XXII, p. 107.
10. LOIZOS, Caroline. 'Play in Mammals', in *Play, Exploration and Territory in Mammals*, ed. P. A. Jewell and Caroline Loizos (London: Academic Press, 1966) p. 4.
11. Ibid, p. 5.
12. Ibid, p. 7.
13. MORRIS, Desmond. *The Biology of Art* (London: Methuen, 1962) p. 144.
14. HUIZINGA, Johan. *Homo Ludens* (London: Temple Smith, 1971) p. 154.
15. Ibid, p. 141.
16. Ibid, p. 21.
17. Ibid, p. 22.
18. LORENZ, Konrad. *On Aggression* (London: Methuen, 1966) p. 32.
19. MORRIS, Desmond. *The Human Zoo* (London: Jonathan Cape, 1969) p. 184.
20. Ibid, pp. 194-5.
21. LOIZOS, Caroline. 'Play Behaviour in Higher Primates. A Review' in *Primate Ethology*, ed. Desmond Morris (London: Weidenfeld & Nicolson, 1967) p. 205.

10

Play and Social Development

The best evidence that the play of young primates is adaptive, and not merely a superfluous activity, comes from the experiments of the Harlows in Wisconsin with rhesus monkeys. In highly aggressive and competitive animals, as we pointed out in the last chapter, ways have to be found to modify the intensity of intra-group aggression so that the group does not destroy itself in uncontrolled strife. Harlow describes the development of a series of 'affectional systems' in monkeys which serve this purpose. 'If affection for members of one's social group has developed through normal mother–infant relationships and normal peer relationships before full-fledged aggression has matured, the later expression of aggression towards in-group members will be greatly ameliorated, and the full force of aggression can be turned against external enemies and predators instead of in-group associates. Failure to develop in-group affection before aggression is fully matured leaves the animal a deviate, a delinquent and a social outcast.'[1] These affectional systems are: 'the mother–infant or maternal affectional system, the closely related and complementary infant–mother affectional system, the age–mate or peer affectional system, the heterosexual affectional system, and the paternal affectional system'.[2] In research designed to analyse the relative importance for future development of these various systems, the Harlows have reared infant monkeys under varying conditions of deprivation. Thus, baby monkeys have been brought up in total isolation; with substitute mothers; with normal access to the mother but no access to other young monkeys; and with normal access to both. The most interesting, and to psychoanalysts, perhaps, the most unexpected, result of this research is the discovery that the 'peer affectional system'—that is, the interaction of the baby monkey with its contemporaries—is more important than the mother–baby relation for determining the animal's future ability to mate successfully, and also, in the case of a female, to become a satisfactory mother. Naturally enough, the baby monkey learns to interact with its contemporaries chiefly through the agency of play.

127

The normal mother–infant relation in rhesus monkeys provides the infant with the basic physiological needs of food and warmth; the basic psychological needs of comfort and close bodily contact; and also serves to protect the developing infant from danger in the external environment. An infant who has received enough of these fundamental requirements from the mother will gradually want to separate itself from her and explore the environment independently; though always with the proviso that he can run back to the mother for support and reassurance if he encounters anything frightening or harmful. In this second stage, the mother encourages separation by mildly punishing the infant and pushing it off if it clings too closely.

Part of the environment which the young monkey explores with interest, if normal development is allowed to proceed, is his own contemporaries. Harlow distinguishes three stages of play, which he names 'rough-and-tumble play, approach-withdrawal or non-contact play, and aggressive play'. Rough-and-tumble play consists of 'vigorous wrestling, rolling and sham-biting responses which involve little or no physical discomfort. Non-contact play is characterized by back-and-forth chasing responses by two or more animals with actual physical contact being kept to a minimum.'[3] Aggressive play, which is a later development, appearing about the end of the first year of life, is accompanied by fiercer bites and rougher handling. Injury is rare; but the play is sufficiently rough for the infant monkey to learn which of its peers is stronger than itself, and which weaker. 'We conceive of aggressive play as having an important, positive social role in which the monkeys learn through early experience to try, test, and accept the differential and changing status positions they will occupy during adolescence and adulthood.'[4]

Play also furthers the development of adult sexual interaction. The pelvic thrusts characteristic of coitus tend to occur in either sex as a reflex response to contact with a warm, soft surface. They are first seen, therefore, in relation to the mother's body. Very soon the male postures of threatening and following, and the female postures of passivity and rigidity, start to develop. Harlow believes that both males and females must learn to accept physical contact with contemporaries if adult mating is to be accomplished satisfactorily.

He also thinks that play modifies the aggressive responses which mature from the second year of life onwards. If aggression is not thus modified, normal heterosexual behaviour cannot develop.

Play and Social Development

Under normal conditions, the infant monkey forms an intense and deep attachment to the mother during the first month of life. Fear of strange objects in the environment is not present at birth, but develops between sixty and ninety days after birth. It seems probable that fear of strangeness is adaptive for the infant which is beginning to explore the environment; since over-boldness might be dangerous in the case of unfamiliar objects. Such a fear is un-necessary whilst the infant is still totally under the protection of the mother. The interesting point here is that other monkeys do not come into the category of fear-producing strangeness, provided the infant has had opportunity to mix with its peers from the be-ginning. Indeed, members of the same social group become, like the mother, providers of security and reassurance.

In human infants, fear of strange persons in the environment is often stated to be a regular development in the seventh or eighth month of life, provided the antecedent care has been normal and satisfactory. But it is not at all easy to be sure of a regular pattern in the development of either fear of strangers or fear of separation from the mother in human infants, as Bowlby has eloquently demon-strated.[5] Infants who have been neglected show a dislike of being alone as early as the sixth to eighth week of life; and so, paradoxically, do infants who have received too much mothering, and who therefore demand almost continuous stimulation from whoever is looking after them.

In rhesus monkeys, aggressive responses and behaviour do not play an important part in behaviour until the beginning of the second year of life. In human children, aggression between peers becomes socially important between the third and fourth year. Before this, it is probable that aggression towards the mother as a response to frustration increases in intensity after the first six months of life. Kleinian analysts assume intensely destructive emotions within the baby *ab initio*, as a deflection outwards of the 'death instinct'. How-ever this may be, Harlow is likely to be correct when he states: 'In all primate species, in all mammalian species, and in many or most vertebrate species there is an orderly development of affection, regardless of the specific form it takes, of fear, and of aggression.'[6] This order can, in monkeys, be experimentally disturbed.

Harlow's formulation may throw some light upon, although it does not solve, the problem of whether love or hate is the primary relation between human beings. Freud, in a paper from which we have already quoted, wrote: 'If we consider that obsessional neurotics have to develop a super-morality in order to protect their object-love from the hostility lurking behind it, we shall be inclined to regard some degree of this precocity of ego development as typical of human nature, and to derive the capacity for the origin of morality from the fact that in the order of development hate is the precursor of love. This is perhaps the meaning of an assertion of Stekel which at the time I found incomprehensible, to the effect that hate and not love is the primary emotional relation between men.'[7]

This sombre conclusion is also implicitly supported by Wynne-Edwards, who believes that all higher animals have had to evolve societies with conventional rules and devices in order to obviate intra-specific destruction. In his view, society itself is an organization of which the chief function is to provide conventional (or, as we might paraphrase, ritualized) competition; a defence, therefore, against the primary hostility between individuals which might otherwise destroy the species.[8]

The truth may not be so simple. If Harlow is right, aggression and competitiveness between peers, which is undoubtedly a necessary adaptive mechanism in primates, including human beings,[9] is modified not only by ritual and convention, but by satisfactory mothering and interaction with peers in early infancy; and these 'love-relationships' are prior to the full development of aggression. In Harlow's experiments, we can see what happens when a baby monkey is brought up in sufficient isolation for its natural tendency to form friendly relations with other monkeys to be suppressed or abolished.

If rhesus monkey infants are separated from the mother at birth and brought up in cages which give no opportunity for physical relations with the mother or with other monkeys, they show a great increase in fear of other monkeys when finally allowed to mix with them. They also show an increase in aggressive behaviour both towards the experimenter who is caring for them, and also towards their own bodies. Isolated animals bite their own limbs as well as the observer's glove. Fear and aggression have not been diluted and modified by either maternal love or by contact with peers.

Interestingly, and, as already suggested, unexpectedly, monkeys who have been separated from the mother but who are allowed to mix with other infant monkeys from an early age, develop pretty well normally. Mixing with contemporaries can largely make up for maternal deprivation. But if mother–infant pairs are isolated for the first seven months of the infants' lives, and the infants are only then allowed to come together, they will not play normally. The best mothering cannot compensate for the deprivation of play with contemporaries.

This 'partial social isolation' in which monkeys are brought up in cages where they can see, but cannot touch, other monkeys, has serious results if it is prolonged beyond the first six months of the monkey's life. Most monkeys so reared are unable to mate. Moreover, if females are made pregnant artificially, they are unable to carry out the maternal role, and neglect or are actually aggressive to their offspring. It is probable that human mothers who 'batter' their babies are suffering from a similar failure to develop normal affectional responses.

Harlow also raised monkeys in total isolation, that is, in a stainless steel chamber in which they could not even see other monkeys, let alone touch them. After six months, such monkeys, when released to mix with controls, were terrified. Not only were they unable to play with other monkeys, they were so helpless in the face of aggression that they were unable to defend themselves, and would have been killed if the experimenters had not removed them. These were the only monkeys who did not even play with themselves, either auto-erotically or otherwise. If this total isolation is carried out not during the first six months, but during the second six months of life, the animals are, instead of being helpless, grossly over-aggressive. This is because they have had an opportunity to develop fear responses (the second in order of the three important responses), but have not had the chance of modifying their aggression by any affectionate attachments. Another result is that such isolates transgress the normal monkey code (also shared by humans) of not attacking the young and helpless when they themselves have become adolescent. Sometimes these animals endangered themselves by attacking an adult stranger, a mistake no normally socialized monkey would make.

Enough has been said to demonstrate the enormous importance of interaction with contemporaries as soon as the infant monkey has gained enough security from the mother to explore the world by itself. And the bulk of this interaction between the young is in the form of play. Is the same true of human beings?

We cannot subject human babies to the kind of total isolation in which Harlow secluded his monkeys; nor would human babies survive if we did so. But we know that children raised in institutions where there is little opportunity to develop close ties of affection with a constant maternal substitute remain 'emotionally cold and isolated, capable of only the most superficial interpersonal relationships'. Such children, like the partially isolated monkeys, show a notable increase in all kinds of aggressive behaviour, including 'temper tantrums, lying, stealing, destruction of property, kicking and hitting other children'.[10]

In dealing with adult neurotic problems, one is more and more forced to the conclusion that isolation, and an inability to mix with contemporaries at an early stage in childhood, are important determinants of adult difficulties. Whether a child becomes a 'scapegoat' or a 'social menace' (to use Harlow's phrase) may be partly decided by genetic factors. It may also, like the monkeys, be determined by the stage in time at which the difficulties or deprivation manifest themselves. Some adult neurotics are chiefly characterized by fear of others; in which case they will seek to ingratiate themselves, by being over-submissive, masochistic and depressed or hysterical. Others are over-aggressive; cannot bear any situation in which they do not feel themselves to be the boss; are touchy, irritable and unnecessarily dominant. Some people alternate the two behaviours, being usually submissive, and then suddenly reversing the pattern (the worm turning) so that if they do show any aggression it is intemperately violent. In either case, the individual is showing that he has not learned how to handle his aggression appropriately. He does not know the form; the form which he should have learned in games with his contemporaries; the games which would have taught him when to assert himself and when to submit; when he would win a contest of strength, and when lose it.

Similarly, isolated children grow up with little knowledge of sex. In the absence of games with contemporaries, their knowledge of their own sexuality and that of the opposite sex remains deficient. Children, if left to themselves, will explore each other's anatomy and play games which are imitations of adult sexual behaviour. They will also explore their own anatomy and discover that pleasure is to be obtained from their own genitals. Analysts know that the child who has never masturbated, and who cannot recall any childhood genital touching, is severely inhibited sexually, and less likely to be able to make a satisfactory adult sexual relationship. The guilt which many children experience about their own sexual impulses, and which causes endless misery and torment in adolescence, is often the product of isolation. How often young people feel themselves to be unique; uniquely evil for having desires which, if they had only had more contact with their peers, they would have realized were perfectly normal.

It is, therefore, reasonable to conclude that, amongst young primates at any rate, play is an adaptive activity. Through play, the young animal learns his place in the hierarchy. He also learns how to make use of his aggression so that he can stand up for himself when it is necessary for him to do so; and to know when it is more politic to withdraw or submit. He also learns to tolerate physical contact with members of his own and the opposite sex, and to engage in physical activities which are the precursors of adult sexual activities. Because play is largely ritualized, it provides an opportunity for learning ways of expressing aggressive and sexual behaviour patterns within a social setting in such a way that actual fights and actual coitus do not occur, but yet the impulses are given partial expression, and peers are seen to behave in similar fashion.

In human children, play is similarly adaptive. Indeed, one of the earliest signs of disturbance of an emotional kind in children is an inability to mix and play with contemporaries. In contrast, psychiatrists learn that if a child has many friends of his own age with whom he plays happily, it is unlikely that there is a great deal wrong with him emotionally, even if the parents have many complaints about him. One frequent characteristic of neurotics is that they are often able to relate satisfactorily to persons who are either much older or much younger than themselves, but unable to make contact with contemporaries.

Play, therefore, is as important for young humans as it is for young rhesus monkeys; and human games show many features of ritualization which have the same functions as those suggested above. The majority of games which children play are ritualized contests; struggles in which the child learns to assert himself and to compete, but in which he also learns to temper his violence according to rules which forbid injury to the opponent. Old-fashioned schoolmasters used to allege that games were a good training ground for character. Boys, they said, learned to be 'good losers'; and also good winners who did not crow too much over defeated opponents. In games, they learned to receive minor injuries without complaint; and to be physically forceful to another person without inflicting serious injury. In football, for example, ritualized attack is allowed in the form of tackling; but the injuries which might be inflicted by kicking or striking with the fist are strictly proscribed.

Sexual games, in Western society, have not yet received the same degree of encouragement and approval as aggressive games, although, judging by some of the literary products of the 'permissive society', they may soon do so. The same is not true of other societies. Amongst the Polynesians, for example, the sexual habits of the Marquesans have been studied in detail by an anthropologist fluent in the language. Marquesan children have, from birth onwards, ample opportunity to observe adult sexual relations. Masturbation in males starts at about the age of three; and young boys of seven or eight gather together in troups for masturbation contests. Female masturbation is much more concealed, but is frequently referred to by males, and undoubtedly occurs often enough, with or without the aid of instruments. 'At the age of approximately seven years, other forms of group sexual activity appear, which are heterosexual. Boys and girls, playing at "mother and father" will often place their genitalia in contact for brief periods. The girl either stands against a tree or lies supine on the ground, with the boy assuming the normal position for coitus. Contact is brief, accompanied occasionally by pelvic movement with much laughter.'[11] The game-like character of this mock coitus is evident from this description.

The Marquesans, compared with ourselves, seem both more tolerant and more sexually successful. Homosexuality is entirely tolerated as a substitute for heterosexual relations; but there are very few habitual homosexuals. Heterosexual relations begin for most girls before puberty; and thereafter they experience little or no difficulty in reaching orgasm quite quickly. Impotence, except among elderly males, is relatively rare. In general, there seems a dearth of the sexual problems so frequently encountered in our own culture, and a frank enjoyment of sex without guilt which we might envy. There can be little doubt that this joyful acceptance of sexuality is related to the tolerance with which manifestations of infantile sexuality are greeted, and, more especially, to the sharing of developing sexual experience between children, and the playing of games with a sexual content.

Play, therefore, if the children are not interfered with by moralizing adults, can have the effect of preparing the child for adult sexual performance, and of making him aware of the importance of his own

134

and other people's sexual feelings. The handling of sexual feelings in adult life, and the proper expression of them, is probably much easier if the child has had some experience, just as the handling of aggressive feelings can be shown to be.

In adult life amongst humans, play continues to serve similar functions. It is obvious that most of the games played by adults are ritualized contests, just as are the games of children. These contests, from football to chess, provide an opportunity for the expression of competitive, 'aggressive' feelings without much risk of injury to the protagonists, although football, especially in South America, arouses such passion amongst spectators and supporters that dangerous clashes sometimes occur. In recent years, especially in the United States, sport appears to have become more violent; and spectacles are now provided which appear to cater to the sadistic interests of the spectators, in much the same way as gladiatorial games enthralled the populace of ancient Rome. But, even though actual injuries do occur, it is still true to say that games are more ritualized than not. Even the most violent game has some rules, and the player of American football is protected by them, just as he is by his helmet and padded armour.

Similarly, as we suggested earlier, the ritual of the 'party' serves to give opportunity for the display of sexuality without much risk of serious involvement, and may thus be regarded as a 'play' activity also. Parties give very little occasion for people to get to know each other intimately, or to conduct any serious conversation; the noise and the numbers are too great. They do, however, give opportunity for sexual display, for flirtation, the exchange of sexual banter and so on. People look forward to parties because they find their sense of self-esteem enhanced by such encounters.

Just as those who have not, in childhood, had much opportunity for aggressive exchange with other children tend to alternate, in adult life, between being needlessly submissive and over-assertive, so those who have had little opportunity of expressing or sharing sexual feelings tend to alternate between suppressing or repressing sexuality and overvaluing it to the point of idiocy. It is those who have had little practice in handling their own sexuality who are likely to 'fall in love' in a devastating manner; and who treat the whole matter of love in an all-or-nothing fashion.

Is it because human beings have, under civilized conditions, too little opportunity of expressing sex and aggression that adults, as well as children, play games? This may be partly true; but to make such a statement without qualification is to oversimplify.

Such a view would closely correspond to Freud's idea that civilization is so intrinsically a source of discontent that men are forced to look outside 'reality' for opportunities to express sexuality and aggression. Thus, as children, they turn to games; and, as adults, to phantasy and its derivative, art: or else, even as adults, continue to play the games they played as children. Just as this view does less than justice to the adaptive function of play, so it also underestimates the adaptive function of art, which, as we pointed out at the end of the chapter on 'Creativity as Wish-Fulfilment', may enhance our grasp of reality instead of merely providing an escape from it.

REFERENCES

1. HARLOW, Harry F. 'The Primate Socialization Motives' in *Social Psychiatry*, ed. Ari Kiev (London: Routledge & Kegan Paul, 1970) Vol. 1, p. 421.
2. Ibid, p. 402.
3. Ibid, p. 406.
4. Ibid, p. 407.
5. BOWLBY, John. *Attachment and Loss* (London: The Hogarth Press and The Institute of Psycho-Analysis, 1969) Vol. 1, pp. 299-330.
6. HARLOW, Harry F. 'The Primate Socialization Motives' in *Social Psychiatry*, ed. Ari Kiev (London: Routledge & Kegan Paul, 1970) Vol. 1, p. 418.
7. FREUD, Sigmund. 'The Disposition to Obsessional Neurosis' (London: The Hogarth Press and The Institute of Psycho-Analysis, 1968) Standard Edition, Vol. XII. p. 325.
8. WYNNE-EDWARDS, V. C. *Animal Dispersion in Relation to Social Behaviour* (Edinburgh: Oliver & Boyd, 1962).
9. STORR, Anthony. *Human Aggression* (Allen Lane, The Penguin Press, 1968) pp. 21-36.
10. MUSSEN, Paul H., Conger, John J., and Kagan, Jerome. *Readings in Child Development and Personality* (London: Harper & Row, international edition 1965) p. 234.
11. SUGGS, Robert L. *Marquesan Sexual Behaviour* (London: Constable, 1966) pp. 45-6.

11

Is Art Adaptive?

In the last two chapters certain comparisons were made between art
and play. At first sight, both activities seem to stand apart from the
'serious' business of life. Both are disinterested, and neither appear to
be directly associated with the immediate satisfaction of biological
needs, in the way that hunting or mating clearly are. Both art and
play are concerned with rule and ritual; and both tend, therefore, to
impose a certain form upon what otherwise might remain chaotic.
Moreover, both play and creativity can be looked upon as adaptive in
the sense of providing additional input to stimulate and alert the
nervous system. In animals like ourselves, whose survival depends
upon flexibility and rapid perception, a constantly alerted nervous
system is obviously valuable, since the system functions more efficiently when in a state of arousal. In addition I showed that, in young
primates at any rate, a good case could be made out for regarding
play as adaptive in that it provided a setting in which aggressive and
sexual impulses could be learned, tamed, and ritualized in such a
way that the individual could preserve his aggressive and sexual
potential, but, at the same time, modify his primitive drives in such
a way that the social group was not disrupted.

It is not immediately obvious that art is as adaptive as we consider
the play of young primates to be. We have seen that, in certain
examples, creative pursuits can be used as an escape from real life;
and we have also examined at some length instances of creativity
being used as a defence; a sublimation of primitive drives, or a way of
avoiding certain pathological states of mind like depression or
schizoid alienation. At the end of Chapter 2, however, it was
suggested that man's imagination did not always spring to life as a
result of 'psychopathology'; and that art was not necessarily either
escape or abreaction. Lionel Trilling's observation that, in certain
works, 'the illusions of art are made to serve the purpose of a closer
and truer relation with reality'[1] was quoted; and it is the way in which
art can both put us in touch with, and enhance our grasp of, reality,
which we shall further explore in this chapter.

137

Our ancestors, at any rate, had no doubt that art served a valuable function. 'According to ancient Chinese lore, the purpose of music and the dance is to keep the world in its right course and to force Nature into benevolence towards man. The year's prosperity will depend on the right performance of sacred contests at the seasonal feasts. If these gatherings do not take place the crops will not ripen.'[2]

When Jung visited the Pueblo Indians of New Mexico, he discovered, to his great excitement, that they daily performed a religious rite which was designed to help the sun to rise. As one Indian told him: 'After all, we are a people who live on the roof of the world; we are the sons of Father Sun, and with our religion we daily help our father to go across the sky. We do this not only for ourselves, but for the whole world. If we were to cease practising our religion, in ten years the sun would no longer rise. Then it would be night for ever.'

Jung goes on to write: 'I then realized on what the "dignity", the tranquil composure of the individual Indian, was founded. It springs from his being a son of the sun; his life is cosmologically meaningful, for he helps the father and preserver of all life in his daily rise and descent.'[3]

This is *methectic* participation; a rite in which the performer participates in a natural phenomenon in such a way that he feels he is actually helping it to occur. I showed in Chapter 8 how ritual can act as a bridge between the inner world of the subject and the external world. We also observed that ritual imposed some order upon what otherwise might appear ill-regulated and beyond control. We all live in a world in which we feel at the mercy of natural events, and indeed are so to a considerable extent in spite of the achievements of science. The volcanic eruption, the typhoon, and the earthquake are almost as far beyond the reach of our influence as they were to pre-scientific man; and even the most sophisticated agnostic is liable to find himself praying if he encounters one of these terrifying phenomena. Primitive man must have felt powerless and threatened to a far greater extent than most of us ever do, since he was confronted by a far wider range of natural happenings which, to him, were unpredictable and inexplicable. How natural that he should engage in ritual which served to give him the illusion that he not only could participate in the course of Nature, but also exercise some control over her arbitrary progressions.

Although music and the dance will not in fact assist the crops to ripen, nor any religious rite control the motions of the earth or sun, it would be a mistake to dismiss all ritual action as serving no practical purpose. In these attempts to make order out of chaos, man was able to enlarge and deepen his perception of the external world, and thus become better able to understand, appreciate, and eventually control at least some of its aspects. At the same time, the rituals which he practised led him to the discovery of what we should now call art.

When primitive man first depicted animals upon the walls of his cave dwellings, his aim was not aesthetic. His painting was a practical rite designed to help him in his pursuit of the animal. In *Icon and Idea* Herbert Read quotes the description given by the anthropologist Frobenius of the hunting preparations undertaken by African pygmies, after he had asked one of them to shoot an antelope.

'As I was eager to learn what their preparations consisted of, I left camp before dawn and crept through the bush to the open place which they had sought out the night before. The pygmies appeared in the twilight, the woman with them. The men crouched on the ground, plucked a small square free of weeds and smoothed it over with their hands. One of them drew something in the cleared space with his forefinger, while his companions murmured some kind of formula or incantation. Then a waiting silence. The sun rose on the horizon. One of the men, an arrow on his bowstring, took his place beside the square. A few minutes later the rays of the sun fell on the drawing at his feet. In that same second the woman stretched out her arms to the sun, shouting words I did not understand, the man shot his arrow and the woman cried out again. Then the three men bounded off through the bush while the woman stood for a few minutes and then went slowly towards our camp. As she disappeared I came forward and, looking down at the smoothed square of sand, saw the drawing of an antelope four hands long. From the antelope's neck protruded the pygmy's arrow.'[4]

This drawing in the sand, therefore, and the whole rite which accompanied it, served a highly practical purpose, as did the cave paintings of palaeolithic art. As Herbert Read points out, the drawing originated from the impulse to 'realize' the object upon which magical powers were to be exercised and which was later to be pursued in reality.

'Realization' in this sense is an active grasping or apprehension, as opposed to a merely passive appreciation. As examiners know well, a student can only be said to have really grasped a subject when he can actively reproduce it; and this is one of the most cogent reasons for preserving the written examination as part of the educational system. We may be able to understand a lecture or a book in passive fashion; but, when we can ourselves lecture or write about a topic, we realize that we know it in a different and profounder sense. The subject has become assimilated; part of our own mental furniture. If a man can draw an animal, he 'knows' its appearance in a far more complete way than if he merely recognized it. It is significant that palaeolithic cave art principally consists of drawings of large animals. Where human forms occur, they are generally two-dimensional and stylized. It is the big game, the dangerous and elusive quarry, which is depicted in concentrated detail.

The preparations described by Frobenius are a kind of ritual, and might be dismissed as nothing but a useless exercise in sympathetic magic. In fact, the ritual is one which enhances the appreciation of reality. The man who had observed the antelope sufficiently closely to be able to make a life-like drawing of it was, in truth, better equipped to pursue and despatch it. In this instance, art is serving the purpose of increasing awareness of the object, and is directly adaptive in that it enhances the chances of survival of the artist. Herbert Read writes: 'Far from being a playful activity, an expenditure of surplus energy, as earlier theorists have supposed, art, at the dawn of human culture, was a key to survival—a sharpening of faculties essential to the struggle for existence. Art, in my opinion, has remained a key to survival.'[5]

This view of art is in striking contrast to that of Freud, who, governed by his concept of the pleasure principle, continued to regard imaginative activity as an escape. Writers, for example, are supposed to liberate tensions in the mind of the reader by enabling the latter to enjoy day-dreams 'without self-reproach or shame'. The writer's art is to soften the 'character of his egoistic day-dreams by altering it and disguising it, and he bribes us by the purely formal—that is, aesthetic—yield of pleasure which he offers us in the presentation of his phantasies'.[6] The idea that phantasy might be used to gain a closer grip upon reality is alien to Freud; and so is the notion that the achievement of aesthetic form might serve a similar function. In another passage Herbert Read writes: 'What man always desires is a firmer grasp of reality. That is a direct consequence of his insecure existence, his cosmic anxiety.'[7] Freud would have agreed that man was insecure and anxious, but, one suspects, would have believed

140

that only science, and not art, could obtain for him 'a firmer grasp of reality'. This is the more peculiar when one reflects that the agents of change in the psychoanalytic process are themselves symbols. For words are representations of reality, rather than reality itself; and yet their judicious selection, as Freud well knew, can profoundly alter a man's psychological attitudes. We have already commented upon Freud's tendency as a thinker to reduce everything to the lowest common denominator. This same characteristic manifests itself in his predilection for reducing feeling and even thought to bodily sensation to the neglect of more 'psychological' phenomena. For Freud, the body appears to have been the one irreducible reality; and all else in man's experience but derivative. This extraordinary concreteness of Freud's thinking so influences his use of language that it prevents his being understood and often alienates people who would otherwise appreciate his genius. For example, when he writes of certain neurotics having a phantasy of a maternal penis, a good many people will be unable to follow him, or will complain that nothing in their own experience corresponds to such a phantasy. If, however, one phrased it differently, and alleged that some neurotics continue to regard the mother as possessing the masculine power and dominance which is generally attributed to the father, many would find such a statement comprehensible, and recognize that confusion as to who 'wears the trousers' might have a deleterious effect upon emotional development. Yet the meaning of the two statements is hardly different.

Another feature of psychoanalytic thought which militates against the view that symbolic activities may have a positive function rather than an evasive one, is Freud's preference for looking backward towards childhood rather than forward toward new developments, For Freud, cure came about by removing blocks due to childhood fixations and misconceptions. The idea that phantasy could lead forward to a new and better adaptation was foreign to his method of interpretation.

The 'realization' of the antelope through drawing has another aspect which is worth consideration. Depicting anything in the external world, whether by painting it, drawing it, sculpting it, or describing it in words, requires that a certain distance be interposed between the artist and the object which he is attempting to portray.

We all know that our subjective involvement with a person interferes with our capacity to describe him. If we want to give a friend a convincing portrait of a favourite child, or of someone with whom we are in love, we find it difficult to do so; and we describe the difficulty by saying that we are 'too close' to the person we are trying to portray. We cannot view a loved person as objectively as we would like to do because we cannot separate ourselves from those we love, and cannot therefore stand back and see them 'in perspective'. Detachment from the object, or 'psychical distance', as it has been called, is a necessary precursor not only of science, but also of art.

In Chapter 6, we saw that the schizoid capacity for extreme detachment could lead, in the case of geniuses like Newton and Einstein, to the creation of a new model of the universe. The new synthesis could only be achieved following an unusually complete detachment from the old and the conventional. On a very much smaller scale, the same psychological mechanism is involved in our standing back from, and thus becoming able to evaluate and depict, any of our human experience. The power of abstraction is the beginning of wisdom. It is a power which is largely, though not exclusively, confined to human beings. Birds, for example, can be shown to possess some capacity for abstraction in their discrimination of pattern and number. But it is only man who can so detach himself from himself and from the world around him as to observe his own emotions objectively and to make symbolic representations of reality.

At the beginning of life, this power of abstraction is lacking. Although some of what we surmise is based upon backward extrapolation, it seems certain that a baby does not at first differentiate himself from either the mother, whose womb he has so recently quitted, or from the world around him of which he seems to himself to be a part. As he gradually comes to define the limits of his own body, he becomes conscious of an external world 'out there' which is differentiated from himself. A great deal of 'growing-up' is concerned with the gradual relinquishment of this initial fusion of object and subject. As Fairbairn puts it: 'The development of object-relationships is essentially a process whereby infantile dependence upon the object gradually gives place to mature dependence upon the object. This process of development is characterized (a) by the gradual abandonment of an original object-relationship based upon primary identification, and (b) by the gradual adoption of an object-relationship based upon differentiation of the object.'[8] This differentiation applies not only to relationships with other people, but also to our relation with the external world and with our own inner world of thought and feeling. As we mature, we become less liable to identify ourselves with our surroundings, with the people we love, and with our own emotions and beliefs. This is partly the consequence of the notable development, in human beings, of memory. On account of memory, we can stand back from our own past experience, look at it objectively, depict it, and, if we possess the necessary skills, transmute it into a work of art. And, as every novelist knows, it is only when time has intervened that this transmutation becomes possible. The more profound an emotional experience, the more essential is it to distance oneself from it, and to recollect it in tranquillity if one wishes to make artistic sense of it. This is why Proust named his great novel *À la Récherche du temps perdu,* and the last, triumphant volume of it, *Le Temps retrouvé.* No artist has ever had a deeper appreciation of the contribution made by memory and time to his own achievement.

The capacity for abstraction gives man a sense of mastery over that from which he is detaching himself. As we have seen, this feeling of power may sometimes be illusory, for incantations grow no crops. Nevertheless, the whole of scientific achievement, and thus the whole of man's actual power over nature, depends in the first instance upon his having separated himself from Nature. In Chapter 6, I briefly glanced at Descartes, whose capacity for abstraction led to a philosophical point of view which is generally accepted as being the basis of modern science. The fact that Descartes' achievement was related to his deprived infancy, and that he could justly be called psychiatrically 'abnormal', does not invalidate our thesis. It is arguable that the greatest innovators possess more than their share of schizoid or other psychopathology; but what we see in them is only an exaggeration of a potential which we all possess, and which, it will be argued, is an essential aspect of our specifically human adaptation.

Man's capacity for abstraction is so fundamental a part of his nature that it can be discerned even in very primitive productions. Max Raphael, quoted by Herbert Read, puts it thus in his book *Prehistoric Pottery and Civilization in Egypt.*

'The beginnings of pottery were rooted in necessity, the beginnings of its ornamentation were rooted in mathematics, in the sense that there was a will to abstraction, i.e. to achieve a certain detachment from the physical quality of the object, to distil and bring forth from amorphousness something simple, limited, fixed, enduring, and universally valid. The neolithic artist wanted a world of forms illustrating not changeable and transient activities and events . . . but rather the relations of people to one another and to the cosmos within an unchanging system. The intention was not to suppress the content of life but to dominate it, to compel it to surrender its physical ascendancy to the power of creative will—to man's drive to manipulate and refashion his world.'[9]

Suzanne Langer, writing on music, makes the same point about detachment. If the artist does not interpose a distance between himself and his material, what he expresses is not music. 'Sheer self-expression requires no artistic form. A lynching-party howling round the gallows-tree, a woman wringing her hands over a sick child, a lover who has just rescued his sweetheart in an accident and stands trembling, sweating, and perhaps laughing or crying with emotion, is giving vent to intense feelings; but such scenes are not occasions for music, least of all for composing. Music is not self-expression, but *formulation and representation* of emotions, moods, mental tensions and resolutions—a "logical picture" of sentient, responsive life, a source of insight, not a plea for sympathy.' When 'psychical distance' has been achieved, 'the content has been *symbolized* for us, and what it invites is not emotional response, but *insight*. "Psychical distance" is simply the experience of apprehending through symbol what was not articulated before.'[10]

Even the use of language itself implies some degree of physical distance. As we pointed out when discussing the use of words in psychoanalysis, words are representations of reality, not reality itself. Using words descriptively, for example, already implies some division of subject from object; a recognition of a thing 'out there' which is separate from the self.

The symbol, therefore, arises as a consequence of distancing or detaching the self from the object. It is also a means by which one apprehends the object. It is by means of symbols that we form concepts; and it is by his use of conceptual thought that man has conquered the world. As Suzanne Langer points out, symbols have a different function from signs, although the two are often confused. 'A sign indicates the existence—past, present, or future—of a thing, event, or condition. Wet streets are a sign that it has rained. A patter on the roof is a sign that it is raining.'[11] But a symbol makes it possible for us to form conceptions of objects. Signs denote objects; but symbols connote conceptions. Once we have a conception, we can use our imagination. The object no longer has to be present; we can think about it in its absence. This is one feature of human psychology which, Suzanne Langer believes, distinguishes us from animals. 'Dogs scorn our paintings because they see coloured canvases, not pictures. A representation of a cat does not make them conceive one.'[12] This statement may not be wholly correct. Adrian Kortlandt, in his experiments with wild chimpanzees, concluded that these animals do recognize and respond to pictures of themselves. But the fact that some animals also may possess a rudimentary capacity for the recognition and formation of symbols does not invalidate the point. Symbols connote concepts; and once we have a concept of a piece of reality, we can play with it, think about it, and, most importantly, relate it to other concepts. It becomes a piece of a mental jigsaw which can, hopefully, be fitted together with other pieces. We shall never finish the puzzle, of course; but even to discover one or two new pieces which interlock gives a sense of exhilaration unmatched by any other experience. This interrelating of concepts is the principal way in which new scientific discoveries are made. It is what Arthur Koestler has named 'bisociation'; and he has examined the process exhaustively in *The Act of Creation*.

The symbol, therefore, increases our grasp and mastery of reality. The way in which this happens in science is clear. Although we remain impotent in the face of great natural disasters, science has enormously increased man's command of his environment. The thesis of this chapter is that artists, also, are continually engaged in attempting the same process. The most obvious way in which the great artists of the world enhance our grip on reality is by means of the word. Novelists of the calibre of George Eliot or Tolstoy, by reason of their greater sensibility, are able to register aspects of reality which have either escaped us, or which, if we have noticed them, we have been unable to 'put into words'. Their verbal gifts make it possible for them to formulate experiences which, with something of a thrill, we may recognize as having shared, but of which we have been unable to make use, since we had not the skill to conceptualize them. The novelist is handing us, ready-made, a concept which we can take over and relate to our own experience.

Proust, for example, is an unrivalled observer of the part which snobbery and status-seeking play in human affairs. Which of us, brought up in an English, 'Christian' tradition, would easily have observed, or invented, the fact that a grandee could think it more important that his wife should be wearing the right shoes to an evening party than that he should delay himself for a few minutes to offer sympathy to a friend who has just revealed that he is dying. This famous scene between the Duc and Duchesse de Guermantes and Swann epitomizes the ruthless heartlessness of human beings; and therefore opens one's eyes to its detection in all sorts of other circumstances.

Similarly, Proust's account of the behaviour of homosexuals, more especially of their recognition of each other, as in the superb scene where M. de Charlus encounters the tailor Jupien, and each discerns in the other the possibility of sensual fulfilment, paves the way to our recognition of similar behaviour in our own acquaintance. Proust himself illustrates the point exactly when he writes, at the end of that same scene: 'Even Ulysses did not at once recognize Athena. But the gods are immediately perceptible to one another, as quickly like to like, and so too had M. de Charlus been to Jupien. Until that moment I had been, in the presence of M. de Charlus, in the position of an unobservant man who, standing before a pregnant woman whose distended outline he has failed to remark, persists, while she smilingly reiterates: "Yes, I am a little tired just now" in asking her indiscreetly: "Why, what is the matter with you?" But let someone say to him: "She is expecting a child," suddenly he catches sight of her abdomen and ceases to see anything else. It is the explanation that opens our eyes; the dispelling of an error gives us an additional sense.'[13]

Or, to take a more recent example, C. P. Snow's series of novels, *Strangers and Brothers*, underlines both man's preoccupation with power, and also the devices to which he has recourse in order to obtain it. Unless, or perhaps even if, one has happened to move in the world of politics and academic intrigue which Snow describes, his depiction will lay bare an area of human motivation which, since it is not confined to the parts of society which the author is describing, but is an universal motive, applies to one's own experience, even if one does not traverse corridors of power more important than those of the parish council.

Every serious reader will be able to recall instances of how a writer has made him aware of aspects of reality which were previously unrecognized by him; and will surely agree that this awareness has increased his understanding and grasp of the world, rather than provided an escape from it.

Nor is it difficult to understand that painters may fulfil a similar function. The revolution in the rendering of colour on canvas brought about by the Impressionists taught people to look at objects in a new way. 'We do not see individual objects each with its own colour but rather a bright medley of tones which blend in our eye or really in our mind.'[14] The creative painter, re-examining his own visual experience, makes us re-examine our own; so that we see, not in terms of the convention we have previously learned, but with a new, and possibly more naïve, vision.

It is well-established that the congenitally blind who acquire sight at first see only chaos; a whirling confusion of colour and shape which makes orientation in the external world at first more difficult rather than more easy. In *Art and Illusion* Gombrich has shown how hag-ridden we are by the visual schemata which we have acquired. In order to apprehend an object visually, it is not enough just to look at it. What we know and have learned, and more especially what we have learned from other pictures, actually interferes with, as well as facilitates our perception. This is of course exactly equivalent to the stultifying effect of a comprehensive scientific hypothesis. The better and the more embracing the old theory, the more difficult it is for men to adjust their minds to embrace the new.

The symbol is a way of attaining insight, but it also limits insight, because no symbol can comprise the whole of the reality which it is enabling us to grasp. Therefore it has to be destroyed by the creator, and an attempt made by him to recapture what Ruskin called the 'innocence of the eye' before he gives us a new scheme by which we can perceive the world. Toleration of the anxiety caused by chaos is, as we shall see, one characteristic of the creative person, who must be prepared to see his grasp of the world broken, before he can renew it.

It is not always appreciated that, for the average person, the undermining and destruction of a cherished vision of reality can be a shattering experience. Such an upheaval is comparable to the disturbance a man suffers when a person in whom he has had 'basic trust' (to use Erikson's phrase) turns out to be unfaithful or untrustworthy. The schema of a loved and loving person, one who understands, and who is unequivocally 'on one's side' may be an illusion derived from infancy. But it is so valuable an illusion that most men cannot dispense with it; and, when it is destroyed, they feel the disillusion and alarm which comes from being thrown back entirely upon one's own resources. Schemata, philosophies, religions, scientific theories, and even aesthetic prejudices, can all act as bulwarks against the basic, cosmic anxiety which we all suffer when we realize how large and how indifferent the world is, and how small and helpless is each individual in it. No wonder we resent having our cherished illusions shattered, our traditional way of looking at things challenged. When the Impressionists first tried to exhibit their works in Paris, they were greeted with storms of abuse. We can only understand such intemperance if we realize that their new vision must have mobilized intense feelings of basic anxiety in the artistic establishment. Similarly, when Ibsen's plays were first produced in England, they incurred bitter and quite irrational criticism. Clement Scott wrote of *A Doll's House*: 'The atmosphere is hideous ... it is all self, self, self:' The *Standard* called the play morbid and unwholesome; and the *People* labelled it unnatural and immoral. The first performance of Stravinsky's *Le Sacre du Printemps* by the Russian Ballet in Paris in May 1913 created a scandal. Part of the audience had so little understanding of Stravinsky's genius that they believed he was making a blasphemous attempt to destroy music as an art; and the performance was ruined by cat-calls and abuse.

All aesthetic considerations apart, perhaps what visual artists are about originally derives from a basic drive to understand and grasp the world through sight. It is an extension, therefore, of the exploratory behaviour so characteristic of primates which we have already had occasion to mention in connection with play. Obviously, the animal which best knows its way about has the best chance of survival. The creature which more fully comprehends the world in which it finds itself has the greater chance both of avoiding dangers and also of obtaining more effectively and quickly what it needs. We only really discover what kind of a visual world we live in when something happens to disrupt it, like the impact of a new discovery in painting, or the assumption of a pair of those distorting spectacles beloved of physiological experimenters. We think we know reality through our eyes; but those delightful, ambiguous figures which can be read as either a vase or two faces, or else as either a duck or a rabbit, demonstrate how much we need schemata before we can apprehend anything which we see. 'The world as we see it is a construct, slowly built up by every one of us in years of experimentation. Our eyes merely undergo stimulations on the retina which result in so-called "sensations of colour". It is our mind that weaves these sensations into perceptions, the elements of our conscious picture of the world that is grounded on experience, on knowledge.'[15]

Is Art Adaptive?

If we turn from the painter's achievement in giving us new schemata by which we may better appreciate, and therefore adapt to, the reality of the external world as apprehended through sight, we may conclude that the aesthetic aspect of painting is also adaptive; though in a less obvious, more internalized, and more 'psychological' sense. In discussing the paintings of apes, we wondered what it was that was so important to the animal that he felt compelled to complete his painting, to 'get it right', even when tempted with food. How can this purely 'aesthetic' activity be adaptive?

Interestingly enough, Desmond Morris, who, as a biologist, might be supposed to be particularly interested in this question, does not answer it, at any rate in *The Biology of Art*.

'We have seen that the reason why apes have not taken their potential aesthetic talents further and put them into practice was clearly because they had no reason for doing so, beyond aesthetic pleasure. It now emerges that man is in a similar position today and yet he still persists with his picture-making activities. But the reason is not hard to find. He has had a long and glorious tradition of picture-making behind him and all the necessary materials are available to him. Both man and the apes have an inherent need to express themselves aesthetically and, given painting materials, will respond in a basically similar fashion.'[16]

But why have apes and men this need, and what purpose does it serve? Dr Morris does not venture a guess. We have seen that both verbal and visual art are either directly and practically adaptive or else can easily be derived from the drive to comprehend and master the environment. In what follows, we shall boldly suppose that even the aesthetic aspect of art has an adaptive function; a notion admittedly speculative, but one which presents a number of engaging possibilities.

REFERENCES

1. TRILLING, Lionel. 'Freud and Literature', in *The Liberal Imagination* (London: Secker & Warburg, 1951) p. 45.
2. HUIZINGA, Johan. *Homo Ludens* (London: Temple Smith, 1971) p. 33.
3. JUNG, C. G. *Memories, Dreams, Reflections* (London: Collins and Routledge & Kegan Paul, 1963) p. 237.
4. READ, Herbert. *Icon and Idea* (London: Faber and Faber, 1955) p. 27.

5. Ibid, p. 32.
6. FREUD, Sigmund. 'Creative Writers and Day-Dreaming' (London: The Hogarth Press and The Institute of Psycho-Analysis, 1959) Standard Edition, Vol. IX, p. 153.
7. READ, Herbert. *Icon and Idea* (London: Faber and Faber, 1955) p. 65.
8. FAIRBAIRN, W. R. D. *Psycho-Analytic Studies of the Personality* (London: Tavistock Publications, 1952) p. 34.
9. READ, Herbert, *Icon and Idea* (London: Faber) p. 41.
10. LANGER, Suzanne, *Philosophy in a New Key* (London: Oxford University Press, 1951) pp. 216, 222, 223.
11. Ibid, p. 57.
12. Ibid, p. 72.
13. PROUST, Marcel. *Cities of the Plain* (London: Chatto & Windus, 1941) Part 1, p. 18.
14. GOMBRICH, E. H. *The Story of Art* (London: Phaidon Press, 1960) p. 387.
15. GOMBRICH, E. H. *Art and Illusion* (London: Phaidon Press, 1962) p. 251.
16. MORRIS, Desmond. *The Biology of Art* (London: Methuen, 1962) p. 151.

12

Man's Inner World: Origin and Function

I ended the last chapter by suggesting that even the purely aesthetic aspect of artistic activity might have an adaptive function. Congo, irritably protesting at his paintbrush being removed before he had finished his picture to his own aesthetic satisfaction, is behaving as if his painting is as 'instinctive' as eating or sex, so that interruption of it in mid-course causes frustration in exactly the same way that interruption of copulation or a meal would do. Congo's pictures, unlike those of more sophisticated human artists, cannot be supposed likely to enhance his or our grasp of the external world. But, as Desmond Morris has demonstrated, Congo and other apes show in their paintings a strong tendency towards balance and control; and even birds show a preference for regular, as opposed to irregular, patterns. We know, from our own experience, that the contemplation of symmetry and order in the external world brings us a sense of peace and fulfilment. Whether we are listening to a Bach concerto, looking at a painting by Giotto, or grasping the logic of a theorem in mathematics, a considerable part of the satisfaction we obtain is derived from our appreciation of order and balance. And if we ourselves, in however humble a way, succeed in creating order where none existed, by making sense out of the obscure, wresting a garden from the wilderness, or even arranging a bowl of flowers in a way which we find satisfying, we achieve a fulfilment which can be as gratifying as the satisfaction of our nutritional or sexual requirements.

In what does this fulfilment consist? We saw, in the last chapter, that we need schemata in order to apprehend the external world. This is not the only world with which man has to contend. We are also faced with the problem of understanding, coming to terms with, and mastering the inner world of our own psyche; and for this we need schemata also. It seems likely that when we either create something ourselves, or contemplate the creations of others, we are attempting to integrate and reorganize our own inner experience. Harrison Gough puts it well when he writes: 'The work of art, for example, reorders and brings into balance the tensions of form and space, and in so doing moderates the inner tensions of the observer, giving him a sense of encounter and of fulfilment.'[1] Just as the discovery of a law of nature brings with it a sense of mastery and the possibility of further advance (it is only when we know about gravitational fields that we can escape from them), so the discovery in art that there can be a logic and symmetry even in the language of the emotions makes us feel that we have some power over our own unruliness, or at least that our feelings need not be totally chaotic.

In order, however, to understand how it is that such reorganization and reordering of inner tensions is felt to be desirable and fulfilling, some digression is necessary. For what is this 'inner world' to which we so glibly refer? Some philosophers, of whom Gilbert Ryle is the best known, deny the existence of any such entity. Even if it does exist, how did it come into being, and has it any function? Dynamic psychologists agree with each other in postulating the existence of an inner realm of the psyche; but disagree as to its contents, structure, and formation. Where Melanie Klein descries 'internal objects', Jung sees 'archetypes'. Where Freud postulates super-ego and id, Fairbairn finds a 'libidinal ego' and an 'anti-libidinal ego'. My task is not to resolve these differences of opinion, although this might not be so difficult as is sometimes supposed, but to convince the reader that there is such a thing as an inner world of the psyche to which one can attribute contents and structure; and to show him further that human beings are so constituted that the understanding, grasping and mastery of this realm of experience is as important as the understanding, grasping and mastery of the external world.

Freud's picture of the mental apparatus, which he freely admitted to be mythological, was of an 'I' or ego, the executive part of the mind, poised uneasily between conscience on the one hand, and instinct on the other, The ego is, as we noted in Chapter 4, subject to the threat of anxiety, against which it attempts to defend itself; and anxiety may menace it from the external world, in the shape of the ordinary dangers of existence, or from within, as a threat from a bad conscience, or as the pressure of instinct demanding satisfaction. The ego, therefore, although representing the will, possesses comparatively little power of independent action since, like a democratic prime minister, it is subjected to many pressures from various sources. Conscience, or the super-ego as Freud called it, is derived from parental training; the incorporated voice of authority which threatens punishment or the withdrawal of love if the code of conduct laid down in childhood is transgressed. Instinct is pictured as emerging from the id; a place of untamed impulse, in which murderous phantasies, perverse desires, possessive love and all the other egocentric passions of infancy, continue to exist unmodified by civilization or the process of growing-up.

This model, although now partly outmoded, is still useful in understanding mental phenomena. What we need to note here is that Freud found it necessary to postulate that there was a largely unconscious part of the mind, but little related to external reality, which was primitive, impulsive, and extreme; and which appeared to have persisted more or less unchanged from the earliest days of childhood. There is implicit in this picture a lack of correspondence between inner and outer, between desires and their fulfilment, which Freud regarded as an inevitable consequence of the impact of civilization upon man's unruliness.

In Jungian theory, the contents of the deeper, 'collective' level of the unconscious are personified as archetypes. These are images, common to all mankind, which reflect man's basic needs and desires, but which are essentially impersonal in that they are not derived from the child's experience of real people. Thus, behind the child's actual interaction with his mother hides the archetypal image of the Great Mother; a figure who may be more infinitely wise, understanding, and compassionate than any merely human mother can be, but who, on the other hand, can also be as destructive as Kali, or as paralysing to all initiative as the Gorgon. Similarly, the contrasexual images of 'animus' and 'anima' exist in the unconscious as personifications of the need of each sex for the other. Such images bear little relation to real people but easily become projected upon real people, with the result that the latter become imbued with magic, and seem to possess the fascination, the glamour, and the compulsive attraction which properly belong to the archetypal image. Jung believed that these images were derived from the inherited structure of the mind rather than from infantile experience; and supported this point of view by showing that archetypal images possessing very similar characteristics could be found in the mythologies and religions of different cultures and different ages. The good and evil mother images, for instance, are ubiquitous; and so are the hero myths which we all enjoyed in fairy stories when we were children. We need not linger at this point to explore the complexities of Jungian theory; but we should note that Jung, like Freud, found it necessary to postulate a level of mind at which there is little correspondence between inner and outer. Jung's collective unconscious is more a mythological world than a seething cauldron of infantile desire; but it is none the less a place of powerful emotions, of compelling, overwhelming experience, which is sharply divided from the external world, but which can on occasion invade external reality, and which in any case underlies man's perception of all objects, both personal and impersonal.

In Kleinian theory, all is derived from infantile experience. According to this point of view, the infant's capacity for phantasy is present from birth, and first manifests itself in hallucinatory images of the breast, which are sharply divided into 'good' and 'bad' according as to whether the infant finds the breast satisfying or frustrating. These images are mental constructs derived from experience; but they nevertheless persist as permanent denizens of the mind, and continue to possess all or nothing qualities of 'goodness' and 'badness' which are obviously equivalent to the absolute goodness of Jung's archetypal mother, and the absolute badness of her opposite, the witch or the destructive goddess. In Kleinian theory, frustrating objects become persecutors; and man's paranoid potential, so easily tapped even in so-called normal people, takes origin from the experiences of the first few months of extra-uterine existence. Whether this is so or not, I concluded in Chapter 5 that schizoid characters clearly demonstrate, in their behaviour and attitudes, the persistence into adult life of various emotional responses which pertain to infancy, including the opposites of omnipotence and helplessness, and the fear of being in the power of malignant persecutors, so clearly exemplified by Kafka. I might have added that schizoid characters are also prone to an idealization of their objects as unrealistic as their paranoid fear of them. When 'falling in love' is, as it can be, an overwhelming or shattering experience, it is as schizoid a phenomenon as its opposite. Absolute trust is, in human affairs, as unrealistic as absolute mistrust.

Other examples of what is meant would not be difficult to find; but enough has been said to show that, however much analysts of different schools may disagree, they are united in believing that there is an inner realm of mind which is separated from external reality, but to which the 'I' or ego of man has to adapt as he has to adapt to the world around him. Although the inner and outer worlds interact, and may on occasion correspond, or appear to do so, they are

154

generally separate. Nevertheless, the inner world of the psyche influences our daily thought, feeling and behaviour in ways of which we are only partially aware. At night, its activity becomes manifest in dreams, which are emotionally, rather than rationally, determined, and which often bring to light incidents and figures from childhood which have been forgotten. In Jungian theory, dreams are believed to have a regulatory function. A one-sided attitude in consciousness— say, for instance, an approach to life exclusively governed by reason— provokes an opposite response from the unconscious, a nightmare of unrestrained emotion, or a passionate outburst of feeling. This idea of the dream as having a compensatory function is interesting in the light of modern research, which has demonstrated that dreams are necessary for health. Because it is now possible to detect when subjects are dreaming, by means of the electro-encephalogram, it can be arranged that a man is deprived of dreams without at the same time being deprived of any substantial amount of sleep. Persons who are prevented from dreaming become disturbed in mind, and eventually mentally ill. This 'therapeutic' effect of dreams is not fully understood; but there is no doubt that if we are not allowed recurrent contact with the inner world of the psyche from which dreams originate, we suffer for it. Since animals appear to dream, we must assume that they too possess some kind of inner world of the imagination; but that possessed by man is probably far richer and more complex.

How does this inner world originate? Analysts tend to assume that it comes about as the consequence of frustration. If, it can be argued, an infant's need was invariably met as soon as it was manifested, there would be no need for the infant to seek imaginary satisfactions. If the breast is always available, there is no reason to hallucinate one. In other words, if there was a perfect match between mother and infant, between object and subject, no inner world would ever be formed, since, in the first instance, this world is presumed to consist of unfulfilled desires and unsatisfied wishes. We know that, in cases like those of Descartes and Newton, where mothering has been notably lacking or rudely interrupted, the result is a schizoid split between reason and emotion, and an added impetus to conquer the world by thought. It is as if such individuals early abandoned any hope of obtaining emotional fulfilment in the real world and therefore banished their feelings to an inner world, largely unconscious, where emotion makes little contact with external reality. In crude and oversimplified fashion one might compare such a manoeuvre to that of the dwarf Alberich in *Das Rheingold*. Disappointed of love from, and rejected by, the Rhinemaidens, he steals their gold, and, with the ring made from it, aims at becoming master of the world.

But these are extreme examples. Deprivation and neglect may accelerate and accentuate the formation of an inner world in which emotional satisfaction is only obtained in phantasy; but such a world is, as we have seen, characteristic of human beings as such, and not confined to the obviously deprived. Of course, no human mother is perfect, and no human infant can therefore expect that its slightest want will receive immediate attention. That is a wish belonging to an inner world of phantasy. But the correspondence between mother and infant is less 'perfect' than might be expected. One of the peculiar features of the human condition is that the young are born into the world not only notably helpless, and therefore notably dependent upon their mothers, but that the relationship between a mother and her infant is easily disturbed. Instead of the perfect match between need and fulfilment which one might expect if Nature arranged matters with the maximum efficiency, it is clear from the subsequent development of infants that, very often, their needs are not adequately fulfilled, or not met soon enough, or fulfilled and then suddenly disappointed, as happens when, for example, a mother has to leave her infant for a protracted period after meeting its needs satisfactorily for the first few months of life.

It is nonsense, however, invariably to blame the mother for what may go wrong with her child's emotional development. Most mothers are, to use Winnicott's phrase, 'good enough', and every psychiatrist will have seen cases in which mothers have been good and devoted, and yet the child has developed into a schizophrenic, or shown evidence of a schizoid or other disorder of character. In Chapter 8, I quoted from Freud's paper on 'The Disposition to Obsessional Neurosis' in which he postulated that the person who later became liable to develop obsessional symptoms had shown, in early childhood, 'a chronological outstripping of libidinal development by ego development'.[2] It is quite possible that intellectually precocious, sensitive infants react to minor frustrations as if they were major tragedies; and that these experiences become indelibly recorded, with a consequent deleterious effect upon the child's future.

We are arguing here that there is something *intrinsically frustrating*

156

about human infancy; that this frustration, because it implies lack of satisfaction in the real world, encourages the development of an inner world of phantasy; and that sensitive, precocious, gifted children, who may be presumed to possess a nervous system which is superior as a recording device, and who later become creative, are more deeply affected and possibly 'imprinted' by their whole experience of infancy.

That human infancy is itself frustrating is a notion not difficult to support: in spite of 'omnipotent' phantasies, how humiliating to be totally at the mercy of adult handling; picked up, fed, cleaned, or played with at *their* convenience; helpless, even when the embracing arms are loving. Swift, admittedly a 'pathological' character, springing from a disturbed background, was surely recording his own impressions of his own infancy when Gulliver, in the hands of the giants of Brobdingnag, recalls: 'That which gave me the most Uneasiness among those Maids of Honour, when my Nurse carried me to visit them, was to see them use me without any Manner of Ceremony like a Creature who has no sort of Consequence.'[3] The more precocious a child, the more quickly and profoundly must he come to realize just how helpless and impotent he is in reality. At birth, and for a long period after birth, the infant nervous system is incompletely developed in such a way that the motor, executive side is far less developed than the sensory, receptive side. The newborn human, unlike the young of many species, can see, hear and smell. He is also sensitive to pain, touch, and change of position. But he is notably lacking in motor coordination, takes a long time to learn to stand and walk, a longer time to control bowels and bladder, and a longer time still to be able to use words with the same facility with which he understands them. There must be many situations in infancy which are intrinsically frustrating because the infant does not possess a mature enough motor apparatus to react with an appropriate response. Pain, for example, makes adults either want to fight or flee, but the human infant can do neither. All he can do is thrash about in impotent rage. Most of us can recall the frustration of not being able to make adults understand because we had not the command of words to do so. Small children appreciate the meaning of what is said to them long before they master the use of language, and suffer frequent humiliation because they know what they want to express, but cannot put it into words. No wonder we all possess an inner world of phantasy; as infants and children, we needed it.

Most people accept that childhood experience is likely to exert a powerful influence upon future development; but many are understandably sceptical about the effects of earliest infancy. Man is distinguished by a highly-developed memory; but very few people can recall events from their childhood which occurred before the period between three and four years old. However, to suppose that the experiences of earliest infancy do exert a potent and permanent effect is by no means as fantastic as it might at first appear, even although these experiences cannot be consciously recalled. Freud assumed that 'infantile amnesia' was the result of repression. That is, he believed that much of infantile experience was concerned with powerful impulses of love and hate directed towards parental figures, and that these impulses were so primitive, violent, and self-seeking that the mind itself banished them and the experiences connected with them to the unconscious. There is, of course, no doubt that repression occurs, and that it is an active defensive mechanism in us all. Dreams, as we previously indicated, do bring to light forgotten and repressed memories of childhood. Moreover, there is some experimental evidence to support Freud's theory. One would expect, according to his hypothesis, that pleasant experiences would be more easily recalled than unpleasant. In one experiment with students who were asked to recall their earliest childhood memories, 50% of the memories were pleasant, 20% neutral, and only 30% unpleasant.[4] It looks, therefore, as if a selective forgetting of the unpleasant does occur; an idea supported by the speed with which we forget pain in adult life. But this may not be the whole explanation. There is another immature characteristic of the human infant which is relevant to the problem of infantile amnesia, and is additional, rather than antagonistic, to Freud's explanation.

The brain of a baby at birth weighs only a quarter as much as it will do when the baby becomes an adult. 'The temporal lobes, which are enormous in the adult human in comparison with other animals, are largely missing. The baby's brain remains in this embryonic stage for about two years.' We know, from neurosurgical experiment, that the temporal lobes are largely concerned with memory. 'Working with patients with epilepsy or brain injuries, Dr Penfield made brain maps. These showed that about one-quarter of the cortex of the left temporal lobe is used by a child for language and becomes his speech centre. It is concerned with memory and the use of words. The remaining three-quarters is used for recording memories of experiences and interpreting them in the light of present events. It is called the interpretive cortex.'[5]

The fact that the part of the brain concerned with later conscious memory is not fully developed at birth does not mean that experience has not been recorded, or that both pleasant and unpleasant happenings have not exerted an effect upon the baby's development. Indeed, what we know from experiments with monkeys, and from the study of institutionally-reared infants, indicates that the psychoanalytic assumption that the earliest months of a child's life are vitally important is correct. At a physical level, we know from the effects of German measles and other noxious agents, that the earlier damage occurs to the brain during the course of his development, the more likely are the effects of such damage to be permanent. The physical mechanism by which events are recorded in the brain is not fully understood, but that it exists is not in doubt; and it is likely that the earliest events leave traces which are just as deep, or deeper, than subsequent impressions. That the temporal cortex is not fully developed for many months after birth is another explanation for childhood amnesia which psychoanalysts do not usually take into account; but they are probably right in thinking that the baby's earliest experiences are registered, though at a lower level than the cortical.

'The experiences of early childhood are firmly recorded in the lower centres of the *old* brain and exert a profound effect upon subsequent behavior. However, they are isolated and inviolable. There is no way for them to become connected with the interpretive cortex, which has not yet developed, and hence they can never be either retrieved as memories or altered by comparisons with subsequent experiences. They are like the patterns of behavior that are inherited as instincts, or are acquired as the result of imprintation.'[5] Here then, is a physiological schema which not only suggests how it might be that an inner world of psychical experience is formed, but also proffers an explanation as to why this world becomes cut off from the external world, and is therefore subsequently unaffected by it. Freud would have been the first to consider, and welcome, an explanation of his theory of repression in physiological and anatomical terms.

What is meant by 'memory' in small infants, therefore, is something different from what is meant by memory in adults, or indeed in later childhood. But experiment has shown that what Crile calls the 'old brain' or the limbic system, not only has some capacity for functioning independently of the 'new brain' or cortex, but is also concerned with the most primitive emotions. Electrical stimulation of this ancient part of the brain can cause erection and ejaculation, aggressive behaviour, defensive-withdrawal behaviour, and feeding behaviour. These various centres are obviously aroused and stimulated in infants in differing ways and intensities according to the varying manner in which they are handled and treated. Pathways and interconnections between cells in the brain, once established, quickly become habitual, and there is no reason to suppose that the limbic system is any different from any other part of the brain in this respect. That is, the brain shows 'memory' at a chemical-physiological level, in that conduction of impulses is facilitated by repeated use of the same pathway of interconnections. But this kind of 'memory' need not be conscious. A child could therefore have experiences of pleasure and pain which he could never consciously recall, but which, from this deep level, continue to influence him.

Does this ancient part of the brain create images? This is a difficult question to answer, but, judging from some of the images which appear in dreams, especially those which seem to come from some unknown source, unrelated to personal memories, it seems quite likely that it does. What is also probable is that it cannot interpret language. As MacLean writes: 'Considered in the light of Freudian psychology, the old brain would have many of the attributes of the unconscious id. One might argue, however, that the visceral brain is not at all unconscious (possibly not even in certain stages of sleep), but rather eludes the grasp of the intellect because its animalistic and primitive structure makes it impossible to communicate in verbal terms. Perhaps it were more proper to say, therefore, it was an animalistic and illiterate brain.'[6]

Here then we have another approach, and another explanation, proffered this time by a surgeon and a neurologist. But whether they are right or wrong, they are recognizing the same problem as did Freud and the other analysts: that is, the existence of an inner world, primitive, passionate, all-or-none in character, which, because it is only tenuously connected with consciousness, has largely to be deduced from indirect evidence.

We have seen that this curious feature of human nature is partly the consequence of the human infant being born into the world in such an immature state, both physically and psychologically. We recognize, and shall further explore in the next chapter, the fact that this immaturity and its prolongation in childhood is adaptive. Man's success as a species has depended upon his cleverness, his capacity to learn, and his ability to transmit his culture from one generation to the next. If he did not have a long period of immaturity during which he could learn, he would be able to do none of these things. The inner world of phantasy, which seems to arise from, or at any rate, to be intensified by, the intrinsic frustrations of human infancy, can be regarded as merely a by-product of this type of developmental pattern. On the other hand, it can be looked on as itself adaptive. If every human being is left with a residue of dissatisfaction which he carries with him from childhood into adult life, and if, moreover, this dissatisfaction is contained in a part of the mind which is buried deep and difficult of access, is it not likely that he will be driven to try and compensate for this dissatisfaction, and to integrate or assimilate this split-off inner world? It is easy to see in the case of 'pathological' characters like Newton and Descartes that their discoveries and philosophical schemata are the consequence of a schizoid split between reason and emotion; and, in each case, there was a cogent reason why such a split should have occurred, in that both were maternally deprived in an obvious way. Einstein's attitude to people strongly suggests that something must have gone wrong with his infantile relation to his mother also; but his biographers are silent upon the point, and we have no evidence of it. In any case, however anxious Einstein may have been to sever all emotional ties, he found a satisfactory adaptation for himself, and was certainly less at odds with other people than either Newton or Descartes. What is being suggested is that these highly creative people are but extreme examples of a general human phenomenon. Man carries with him throughout life a discontent, varying in degree, but always present, as a consequence of the intrinsic frustrations of his infancy. This drives him to seek symbolic satisfactions: ways of mastering the external world on the one hand, and ways of integrating and coming to terms with his internal world on the other. It is by means of his creativity, both in art and science, that man has survived and achieved so much. His prolonged and unsatisfactory infancy is itself adaptive, since it leaves him with a 'divine discontent' which spurs him on to creative achievement.

REFERENCES

1. GOUGH, Harrison G. 'Identifying the Creative Man', *Journal of Value Engineering*, Vol 2, No. 4. 1964, August 15, pp. 5-12.
2. FREUD, Sigmund. 'The Disposition to Obsessional Neurosis' (London: The Hogarth Press and The Institute of Psycho-Analysis, 1958. Standard Edition, Vol. XII, p. 325.
3. SWIFT, Jonathan. 'A Voyage to Brobdingnag' in *Gulliver's Travels and Selected Writings in Prose and Verse;* ed. John Hayward (London: Nonesuch Press, 1963) p. 115.
4. HUNTER, I. M. L. *Memory* (Harmondsworth: Penguin Books, 1964) pp. 271-3.
5. CRILE, George. *A Naturalistic View of Man* (New York: World Publishing Company, 1969) pp. 11, 30, 31.
6. MACLEAN, Paul D. Quoted in *The Ghost in the Machine* by Arthur Koestler (London: Hutchinson, 1967) p. 287.

13

Divine Discontent

In the last chapter, I pointed out that the human infant, although well-equipped to perceive and register sensory experience, is born in a particularly dependent and helpless condition, and remains in this state for a relatively longer time than the young of many other species. We boldly supposed that the discontent thus engendered might itself be adaptive, since frustration encourages the formation of an inner world of the imagination; and this, in its turn, promotes the creative discovery of symbolic achievements and satisfactions. If this hypothesis is correct, we should expect to find that the prolongation of human 'immaturity' would not be confined to infancy, but that it would be extended into later childhood. That this is in fact the case is not difficult to demonstrate. Moreover, 'immaturity' continues to be as adaptive in later human childhood as it was in infancy.

At the anatomical level, it has long been recognized that human beings continue to display, in adult life, characteristics which, in other species of primates, belong to the foetus, and which generally disappear or are superseded in the mature animal. This peculiarity of man is so pronounced that it is variously referred to as 'neoteny', 'foetalization', or 'paedomorphosis'. According to Julian Huxley, the distribution of hair on man is 'extremely similar to that on a late foetus of a chimpanzee, and there can be little doubt that it represents an extension of the temporary anthropoid phase into permanence'.[1] So, also, is the flatness of the human face, and the absence of heavy brow ridges. The small size of man's teeth, and their late eruption, is another infantile feature to persist. The angle formed betweeen the base of the skull and the spine is especially characteristic. This, in man, is almost 90°, so that the skull is balanced on top of a vertically disposed spinal column. In apes this arrangement is found only in the foetus. The adult ape carries its head much further forward relatively to the spinal column, and needs, therefore, a more massive musculature at the back of the neck to support it; an anatomical feature immediately obvious to anyone who has tried to draw, or to

163

imitate the posture of, a gorilla or an orang-outang. These anatomical immaturities are matched by a generalized retardation of the rate of man's growth and development, which, relative to the length of the total life span, has been very much slowed down. In most other animals, the period from birth to the onset of sexual maturity comprises something between a twelfth and an eighth part of the whole duration of the animal's existence. In man, this period is so extended that it forms no less than a quarter of his life. Many parents, reflecting ruefully upon the emotional and financial commitments involved, might be glad to see their offspring mature and become independent at a very much earlier age. But if they did so, they would bypass much of what makes them human and civilized; for the price of culture is delayed maturity.

Just as the attainment of sexual maturity is held back, so also is the completion of growth of the brain itself. A young chimpanzee completes its brain growth within twelve months of birth; most monkeys take but six months to do the same. Man, on the other hand, has a brain at birth which is relatively much smaller, since it is only 23% of its adult size; and his growth in general is not complete until more than twenty years after birth.

This prolongation of anatomical and physiological immaturity is matched by a corresponding extension of the period during which the human child is dependent upon adults. The biological purpose of this prolonged childhood is not in doubt. Man's specific adaptation to his environment is based upon his capacity to learn, his flexibility, and the fact that his culture can be transmitted, partially 'ready-made', from one generation to the next. Natural selection determined that man should inherit the earth, not because he is well-armed, for he is actually weak and ill-protected, but because of his cleverness. His adaptation has been through the use of his brain, more especially through the use of those parts of that hypertrophied organ which are connected with speech. To use his brain to the full, man had to linger in the childhood position. For children, far more than adults, are flexible, malleable, and adaptable. For purposes of learning, therefore, it is clearly advantageous that a man should remain a child for relatively longer than the young remain immature in other species. Konrad Lorenz has called man 'the specialist in non-specialization'. His persistent immaturity aids him in this respect; for it is the 'grown-up' who becomes fixed in his ways, and who is unable to grasp new ways of approaching problems.

One interesting way in which this persistence of childhood characteristics shows itself is in man's continuing predilection for games. Although animals of various species continue to play when adult, they generally do so much less than when they were infants. But man continues to play all kinds of games in adult life to a far greater extent than might be expected. This is relevant to his creativity. As many scientists will attest, new ideas come from 'playing around' with old ones. We should be less than human if our imagination were not playful as well as serious; and some of our most creative and original minds, for instance, Arthur Eddington and J. D. Bernal, have shown a Carroll-like turn of phantasy which is closely connected with their scientific inventiveness. Eddington's wit and imagination are evident in *The Nature of the Physical World*; the famous set of Gifford lectures in which he expounded the foundations of modern physics to a lay audience.[2] Other scientists have not disdained science fiction; for example, Fred Hoyle in *The Black Cloud*. The borderline between playful and serious in scientific creativity is not sharply defined, and what one generation may dismiss as mere phantasy can be translated into reality by the next. The scientific romances of Jules Verne and H. G. Wells, both of whom wrote of journeys to the moon, have turned out to be more realistically achievable than either author probably expected.[3]

Another childhood trait which is persistent in man is his curiosity. Most animals, on reaching sexual maturity, show less of this than they did when juvenile. 'Inquisitive behaviour wanes or disappears completely in all learners after sexual maturity.'[4] This is not so with man, who continues to show extreme curiosity and inquisitiveness long after he is grown-up. If he did not do so, we should presumably have no scientific laboratories. Once established, curiosity may remain into extreme old age, and, indeed, often appears to be the spice of life which 'keeps people going'. An enhanced ability to imagine the future is characteristic of the human species, and curiosity about whether or not one is right in one's predictions is one motive for staying alive.

There can be no doubt that man has been so signally successful because he has remained 'immature' and therefore flexible and able to continue learning. There is something about being adult which is inimical to learning. Intelligence, which can largely be defined in terms of responding to, and grasping the essentials in an unfamiliar situation, starts to decline within a few years of its peak having been

165

attained. As measured by intelligence tests, intelligence begins to diminish as early as the middle or late twenties. It may be that this decline is psychologically, as well as physiologically, determined. Human beings can, of course, go on learning all their lives; and the greater difficulty which the middle-aged experience in tackling new tasks has often been exaggerated. One result of man's prolonged childhood is the fact that he can easily regress to being a child again when this is appropriate. Authority figures have become so much incorporated into his inner world that they are easily projected upon teachers and bosses. And so, a middle-aged man may sit contentedly in an evening class like any schoolboy without loss of face, and may accord to a teacher much younger than himself the same respect he felt for a schoolmaster when he really was a child. This learning situation, however, requires some such regression psychologically if it is to prove effective; and those who cannot temporarily relinquish adult status are likely to prove poor pupils. The student unrest, which seems a recurrent problem in all civilizations which demand higher education, is related to this psychological problem. We require students to be adult, responsible and independent. Yet, at the same time, we keep them artificially in a 'young' situation in which they are supposed to sit at the feet of professors and be under instruction. Since these requirements are to some extent incompatible, especially at an age when adulthood has not yet been firmly established, it is not surprising that the result is conflict. It is much easier to regress to a childhood 'learning' situation without loss of face if one has been, for some years, an established adult. Although the practical difficulties are considerable, there is a good deal to be said for letting a year or two intervene between leaving school and proceeding to university, during which the adolescent may win his adult spurs. He is often then better equipped emotionally to accept going back to being a student. Indeed, this happened during the years following the 1939–45 war; a period notable for creative achievement by undergraduates.

It is, of course, sexual maturity which is generally held to mark the attainment of adult status. In peoples more primitive and perhaps more emotionally realistic than ourselves, the passage from being a child to becoming an adult is marked by ritual observances. Such rites linger on in Western society in attenuated and spiritualized form in the ceremonies of confirmation and Bar Mitzvah. Perhaps the achievement of an university degree or higher certificate of education ought now to be invested with the significance which used to pertain to the rites of religion. In any event, our ceremonies are ill-attuned to the realities of our culture; since, although a young person may become sexually active shortly after puberty, the exigencies of civilization demand that he shall continue to be educated, and hence to remain in the dependent position, for far longer than his sexual status would warrant in a primitive society.

It would be easy to blame the sexual problems of modern Western man upon his culture; and indeed I did so in Chapter 10, in which I contrasted our own attitude to childhood sexuality unfavourably with the more liberal practices of the Marquesans. There is indeed much room for improvement in this respect in our society, But this cannot possibly be regarded as the whole story: and reformers like Wilhelm Reich, who hoped that, if the sexual mores of Western society could be transformed, we should abolish neurotic problems, must be dismissed as Utopian. There is something very peculiar about man's sexual development; and the sexual difficulties which dog him are, to a considerable extent, not the result of cultural prohibition, but implicit in this peculiarity of his species.

Freud, with his usual prescience, was well aware of this. In his last, unfinished book he wrote: 'It has been found that in early childhood there are signs of bodily activity to which only an ancient prejudice could deny the name of sexual and which are linked to psychical phenomena that we come across later in adult erotic life—such as fixation to particular objects, jealousy and so on. It is further found, however, that these phenomena which emerge in early childhood form part of an ordered course of development, that they pass through a regular process of increase, reaching a climax towards the end of the fifth year, after which there follows a lull. During this lull progress is at a standstill and much is unlearnt and there is much recession. After the end of this period of latency, as it is called, sexual life advances once more with puberty; we might say that it has a second efflorescence. And here we come upon the fact that the onset of sexual life is *diphasic*, that it occurs in two waves—something that is unknown except in man and evidently has an important bearing on hominization.'[5] In a footnote, Freud refers to a hypothesis that man was descended from a mammal which reached sexual maturity at the age of five, but supposes that this straight line of development was interrupted by some unspecified external influence.

Freud was not entirely correct in supposing that this phenomenon was 'unknown except in man', although it is certainly much more fully developed in the human species than in any other. In passing, we may observe that one of the major intellectual losses of our time is the fact that Freud was born too soon. Had he been familiar with modern biological and ethological thought, we should have had a different and even more complete synthesis from him, in which biology and psychology would be more satisfactorily reconciled than is at present possible. Alex Comfort makes the same point as Freud in rather different words: 'After a rather rapid epoch of development and growth which leaves the human child, at about the fifth year, walking, talking and weaned, but still wholly unable to fend for itself, the curve flattens out. Growth progresses at a slower tempo, until just before puberty, when it undergoes a spurt. Full size, sexual maturity, and adult intelligence are then reached relatively quickly. It is as though a 'shelf' or plateau had been inserted into the human growth curve, so as to lengthen childhood disproportionately. Traces of this shelf can be seen in lower primate growth curves, but its full development is seen only in Man.'[6]

As we have seen, one purpose of the latency period is not in doubt. By keeping the human child dependent for an unusually long period, Nature is providing the necessary time for learning and the transmission of culture to occur. If a child became sexually mature at the age of five, or even at eight or nine, an age which is actually more in line with the extrapolation of the infantile growth curve—no one can doubt that its capacity to learn and to acquire culture would be much reduced. Moreover, the latency period is the time during which external regulation by parents is replaced by the internal control exercised by the super-ego. This replacement is accompanied by a diminution of the spontaneity which is so typical, and so charming, a feature of early childhood. Many enthusiastic reformers have hoped that this spontaneity could be preserved by the employment of more liberal methods of education; but this can only be achieved to a very limited extent. For acting upon, or expressing, immediate impulse, which is the essence of spontaneity, has its dangers as well as its charms. The majority of crimes of violence, dangerous driving offences, and sexual offences are committed by psychopaths who have failed to develop an internally-controlling super-ego, and who therefore act upon the impulse of the moment, good or bad, with all the spontaneity of childhood.

According to Freud, the beginning of the latency period is marked by the passing of the Oedipus complex. In other words, the infantile passions of love, hate, jealousy and sensual involvement which have hitherto been directed towards parents, undergo a decline in intensity. Looked at biologically, the Oedipus complex appears to be a peculiar phenomenon, of which the function is not immediately obvious. At first sight, it seems unadaptive, since it is primarily concerned with physical impulses towards parent figures which cannot normally be satisfied and which, even if they could, would not result in procreation. Animals other than man show comparatively little evidence of infantile sexuality (though Jane Goodall reports otherwise in male chimpanzees). Yet, as Freud demonstrated, the human child exhibits immature precursors of adult sexuality, manifesting themselves in the oral, anal, and phallic modes; and these impulses are primarily directed towards, or concerned with, the parent of the opposite sex. Alex Comfort makes the interesting suggestion that this apparently premature flowering of the sexual impulse occurs because human sexuality has been 'brought forward' into prereproductive life; a biological device which is perfectly feasible. Because of the long period of human immaturity, and the adaptive necessity of learning, some arrangement was necessary to ensure that the young male should continue for a long period to love the mother in order to stay with her, whilst at the same time avoiding her as a sexual object. The most characteristic feature of the whole complex of Oedipal reactions is that a passionate attachment to the parent of the opposite sex goes hand in hand with an almost equally powerful warning-off device; which psychoanalysis has summarized under the comprehensive term 'castration complex'. It is certainly true that most adult sexual difficulties can ultimately be explained in terms of an over-emphasis upon the warning-off mechanism at the expense of the attachment mechanism. Thus, the male who as a child has been rebuffed and not given enough physical affection from the mother will, in adult life, find that fear of the opposite sex predominates over their attractions. The consequence of this may be impotence, homosexuality, or one or other of the other sexual perversions, most of which are rather complicated devices of reassurance designed to allay fear and thus make possible the expression of sexuality. In similar fashion, feminine homosexuality and frigidity are generally traceable to a persistent fear of the male, who continues to be regarded unconsciously as a powerful and punitive 'father' who is therefore potentially hurtful and damaging.

Our hypothesis that the early childhood, as well as the infancy, of human beings is intrinsically frustrating is amply supported. The 'bringing forward' of sexuality into prereproductive life, in addition to reinforcing dependency, creates a situation in which the child experiences powerful impulses of an instinctive kind which must remain unsatisfied unless the taboo on parent–child incest is infringed. That there are cogent reasons for upholding this taboo is familiar to psychiatrists who have seen the malign effects which parent–child incest sometimes has upon the child's struggle to attain independence and maturity.

In discussing the frustrations of infancy, I was chiefly concerned with the kind of 'psychopathology' which underlies a schizoid or manic-depressive character structure, and which contributes to the formation of an inner world of the imagination. In Chapters 6 and 7, I looked at the kinds of creative solution to which persons with these character structures are impelled. The Oedipal phase of childhood with which I am now concerned is the period from which hysterical and obsessional character structures take origin; and the kinds of creativity preferred by people with these personality traits have been discussed in Chapters 2 and 8.

The fact that the Oedipal phase of childhood is frustrating has the effect of forcing passion into channels other than those leading towards parents. One of the most interesting features of human psychology is the capacity of human beings to become passionate about things other than people. This capacity originates very early, before the time at which the Oedipal reactions are supposed to be fully operative. But it is obviously reinforced by their frustration; and when the latency period supervenes, and the Oedipal emotions are somewhat abated, ample opportunity is afforded for these less personal passions to become more firmly established. The study of creative people reveals that their predominant interest generally becomes established early in life. As Rosamond Harding writes in *An Anatomy of Inspiration*: 'In the man or woman of genius there are always present great technical skill and originality. The technical skill is usually built up from childhood. The future poet scribbles verses as a child, the future artist begins to draw as soon as he can hold a pencil.'[7] Even those who, like George Eliot, do not really begin their creative career till middle age, show, in childhood, foreshadowings of the future. Although 'scenes from Clerical Life' did not appear in Blackwood's magazine until the novelist was 38, it is known that she wrote both fiction and verse in childhood. Picasso could draw before he could speak; and the first noise he learned to make was 'piz', short for 'lapiz', a pencil. At four years old, Mozart was already composing. At the same age, Bela Bartok could play from memory forty songs—with one finger!

If it is agreed that the discontents of infancy serve an adaptive purpose, there will be no difficulty in accepting that the intrinsic frustrations of the Oedipal situation do the same. Similarly, we can see that the persistence of pregenital traits which are usually, and pejoratively, labelled neurotic, may also promote the human tendency towards creative, symbolic endeavours and syntheses.

When Freud first discovered that neurosis was invariably accompanied by a disturbance in the sexual life of the patient, and that this disturbance was the consequence of a failure to outgrow certain infantile, pregenital fixations, he was set upon a path which led towards the assumption that if the patient, by means of psychoanalysis, were able to overcome these fixations, and attain a normal, fully satisfying genital relationship, he would be entirely cured. 'Genital primacy', although recognized to be something of an ideal which is no more completely attainable than emotional maturity, integration, self-realization or enlightenment, still remains the implicit aim of psychoanalysis; and psychoanalysts continue to believe that a fully adult, satisfying sexual relation brings such fulfilment that a man has no need to look beyond this to find happiness. It is true that Freud added to his criteria of happiness the ability to work, but work was not a subject which he explored with the same devotion he accorded to sex. Since, according to his own admission, sex gave him little fulfilment during the second half of his life, and work obviously brought him a great deal, this neglect is somewhat surprising.

Although Freud assumed that, ideally, the various stages of infantile sexuality ought to be passed through and overcome, he did, of course, realize that this was an ideal seldom achieved; and would no doubt have alleged that most men were to some degree 'neurotic' on this account.

'The complete organization is not attained until puberty, in a fourth, genital phase. A state of things is then established in which (1) some earlier libidinal cathexes are retained, (2) others are taken into the sexual function as preparatory, auxiliary acts, the satisfaction of which produces what is known as fore-pleasure, and (3) other urges

171

are excluded from the organization, and are either suppressed altogether (repressed) or are employed in the ego in another way, forming character-traits or undergoing sublimation with a displacement of their aims.'[8] (The word cathexis is best defined as emotional investment. A person or object which becomes of emotional importance is said to be 'cathected' by the subject. In this passage, Freud means that the mouth, the anal region, and so on continue to retain some emotional significance, even though puberty has been reached.)

From this account it is clear that Freud realized the likelihood that most men carry with them into adult life some remnants of unsatisfied (and possibly unsatisfiable) impulse from their infantile pasts. He goes on: 'This process is not always performed faultlessly. Inhibitions in its development manifest themselves as the many sorts of disturbance in sexual life. When this is so, we find fixations of the libido to conditions in earlier phases, where an urge which is independent of the normal sexual aim is described as *perversion*.'[9]

In spite of this realization, psychoanalysts continued to believe that, given ideal conditions of emotional development, all pregenital and Oedipal impulse should be finally discharged in one way or another, and that true happiness was only attainable through sexual pleasure. The idea that there might be a positive function in the persistence of infantile and childhood emotional traits seems to have escaped them. So has the notion that, even if the genital phase has been reached, and a satisfying sexual relationship established, this state of affairs might still not provide complete fulfilment for, or resolution of, the discontents of man.

In Chapter 1, I quoted from K. R. Eissler's book on Leonardo his view that a genius would not be capable of his creative achievements if he was enjoying an adequate sex life. 'The energy flow into the object relation would be diverted from the artistic process. Consequently, only the blockage of a permanent object attachment can produce that intense hunger for objects that results in the substitute formation of the perfect work of art.'[10]

Implicit in this statement is the idea that 'object relations' are so satisfying that a man needs nothing else for happiness; and also that all pregenital impulses can be comprised in an adequate object attachment. Yet, as we have seen, both these assumptions are questionable. There are plenty of examples of artists who appear to have enjoyed fully satisfactory sexual relationships, and yet have found it necessary to pursue their art with vigour. In Chapter 2, I quoted from the Wittkowers' study of artists *Born under Saturn*. They demonstrate that every variety of the erotic life, including happy marriage, can be found amongst artists. And it is not difficult to demonstrate that the oral, anal, and phallic phases of childhood are never fully integrated by anyone, but continue to exert an effect upon adult behaviour. The oral phase, for example, manifests itself in innumerable ways, from smoking and the chewing of sweets for pleasure rather than for food, to unassuageable 'oceanic' longings for losing oneself. Civilization could hardly continue were we not persistently 'anal'; with a consequent need for order, with a strong distaste for dirt, and with an urge to organize and control. And which of us is free from the traits of exhibitionistic display so characteristic of the phallic phase? We all like to boast, to show off, and to impress others with our achievements—our 'potency'. In short, none of us ever completely integrate our infantile libidinal phases into an adult love relationship.

Congo, when he was given two females, ceased to paint. Perhaps chimpanzees are more adept than man at integrating their infantile sexuality and finding fulfilment in an adult 'object relation', (or, in this case, two object relations). Whether this is so or not, there can be little doubt that man is so constituted that he is compelled to seek symbolic solutions and syntheses, and that this trait originated as an adaptive device which better fitted him to master the world in which he found himself. Necessity is one parent of invention; the other is the discontent which is a consequence of man's prolonged immaturity.

REFERENCES

1. HUXLEY, Julian. *The Uniqueness of Man* (London: Chatto & Windus, 1941) p. 13.
2. EDDINGTON, Arthur S. *The Nature of the Physical World* (Cambridge University Press, 1928).
3. HOYLE, Fred. *The Black Cloud* (London: Heinemann, 1957).
   VERNE, Jules. *From the Earth to the Moon*.
   WELLS, H. G. *First Men on the Moon*.
4. HASS, Hans. *The Human Animal* (London: Hodder & Stoughton, 1970) p. 93.

5. FREUD, Sigmund. 'An Outline of Psycho-Analysis' (London: The Hogarth Press and The Institute of Psycho-Analysis, 1964) Standard Edition, Vol. XXIII, p. 153.
6. COMFORT, Alex. *Nature and Human Nature* (London: Weidenfeld & Nicolson, 1966) p. 17.
7. HARDING, Rosamond E. M. *An Anatomy of Inspiration* (Cambridge: Heffer, 1940) pp. 1-2.
8. FREUD, Sigmund. 'An Outline of Psycho-Analysis' (London: The Hogarth Press and The Institute of Psycho-Analysis, 1964) Standard Edition, Vol. XXIII, p. 155.
9. Ibid, p. 155.
10. EISSLER, K. R. *Leonardo da Vinci. Psychoanalytic Notes on the Enigma* (London: The Hogarth Press and The Institute of Psycho-Analysis, 1962) p. 287.

14

Disposable Passion

In the last chapter I noted in passing that one peculiarity of human beings is the capacity to become passionate about the impersonal and the abstract as well as about other members of the human species. It is true that the chimpanzee Congo displayed this capacity in rudimentary form; but, as we have seen, his interest in painting did not survive his attainment of 'genitality'. This is not so with human beings, who continue, as a rule throughout life, to be enthusiastic about all manner of things which are not obviously or directly connected with the physical passions. In this book, I have been chiefly concerned with the arts and with scientific hypotheses; and we have seen that the passion with which men pursue either or both is biologically explicable. But science and the arts are, of course, not the only areas to become invested with emotional energy. Men become passionate about an enormously wide range of ideas and subjects, from religion to sport, from gardening to the niceties of linguistics. Nor does this apply only to the creative and original. The man who is no more than a spectator, a listener, or a passive participant may invest a considerable amount of libido in whatever field has happened to engage his interest. This book is primarily directed towards examining what forces drive the highly creative; but it is clear that the capacity for investing things other than the body with emotional energy is not confined to them. If it were so, they would have no one to appreciate their discoveries and creations.

The human being, one might suppose, is more entirely a 'physical' being during infancy than at any subsequent period of his existence. Yet the human tendency to shift libidinal interest from the body on to something else is evident from an extremely early age. D. W. Winnicott was the only psychoanalyst to pay much attention to this; and he did so in a series of interesting papers devoted to the study of what he calls 'transitional objects'. A transitional object is so-called because it 'represents the infant's transition from a state of being merged with the mother to a state of being in relation to the mother as something outside and separate'.[1] Objects of this kind may be soft toys, blankets,

175

sheets, or indeed almost anything that can be sucked and cuddled. Such an object becomes intensely important to the child, who will not willingly be parted from it, especially on going to sleep at night, and also at other times when he may be feeling lonely or anxious. Most mothers recognize the importance of such objects, allow their children to possess and use them, and fall in with the child's reluctance to have the object washed, removed, or altered in any way. As Winnicott said: 'It is true that the piece of blanket (or whatever it is) is symbolical of some part-object, such as the breast. Nevertheless, the point of it is not its symbolic value so much as its actuality. Its not being the breast (or the mother), although real, is as important as the fact that it stands for the breast (or mother).

'When symbolism is employed the infant is already clearly distinguishing between fantasy and fact, between inner objects and external objects, between primary creativity and perception. But the term transitional object, according to my suggestion, gives room for the process of becoming able to accept difference and similarity. I think there is use for a term for the root of symbolism in time, a term that describes the infant's journey from the purely subjective to objectivity; and it seems to me that the transitional object (piece of blanket, etc) is what we see of this journey of progress towards experiencing.'[2]

In Chapter 12, referring to the formation of the infant's inner world of the imagination, I discussed the hypothesis that, because the breast is not always available, the infant tends to imagine, or 'hallucinate' it; and I also said that such images, 'good' and 'bad', both of the breast and later of other things and of whole people, tend to persist unchanged in the inner world of the child as 'internal objects'. The most interesting thing about transitional objects is that they are *not* internal objects, because they obviously have a real existence outside the child. Yet, on the other hand, they are equally *not* the mother or the breast for which they act as symbols. They are intermediate between the inner, subjective world of the imagination and the real, external world which may be presumed to be that which is shared with everyone else. They are also objects which have become invested with emotion—comfort, support, protection—which is associated with the presence of the mother and with physical contact with her. They are the earliest example, in terms of human development, of the tendency to invest something other than a person or a body with passion.

The kind of passion with which an infant invests a transitional object is of course 'pregenital' rather than genital. The object represents or symbolizes the infant's oral needs; for the breast itself, and for the comfort and security which are its emotional accompaniments. What is interesting is that phantasy, or the use of its own body, is not enough to bring satisfaction. Thumb-sucking, or, at a later stage, playing with the genitals, may appear to bring comfort to infants who do not make use of transitional objects. In this largely unexplored area of human behaviour it is difficult to be sure why some children do, and others do not, become emotionally attached to objects in the way described. However, it seems highly probable that the use of transitional objects is a sign of health. There is always something unsatisfactory and even dangerous in possessing an inner world which is utterly unconnected with the outer world. For the schizoid person, the inability to find any connection between inner and outer is a perpetual threat; for the failure to do so has the result that life becomes meaningless and futile. If there is no subjective investment of the external world with emotion, from the subject's inner world, reality appears quite flat and dull; as meaningless as music to the tone-deaf, or as red–green contrasts to the colour-blind. Since the transitional object is a link between inner and outer worlds, belonging wholly to neither, yet clearly pertaining to both, it may be presumed to be an advance upon phantasy which has no relation at all to the world outside the subject.

It is in schizophrenia that the inability to make any link between inner and outer worlds is seen in its full malignancy. The schizophrenic becomes 'mad' when he substitutes his inner world for external reality, and it becomes obvious that ordinary people can neither share nor understand his way of looking at things. There is generally a long precursory history of failure to find satisfaction in the external world, and a correspondingly intense preoccupation with phantasy. Interestingly enough, it has long been recognized that schizophrenics have a particular difficulty in making use of symbols which might create for them bridges between what goes on inside them and what happens outside. Tests emphasizing the metaphorical use of language reveal the schizophrenic's inability to free himself from the concrete. Thus, if asked the meaning of the proverb 'A rolling stone gathers no moss', the schizophrenic will reply: 'A stone rolling down hill doesn't stop long enough for moss to grow on it.' All he can see is the literal picture conjured up by the words.

The link which would bridge the gap between the behaviour of the stone and the restless, unsettled behaviour of some human beings, is lacking.

As we have seen, some split between the inner world and the outer world is common to all human beings; and the need to bridge the gap is the source of creative endeavour. When the gap is particularly wide, as in the examples of Newton, Einstein and Descartes, we refer to the person as schizoid. Only an all-embracing scheme of things is sufficient to heal so wide a rift as they present. For them, hypotheses served an analogous function to that performed by a transitional object for the infant. Because their theories related both to their own internal worlds, and also to the external world, we rate them as men of creative genius. If there had been no such link with reality, their hypotheses would have been indistinguishable from psychotic delusions.

Various examples of the human tendency to invest things other than people with passion can be found in the sexual perversions. This topic is relevant to our main theme in that Freud wrote: 'The forces that can be employed for cultural activities are to a great extent obtained through the suppression of what are known as the *perverse* elements of sexual existence.'[3] Winnicott, in various places in his writing, linked transitional objects with fetishes; and indeed, the former can sometimes become the latter, although at a much later stage of childhood development. Elsewhere, it has been described how a child who was much neglected by his mother used to steal bangles from her dressing-table, and obtain vicarious comfort by taking these trinkets to bed with him. In adult life, it became obligatory for his girl-friends to wear such bangles if he were to achieve full sexual arousal.[4]

At first sight, a good deal of perverse sexual phantasy might be thought to be a rudimentary form of creativity. I pointed out in Chapter 2, that the writings of Ian Fleming contain much sado-masochistic material. I also noted that perverse interests can be detected in the novels of Conrad; his fear of dominant women, and his fetishistic preoccupations with shoes and hair. But, whereas the perverse elements are overt in the writings of Ian Fleming, and still more so in frank pornography, they have to be untangled and disinterred from the novels of Conrad, because Conrad has made them part of a greater whole. There is a real difference between a work of art and a masturbatory phantasy, however much the same elemen-

tary units of human experience may enter into both. Velasquez'
Rokeby Venus and Goya's *Naked Maja* are both paintings celebrating
the delights of the nude female body, but it is improbable that many
people are impelled to masturbate while looking at these pictures.
Yet this is the express function of the nudes in pornographic magazines. The latter are, in spite of being photographed, not real people
at all but personified phantasy. Pornographic images lead away from
reality, not towards it; whereas great art enhances our appreciation
of reality, and, in the instances of the *Rokeby Venus* and the *Naked
Maja*, make sexuality itself part of a greater whole in which sensuality
is combined with beauty. There are, of course, examples of pictures
which are neither art nor pornography, but something intermediate.
The paintings of Sir William Russell Flint, for example, are titillating
but not crude enough to be labelled pornographic; skilful, but lacking
any spiritual or aesthetic content which could transmute them into
art.

Although the sexual perversions might be regarded as embryoni-
cally creative, in that much of their content is symbolic, and an
attempt to displace libido from the body on to an idea, yet they are in
fact totally sterile. No literature is more stereotyped, repetitive, and
ultimately boring than pornography. It might be argued that the
various forms of sado-masochistic, fetishistic and other types of
perverse sexual phantasy provide a link between the inner world of the
subject and the real world; thus fulfilling what we have stated to be a
valuable function, shared by transitional objects, scientific theories,
works of art and other things. But, in practice, this is not so, since
the end result is masturbation, not a relationship; and this is often
the case even when the perverse phantasies appear to be used to
enhance an apparently adult sexual relation. A good deal of sexual
intercourse is more like masturbation than the real thing.

In this connection, an observation of Winnicott's is important. He
recognizes that there is a close connection between creativity and
play; and allocates both to the 'transitional' world between subjective and objective, with which we have been concerned in this
and the previous chapter. He is equally dissatisfied with the simplistic
psychoanalytic view of sublimation; the idea that creative activity is
a straightforward substitute for instinctual expression. Here is what he
writes about play and masturbation. 'In psychoanalytic writings and
discussions, the subject of playing has been too closely linked with
masturbation and the various sensuous experiences. It is true that

when we are confronted with masturbation we always think: what is the fantasy? And it is also true that when we witness playing we tend to wonder what is the physical excitement that is linked with the type of play that we witness. But playing needs to be studied as a subject on its own, supplementary to the concept of the sublimation of instinct.

'It may very well be that we have missed something by having these two phenomena (playing and masturbatory activity) so closely linked in our minds. I have tried to point out that when a child is playing the masturbatory element is essentially lacking; or, in other words, that if when a child is playing the physical excitement of instinctual involvement becomes evident, then the playing stops, or is at any rate spoiled.'[5]

Masturbation, therefore, acts as a short circuit. In so far as either art or play are sublimatory—and no one is attempting to deny that this is part of their function—masturbation is inimical to the process. It does not relate phantasy to external reality; but throws the subject back still more upon himself and his inner world. In clinical practice, it is not uncommon to come across persons whose sexual lives are confined to phantasy. Often these phantasies are of such elaborate complexity that one cannot help feeling that they contain the germs of a novel or some other creative production. But the fact that they cause direct physical excitement which is discharged in masturbation means that they never undergo the process of transformation and integration which might transmute them into works of art. This is the explanation of Freud's dictum quoted above. It is the *suppression*, rather than the *expression*, of 'the perverse elements of sexual existence' which may provide some of the motive force for culture. The distaste or contempt with which various peoples throughout the world regard masturbation is not necessarily based upon a puritanical condemnation of sexual pleasure, but rather upon a half-formulated recognition that it is a childish way of short-circuiting and discharging impulses which could be integrated in a creative way if they were not so dissipated. 'Composition is born out of containment, out of imposed discipline.'[6]

In view of what has just been said about masturbation, some might suppose that an adult, heterosexual relationship was itself 'anti-cultural'. Indeed, this is the view of the psychoanalyst Eissler, whom I have already quoted as alleging that, if a genius had achieved such a relationship, he would be incapable of his creations. Yet, as we have seen, this is not in fact the case. Indeed, the very opposite might be argued. People whose sex lives are unhappy tend to be obsessed with sex to the exclusion of everything else. It is hard for them to concentrate, to escape the persistent intrusion of sexual phantasy, and especially difficult for them to engage in creative work, since this requires discipline imposed by the self rather than by any external authority. It is true that many creative people have not been sexually happy; but many have, and those that have not might well have achieved more had their sexual emotions found a satisfactory release. It is not the suppression of *adult* sexuality which leads to creativity but of its childhood precursors; and where Eissler is in error is in supposing that these precursors can ever find satisfaction in an adult sexual relation. Thus, a man can have a happy and fully satisfactory heterosexual relationship, and still be impelled to create because of the childhood residue of dissatisfaction which he carries with him into adulthood, and which can never find resolution except in symbolic ways.

Freud's pregenital stages leave their traces in all of us. As we have seen, the infant begins life unable to differentiate himself from the mother of whom he was so recently a part. The persistent desire of human beings to 'lose themselves' in a larger whole can be traced to this source. To be 'carried away'; to lose one's identity; to be relieved of the burden of striving; even to die, and thus be reunited with the stuff of the universe from which one sprang are universal, if regressive, longings; and they have often been the motive force for art:

> From too much love of living,
> From hope and fear set free,
> We thank with brief thanksgiving
> Whatever gods may be
> That no life lives for ever;
> That dead men rise up never;
> That even the weariest river
> Winds somewhere safe to sea.[7]

Swinburne's lines are so well known as to seem banal; but they illustrate perfectly that variety of the death-wish which is really a longing to give up the effort of maintaining a separate existence and to be merged once again with the maternal sea. It is an example of a wish which can only be dealt with symbolically, so long as life itself persists; but it is not difficult to trace its influence in art. Similarly, nostalgia for the past, particularly for an imagined childhood

181

'innocence', represents a wish which can never be fulfilled once adult existence is established, but which has inspired innumerable artists, from Schubert downwards. Such wishes are derived from Freud's 'oral' stage; and, in conventional psychoanalytic psychopathology, so are the schizoid and manic-depressive phenomena already noted in earlier chapters.

To Freud's 'anal' phase belong the organizational aspects of creativity; the desire to make order out of chaos; the wish for complete control; the need to exclude the irrelevant, the disorderly, and the distasteful; and the striving after perfection. In Chapter 8, we examined the relation of creativity with the obsessional character. Life itself can never be as ordered as our childhood striving for security would have it; but, in the symbolic realm, we can achieve a nearer approach to this perfection than is possible in reality.

The 'phallic' phase persists in the exhibitionistic aspect of creativity; in the desire to assert, to prove the self, to compete, and to display. Very few human beings, if any, reach such complete confidence in their adult being as not to retain some of these childhood 'phallic' wishes; and the symbolic sphere provides vehicles for their expression which 'real' life often fails to do.

I began this chapter by observing that the discontent which man inevitably bears within him has the effect of compelling him to seek symbolic resolutions, and thus to become passionate about all manner of things other than the obviously instinctual. These need not, of course, be creative on the highest plane. Even so mundane a pursuit as stamp-collecting can provide opportunity for the wish to arrange, order, and control, as well as for competition and display, and thus may be engaged in with emotional intensity. The capacity for 'disposable passion' can, at first sight paradoxically, apply to sexual love itself; which often becomes imbued with emotions more properly pertaining to the unresolved difficulties of childhood than to an adult sexual relationship. Indeed, most marital problems derive from the fact that one or both partners expect of the other something which might properly have been demanded of a parent by a child, but which should not be asked of one adult by another. An obvious example is the common situation in which one partner is so dependent as to ask for a great deal of emotional support and reassurance, but is not mature enough to provide any in return.

If no one ever tried to make up for the disappointments of childhood by means of marital and other relationships in adult life there would be a great deal less work for psychiatrists and marriage guidance counsellors. Unfortunately, it requires more self-knowledge than most people possess to know when this process is happening; nor is it generally realized that such disappointments are best, and possibly only, resolved symbolically. In this connection, it is worth reiterating that psychoanalysis itself is a symbolic process. The analyst cannot actually replace a parent or make up for the past; he can only provide symbolic solutions. Nonetheless, these may be highly effective.

Passionate infatuation, the state of being romantically 'in love', is also a condition in which an ostensibly adult love relationship is endowed with various elements of emotion which do not necessarily or properly belong to it, and which ultimately derive from childhood. It is not disputed that a love relationship, based on a realistic appraisal and acceptance of another person, is one of the chief sources of human happiness. But being 'in love' is very different from this, and is a condition of mind generally recognized to be unrealistic. Indeed, Freud went so far as to call this exalted state 'the psychosis of normal people'. He saw that just as the schizophrenic substitutes his inner world for the real world, and thus becomes 'mad', so the infatuated lover projects upon the object of his love an image derived from his own inner world which bears little relation to the reality of the person who receives the projection. The lover is also 'mad', although in a more limited sense; mad about a person, and deluded in thinking that this one person is the answer to life and to all his emotional needs.

In Chapter 12 I referred to one feature of the inner world, present in all of us, but closer to the surface and less modified by reality in the characters we call schizoid. This is the sharp division of images of persons into good and bad, black and white, heroes and villains, saints and devils. These images, it is believed, are either inborn, archetypal data; or else derived from a very early stage of infantile experience, before the child realizes that the good mother who nourishes can also be the rejecting mother who frustrates. These images have no place in reality; but the infatuated lover projects upon his loved one an idealized picture of a person impossibly good; possessing not only beauty, but unselfishness, compassion, understanding, wisdom, and the capacity for absolute acceptance, together with any other virtue one cares to name. Obviously, no real human being can live up to such an ideal; but such projected figures have a compelling emotional power, since they touch the depths of our being; and when we see them personified on the stage, or read of them in poetry, they seem eternal and out of this world, as indeed they are. Othello, idealizing Desdemona, is himself an ideal, heroic figure, in that he has no doubts, no worldly-wise reflections upon the nature of women, no cynicism. Iago, his opposite, is 'ideally' villainous, moved by pure malice, with no virtues whatever to modify or dilute his envy, hatred and absolute disbelief in goodness. In a sense, it is curious that we are often more moved by personifications of impulse than by real people; but that is because the impulses are really our own, whereas another person is always something 'other', as well as being more complicated than these images. The lover is always in love with his own subjective feeling, rather than with the person who carries his projection.

There is actually something both childish and intrinsically humiliating in being passionately infatuated, however exalted the lover may feel for the moment; for he is, inevitably, dependent upon, and at the mercy of his idealized object. No one is so vulnerable as the person in love, unless it be the newborn; and although most people have an intuitive realization of this, which causes them to treat those in love with them gently, this is not invariable. There are few experiences so catastrophic as the disillusion which follows upon an idealized person suddenly becoming cruel and exploiting the vulnerability of the person in love.

Romantic infatuation is relevant to creativity in that it is sometimes possible to see the former replacing, or interfering with, the latter. Real love between real people does not interfere with creativity; but 'the psychosis of normal people' may certainly do so. Although romantic love has been the inspiration of much that is creative, especially lyric poetry, in instances where there is little chance of the love finding any fulfilment, an infatuation can seem to promise so complete an answer to life that everything else, including creative pursuits, become superfluous. Indeed, this seems regularly to be the case whilst the infatuation runs its course. It is only after disillusion has supervened that the creative task of symbolization and integration can be resumed. One musician, to whom music had been of vital importance since early childhood, was incredulous of his own experience when he found that a passionate infatuation made music, for a brief period, almost meaningless to him. Once the infatuation had passed, things resumed their proper place once more, sexual love being important but not overwhelming, and music once again becoming a repository for the ideal, and a link between inner and outer.

Robert Browning wrote only one poem during the first three years after his marriage to Elizabeth Barrett.[8] Admittedly, he seems to have treated her more like a mother than a wife ('You shall think for me, that is my command!' he wrote[9]); but, even so, it is a remarkable instance of the idealization of a person interfering with creative production. There is evidence to suggest that Elizabeth Barrett was impatient with her husband's subservience, and would have preferred that he should have been less attentive and more productive. For a time, however, it appears that his relationship with her, comprising as it did both the infantile and adult components of love, filled his life to such an extent that everything else, including any relationships with other people, appeared unnecessary. Inspiration, in the case of men, is commonly personified as a female figure. It is not uncommon, but usually disastrous, for creative people to confuse their mistress with their muse. The former belongs to the external world, the latter to the inner: and it is generally best to keep both ladies separate and in their respective places.

It is well known that romantic love flourishes most vigorously when obstacles are put in the way of its fulfilment. It is thus encouraged by a Puritan culture, or by one in which mingling between the sexes is discouraged. It seems scarcely possible that it can exist in cultures like that of the Marquesans, in which there is little bar to the expression of sexuality. Be that as it may, the Western romantic tradition that being 'in love' is *the* solution to all emotional problems is unrealistic and harmful; but it is an illusion fostered by innumerable novels, films, and women's magazines.

Although Freud himself was anything but a romantic, both he and subsequent psychoanalysts have, as we have seen, made something of an ideal of genitality—Freud's final stage of sexual and emotional development—in which all 'pregenital' sexuality can theoretically be comprised, and which, again theoretically, seems to promise an end to man's discontent. It is probable that some psychoanalyses go on so long—and some last twenty years or more—because both parties are aiming at an impossible ideal. It might be that better therapeutic results would be achieved if more attention was given to the possibility of resolving neurotic problems in creative ways. This is especially true for schizoid and obsessional character disorders.

Of course, most neurotic patients cannot be turned into artists. In

Chapter 1 I quoted Freud's remarks from 'Civilization and Its Discontents' in which he points out that the artist's joy in creating or the scientist's in solving problems can only be experienced by very few people possessing special gifts. This is true; but perhaps Freud paid less attention than he might have done to the many pursuits open to men which do not require special endowments and which yet provide symbolic resolutions and satisfactions. Even the uneducated and unintelligent develop passions for sport; and the current enthusiasm for Association football which has swept the world unites supporters from every walk of life, cutting right across the barriers of class and intelligence.

In mental hospitals, art therapy, music therapy, and occupational therapy are used increasingly; but they still tend to be treated as poor relations, mere adjuncts to the therapeutic ministrations of the psychiatrist. If the point of view advanced in this book is accepted, it follows that a great deal more attention and research will have to be devoted to such ways of encouraging symbolic resolutions of emotional problems. This is especially so in the case of the poorly endowed. Genius can make its own way; the gifted may need no more than encouragement. It is those who are not so gifted who need help and teaching.

A recent book by an American composer, Paul Nordoff, and an educationalist, Clive Robbins, demonstrates convincingly that music can have an important therapeutic role to play in the treatment of severely handicapped children.[10] Some autistic children who did not communicate by means of speech, and who appeared to be almost wholly cut off from human contact, were able to learn to communicate through participating in musical performance, and showed improvement both in spirits and behaviour as a result. Other brain-damaged children, unable to control their chaotic and often violent emotions, became able to express these emotions in orderly fashion by means of the rhythmic framework provided by music, and thus gained a sense of mastery over the chaos of their inner worlds at the same time as finding an emotional outlet. In addition, for children who have lost faith in the emotional reliability of adults, or who have never experienced 'basic trust', music can become a stabilizing influence; a recurrent emotional experience which can be trusted because it is not directly human.

In the same way, painting and modelling can be used fruitfully even by those who have little innate ability. A painting can often express what cannot easily be put into words; and many patients who produce such paintings gain benefit from the act of doing so, even if no attempt is made by a therapist to interpret the content of what they have produced. To bring what is inside one into the external world, in however rudimentary a fashion, is itself a valuable exercise, and does not necessarily require explanation or intellectual comprehension.

REFERENCES

1. WINNICOTT, D. W. *Playing and Reality* (London: Tavistock Publications, 1971) pp. 14-15.
2. Ibid, p. 6.
3. FREUD, Sigmund. 'Civilized Sexual Morality and Modern Nervous Illness' (London: The Hogarth Press and The Institute of Psycho-Analysis, 1959) Standard Edition, Vol. IX, p. 189.
4. STORR, Anthony. *Sexual Deviation* (London: Heinemann, 1965) p. 44.
5. WINNICOTT, D. W. *Playing and Reality* (London: Tavistock Publications, 1971) p. 39.
6. READ, Herbert. *Icon and Idea* (London: Faber and Faber, 1955) pp. 49-50.
7. SWINBURNE, Algernon Charles. *Collected Works.*
8. MILLER, Betty. *Robert Browning. A Portrait* (London: John Murray, 1952) p. 145.
9. Ibid, p. 128.
10. NORDOFF, Paul and Robbins, Clive. *Therapy in Music for Handicapped Children* (London: Gollancz, 1971).

15

The Creative Ego and Its Opposites

In my examination of creativity, I have so far been principally concerned with motive; that is, with the psychodynamic forces within the personality which impel men to create. I began by demonstrating that a man may be driven to produce an original conception by his need to defend himself against depression; or by the feeling that he must restore what he has in phantasy destroyed. He may be impelled by the need to reunite himself with a world from which he feels alienated, and thus come to build creative bridges between subjective and objective. He may experience a compulsion to impose order upon a world which he feels to be chaotic or, more simply, wish to compensate in phantasy for what he feels to be missing in reality. Depressive, schizoid, obsessional and hysterical mechanisms all undoubtedly play their part in the creative process, and can be seen to operate with especial clarity in the exceptional individuals whom we have so far considered.

But 'psychopathology' is ubiquitous in that these same mechanisms can be detected, in varying degree, in all of us; and creativity, although perhaps the best, and certainly the most interesting, technique of attempting to resolve internal conflict, is not the only way of so doing. The hypomanic may simply become an overactive business man; the schizoid a solitary who never reveals his phantasies; the obsessional a bank clerk who prides himself upon his punctilious accuracy; the hysteric a reader and viewer who loses herself in the day-dreams of others. Moreover, as shown in the last chapter, there are various ways of providing symbolic expression and resolution of the tensions and conflicts which beset us all which cannot be called creative, unless the word is stretched to include much which is neither new nor original. Therefore, it is not only the psychopathology of creative persons which is of interest: the ego, too, is important; that is, the conscious, controlling, executive part of personality which, to a variable extent, stands in contrast to the more dynamic, emotional aspects to which I have so far accorded most of my attention. It is this part of personality which has been the chief object of study by those psychologists who work in laboratories and research institutes, as distinguished from psychiatrists and psychoanalysts who spend their professional lives in the consulting room. Most of the traits of personality discussed below have been defined as characteristic by means of psychological tests.

Most authorities who have studied creative people agree that one of their most notable characteristics is *independence*. This shows itself particularly in the fact that they are much more influenced by their own, inner standards than by those of the society or profession to which they happen to belong. In a study of architects in which the subjects were divided into three groups according to their creativity, the most creative group were primarily concerned with meeting an inner artistic standard of excellence which they discovered within themselves; the least creative group with conforming to the standards of the architectural profession.[1] It is not unlikely that this trait of independence may be related to the precocity of ego development noted by Freud in obsessionals, and discussed in Chapter 8. To be primarily 'inner-directed' argues the early development both of the ego and also of a sensitive super-ego; a conscience providing an inner standard to which reference is made, and which is likely to demand a higher performance than any collective, professional group could ask. At any rate, this is a possibility worth further investigation.

Another interesting aspect of this trait of independence is the fact that the highly creative belong to fewer organizations and social groups than do their less creative contemporaries. At first sight, this might simply be attributable to impatience. The highly original person is likely to find his less gifted colleagues boring; and also, if he has realized his own potential, is less in need of the support and reassurance which most people require from social groups. However, this is not the whole story. It must not be forgotten that new ideas are sensitive plants, easily damaged or destroyed by premature criticism; and the reluctance of creative people to share their ideas before they are completely formulated is well-founded. Moreover, as I pointed out in Chapters 5 and 6, schizoid characters, amongst whom some of the most original minds are to be found, carry within them a fear of the influence of others which is often so intense as to warrant being called paranoid.

It has often been pointed out that creative people are sceptical, and reluctant to acquiesce in the findings of authority just because these have become generally accepted. There are also those who rebel for the sake of rebelling, and who have no creative alternative to offer, but these need not concern us. The point is that independence is seldom a simple trait. It is compounded of both strength and weakness, aggression and fear. As Hartmann points out, 'in certain situations the resistance against contamination can be considered an indication of ego strength';[2] and, as we shall see, 'ego strength' is acknowledged by research workers to be a notable characteristic of the creative. Tests which demand a perceptive appreciation and appraisal of the needs of others reveal that creative people are emotionally and socially sensitive. In view of what we surmise about their precocity, this is not surprising. But initially it may seem odd that people who tend to be non-joiners can also be described as *socially* sensitive. However, if we are right in supposing that the creative are often fearful of undue influence it is understandable that it may be their very sensitivity to what others are thinking and feeling which makes them shun too much company. Moreover, some creative people seem to have only a tenuous sense of their own identity. Indeed, their work may be an expression of their search for identity. Sensitive people, and especially those with a predominantly depressive psychopathology, very easily identify themselves with others; and, lacking certainty in their own uniqueness, feel an especial need to assert and preserve what is felt to be precarious.

It would be generally predicted that creative artists must be aesthetically sensitive. Concern with form and elegance is an obvious prerequisite for achieving form and elegance; and these are essential features of creative achievement in the arts, without which no art exists, but only self-expression. However, it may surprise some people to learn that a psychological test designed to detect in artists preference for good form and design is 'the most powerful single test yet discovered as a predictor of creative potential in any field of endeavour . . . One would not be surprised to see such a test correlating with creativity in the arts and perhaps in literature but we need to note that the test is an equally good predictor of creative potential in the physical sciences and engineering.'[3] That there are aesthetic aspects to science is well-recognized. Mathematical theorems and proofs can display both economy and beauty, as G. H. Hardy demonstrates with his examples in *A Mathematician's Apology*.[4] But it is interesting that a feeling for aesthetic form is so important a part of the creative scientist's equipment. Is such a feeling possessed to an unusual degree by those whose need is to arrange and find order? Or are the need and the ability unrelated? Perhaps there exist people whose pattern-making ability and sense of form is acute, but who never feel impelled by inner tension to make use of it. It is certain that there are many who are anxious and obsessional, whose compulsion to arrange and order never goes beyond ritual tidiness and cleanliness.

An ability to recognize, and a tendency to prefer, what is generally agreed to be good form and design is one trait shared by the creative in various fields. Another, which on the surface seems opposed to this, is a preference for complexity, asymmetry, and incompleteness. Tests which offer the subject a choice of patterns show that creative people reject the simple and the already completed in favour of the complicated and unfinished. This preference has a positive correlation with independence, originality, verbal fluency, breadth of interests, impulsiveness, and expansiveness; all traits which, as one might expect, tend to be associated with creativity. It is negatively correlated with conservatism, control of impulse, social conformity, and rigidity.[5] These latter traits, however, are possessed in high degree by many obsessional neurotics, whose anxiety makes them over-cautious, and therefore conservative, controlled, conformist and notoriously rigid. Yet, as we have seen, there is a definite association between the rituals of the obsessional, and the pattern-making of the creator; and some rigid and inhibited obsessionals, like Ibsen, are also highly creative. It may be that incompleteness and complexity are preferred by creative people because they are thereby stimulated to produce a new order of their own; just as a scientist is stimulated to produce a new hypothesis by the fact that will not fit, that is, by the incompleteness of the current hypothesis. Moreover, the creative person's independence is likely to make him dissatisfied with completed patterns, since they have been finished, not by himself, but by another. Although the creative often complain of the laboriousness of their work, and appear to long to have it finished, many are only happy when they are working at some new problem, and require recurrent challenges as a stimulus. It is the uncreative and the passive person who prefers simplicity in his patterns, and who is relieved that someone else has done the work of arrangement for him.

In this connection, it is relevant to note that the ability to tolerate tension and anxiety is characteristic of the creative. It has been implied at many points in this book that the motive power of much creative activity is emotional tension of one kind or another, although some care has been taken not to label this tension as invariably neurotic

191

since, in my view, a good deal of it is adaptive, and therefore part of the human condition. However, the need to seek relief from tension is also natural enough; and what seems remarkable about creative people is their ability to postpone this relief, to reject facile solutions, and to wait until they themselves have arrived at a more satisfying synthesis. Keats put it well in one of his letters.

'I had not a dispute but a disquisition with Dilke on various subjects; several things dove-tailed in my mind, and at once it struck me what quality went to form a Man of Achievement, especially in Literature, and which Shakespeare possessed so enormously—I mean Negative Capability, that is, when a man is capable of being in uncertainties, mysteries, doubts, without any irritable reaching after fact and reason—Coleridge, for instance, would let go by a fine isolated verisimilitude caught from the Penetralium of mystery, from being incapable of remaining content with half-knowledge.'[6]

Goethe remarked that 'the first and last task required of genius is love of truth,' a trait which must surely be closely related to being incapable of remaining content with half-knowledge. Ernest Jones, who quotes Goethe's dictum in his lectures on 'The Nature of Genius',[7] refers to Freud's passion for pursuing the truth to the limit as one of his most striking characteristics. As one would expect a psychoanalyst to conclude, Jones believes that Freud acquired this passion in infancy. Freud had a younger brother, Julius, born when he was eleven months old, who only survived until Sigmund was aged nineteen months. Apparently Freud, who was jealous of, and hostile towards, the interloper, continued to blame himself for his brother's premature death as if his own resentment had been responsible for it. 'He had had, therefore, very good reasons for wanting to know how such things happened, how it was that intruders could appear and who was responsible for their doing so ... Only in knowing the truth could there be found security, the security that possession of his mother could give.'[8]

Whether or not this is the true explanation in Freud's case is open to question; but there can be little doubt that the love of truth is often motivated by the search for security. The 'Eureka' experience of having arrived at a new and truthful insight into some aspect of reality is accompanied by an increase in the feeling of personal security, since it implies a corresponding increase in mastery over the external world. Increments in understanding are generally felt as increments in power, even when the latter is not actual, but imagined.

Goethe is surely wrong when he supposes that love of truth is both the first and last task required of genius; for there are many other aspects to creation; but it is obviously a factor of considerable importance, and one which fits the main hypothesis of this book, since it is easily related to man's need to adapt to the world about him by creative use of his intelligence.

The use of the word 'intelligence' requires some comment upon the vexed question of the relation between intelligence and creativity. Frank Barron, in his book *Creative Person and Creative Process*, summarizes the findings of current research by stating: 'For certain intrinsically creative activities a specifiable minimum IQ is probably necessary to engage in the activity at all, but beyond that minimum, which is often surprisingly low, creativity has little correlation with scores on IQ tests.'[9] So long as that dubious abstraction 'intelligence' is defined in terms of scores on IQ tests, this lack of correlation will continue: but psychologists are increasingly coming to realize that such a definition of intelligence is too limited. It is not possible to perform well in an IQ test without being intelligent; but it is possible to perform badly and yet to display considerable intelligence in appraising and adapting to new, real-life situations. In recent years it has been fashionable to dissociate intelligence and creativity to the point where one might suppose that the possession of a high IQ was a bar to originality. This notion sprang from the distinction, originally proposed by Getzels and Jackson, between children who possessed high creativity and low IQ, and children who exhibited high IQ and low creativity. This distinction is less valid than was originally supposed, since the authors neglected to study the much larger group of children in their sample who scored highly on both counts.

I have been at pains to point out that the motive power for creation comes from inner tensions which are characteristic of the human species but which need bear no relation to intelligence. But, although a person of low intelligence may have an original idea, it is unlikely that he will be able to elaborate or present it in any effective way. High intelligence is invaluable for most creative endeavours. It is now thought that the occasional 'idiots savants' who were found amongst children in mental deficiency hospitals, and who might show considerable inventiveness, or even the ability to engage in such intellectual activities as chess, were either schizophrenic, or else deaf, and thus not necessarily deficient in intellectual ability, although precluded from using this ability to the full except in limited areas.[10]

High intelligence unaccompanied by originality or much creative drive will be familiar to those who have mixed in academic circles. Many dons have been, in youth, great passers of examinations; and have, therefore, been appointed to the staffs of universities. Instead, however, of devoting their time to original work, many spend the rest of their careers in sterile argument, in compiling books from the work of others, or in the absorbing trivia of academic politics. The drive to create springs mostly from internal discomforts, at least in our well-padded culture; but it might be interesting to see whether more original work might be produced if university fellows and professors were a little less secure in their positions. Industry, also, complains that the bright research scientist often seems to cease producing original work when his future is assured. But these speculations are of minor import. The really original person is invariably 'inner-directed' and no amount of material comfort or security of tenure will deter him from pursuing his quest.

One observation consistently reported by psychologists using various tests is that their male creative subjects show high scores on scales measuring 'femininity'. 'The evidence is clear. The more creative a person is the more he reveals an openness to his own feelings and emotions, a sensitive intellect and understanding self-awareness, wide-ranging interests including many which in the American culture are thought of as feminine. In the realm of sexual identification and interests, our creative subjects appear to give more expression to the feminine side of their nature than do less creative persons.'[11] Whether creative women show more masculine interests than average is not so well established; but, judging from history and personal acquaintance, it seems likely. George Sand is a good example. Balzac wrote of her: 'She is not lovable and consequently she will only be loved with great difficulty. She is a bachelor, an artist, she is great, generous, devoted, chaste; she has a man's features; ergo she is not a woman . . . In fine, she is a man, and all the more so since she wishes to be one, since she has gone outside the position of a woman, and is not a woman.'[12]

This finding of more than usually overt bisexuality is interesting on a number of counts. Many creative people refer to their productions as 'children', and compare the creative process to that of conception, gestation, and birth. 'Brain-children' are rated as highly or more highly than actual children by artists; a fact recognized by Ibsen when he makes Hedda Gabler say, whilst burning Eilert Lovborg's manuscript: 'I'm burning your child, Thea! You, with your beautiful wavy hair! The child Eilert Lovborg gave you. I'm burning it. I'm burning your child!'[13] Wagner, who wrote his own libretti, makes a similiar comparison in *Die Meistersinger* in the scene where Walther, the hero, sings to Hanns Sachs the first verse of a song which has come to him in a dream. This song will later become the 'Prize Song' and win him his heart's desire, the hand of Eva. First, Sachs holds forth on the importance of dreams. They are, he says, the source of all that is best in poetry, which is simply dream made manifest. Then he directs Walther in how to shape his inspiration. In order to win the prize, he must to some extent conform to the rules laid down by the Mastersingers, although Sachs is secretly in agreement with Walther's intolerance of their restrictions. To this end, the second stanza of the song must match the first. These are the 'parents'; and their similarity is designed to indicate that Walther's heart is set on marriage. The third stanza is the 'child'. It must, like human children, resemble the parents; and yet it must also be different, an individual in its own right. In the famous quintet, the new song is named and christened in front of witnesses; and Sachs tells them that this is the habitual procedure adopted by the Mastersingers whenever a new 'Master-song' has been created.[14] Wagner was an intolerable human being in many ways; but he had a good deal of insight into his own creative processes, and anything he writes on the subject is usually worth attention.

It is a truism to say that we are all bisexual; but the evidence does suggest that, in the case of creative people, the contra-sexual side is closer to the surface, more in evidence, and less shunned than is the case amongst the average. This may in part be the result of the tenuous sense of identity to which we have briefly referred, which seems characteristic of some artists. For most people, the feeling of being unequivocally masculine or feminine is so important a part of identity that they are threatened if this feeling is called in question.

Another personal observation is more speculative. Many artists display more than the average share of vanity. They are, to use jargon, narcissistic. Wagner is a supreme example. This may be related to their franker admission of, and closer relation with, their own femininity. Most men project the whole, or nearly the whole, of their feminine side upon a woman. The artist tends to contain it more within himself. We have seen that a man in love may confuse his mistress with his muse. Some artists engage in the opposite manoeuvre, and are so in love with their muse that they fail to attribute as much value as perhaps they should to the real woman with whom they are living. In this way they somewhat resemble the hypothetical hermaphrodites described by Plato in *The Symposium;* and it will be recalled that those 'complete' creatures were bisected by Zeus who was enraged with them because of their 'hubris'. Hubris is closely akin to narcissistic vanity. Artists who are primarily in love with their own creative power are, of course, less vulnerable on this account, since they are less affected than most of us by the bestowal or withdrawal of love. They are also less agreeable; since most of the pleasantness of ordinary human beings is related to their need for approval and affection, which makes them anxious to please, and reluctant to offend, their fellows.

The male–female dichotomy is but one of a pair of opposites which show themselves more obviously in creative people than in the average person. All psychodynamic psychologies assume divisions and opposites within the mind. They would not be dynamic if they did not, since they are concerned with the interaction of opposing forces. As we have seen, Freud's scheme of ego, super-ego and id is one way of describing some of these forces; but there are many others, and we have, at various points, found it useful to employ the concepts of internal objects and unconscious phantasy. Because we all possess inner worlds of the psyche which do not correspond with the external world, or with the attributes of the conscious part of the personality which relates to the external world, we are all divided selves. But most people are, for most of the time, rather unaware of the divisions within them. Just as the average man is unaware that he possesses a feminine side, and identifies himself wholly with his masculinity, so he is also unconscious of the fact that other characteristics, including some upon which he may pride himself, are counterbalanced by their opposites within.

There is good reason to suppose that creative people are distinguished by an exceptional degree of division between opposites, and also by an exceptional awareness of this division. The male–female pair of opposites is one example. Another, which I have touched on several times, is the contrast between obsessionality and the preference for asymmetry and complexity. How can a man be both compulsive, rigid and inhibited; and at the same time flexible, fluent and expansive? Clinicians familiar with the treatment of obsessional neurotics know that their compulsive tidiness and insistence upon order is

196

often more superficial than appears. Everything may be put away in drawers, for example, but the drawers themselves may be chaotic. In obsessional neurotics, ritual tidiness is indeed a defence; and it is needed as such because the inner world of the obsessional is more disordered, more unruly, and more aggressive than that of the average man. The same is true of the creative who display obsessional traits—and we have seen that many do—but their awareness and tolerance of their own internal chaos is far greater than that of most neurotics, and their rituals creative rather than sterile. This latter statement is, of course, something of an over-simplification. Dr Johnson displayed a number of compulsive habits—touching rituals and the like—which were anything but creative. Creativity and neurosis are not the same thing; but this is not to say that they can never co-exist.

The increased awareness of opposites within, which characterizes the creative as opposed to the neurotic, may have its origin in the rather general enhancement of reaction to all stimuli which is also typical. Sensitivity to what is going on around, which may account for the premature development of the ego to which reference has already been made, is surely likely to be matched by a corresponding sensitivity to stimuli from within.

In his lecture on 'The Nature of Genius' Ernest Jones draws attention to a pair of opposites closely related to, if not identical with, those which we have just been discussing. 'For there is every reason to suppose that men of genius are characterized by possessing exceptionally strong emotions and usually a correspondingly strong capacity for containing them.'[15] This was particularly so in the case of Freud himself, of whom Jones writes: 'By nature Freud was endowed with unusually strong emotions; he could both love and hate passionately. But that gift went with an equally strong self-control, so that the emotions were hardly ever displayed to outsiders.'[16] Exceptionally strong emotions require exceptionally strong defences against their untoward or inappropriate emergence; hence the connection with obsessional rituals, and the significance of Freud's own remark that, were he to become neurotic, his neurosis would be of the obsessional variety.

Many of the tests used to detect creative potential are concerned with disclosing what might be called 'imagination'. Thus, tests which require the subject to think of as many uses for an object as possible, or give as many meanings as he can to a list of words, or, better still, to complete stories in different ways, give scope both for fluency and invention. Creativity, however, is not merely a matter of being able to give free rein to the imagination, a fact conveniently forgotten by contemporary educators who emphasize freedom at the expense of discipline. As a psychologist who has criticized some of the contemporary approaches to creativity testing points out: 'Constructive creativity may well demand the fluency and imaginativeness required by many of the tests but it demands also some degree of self-criticism and judgment.'[17] Once again, we encounter the fact that the simultaneous operation of opposites is a *sine qua non* of creativity.

Another way of looking at these same opposites is to study content and form. Form without emotional content is sterile: emotion without formal containment is mere 'self-expression'. One of the most interesting pieces of research that could be undertaken would be to study how far inspiration appears to the creative in unorganized, uncontrolled form, and how far form and content appear together. The great originals vary very much in this respect; and I have already commented upon the contrast between Beethoven and Mozart. The former was compelled to make numerous attempts at reshaping his musical ideas before they assumed their final form. The latter was able to avoid this labour, since form and content appeared to him as a single inspiration.

I have already commented upon the scepticism of the creative, in connection with our discussion of their independence. The opposite of scepticism is credulity, and this trait, also, is rather often found in the creative. Ernest Jones thought that both traits were strongly present in Freud, whom he criticizes for being naïve and credulous about other people, whilst at the same time sceptical of authority.

More important, perhaps, are the opposites of activity versus passivity; a pair which can, if one so wishes, be linked with the masculine–feminine opposition already discussed.

Creative people are of course competent executants. If they were not they would not produce anything, but merely dream of it, like those novelists manqué so familiar to anyone who has any acquaintance with the world of literature. Ego-strength, a characteristic of creative persons upon which we have already remarked, is perhaps not easy to define; but the notion does include the idea of a will which can be voluntarily brought into operation to achieve whatever end is contemplated; a high tolerance of anxiety, and a firm grasp of reality. Perhaps 'personal effectiveness' is the best shorthand phrase to designate ego-strength; and tests designed to measure it, such as the

California Psychological Inventory, developed by Harrison Gough, show that the more creative possess more of it than their less creative peers. Dominance, self-acceptance, responsibility, self-control, tolerance, intellectual efficiency, are among the traits measured by tests of ego-strength; and it will no doubt surprise those who think of creative people as long-haired dreamers to realize that they rate highly on all these measures. And indeed our day-to-day experience of other people justifies this surprise to some extent; for we do not normally expect the man of action or the powerful executive to be, at the same time, at home in the world of the imagination, nor to be capable of the passivity which is generally acknowledged to be necessary if a new idea is to make its unpredictable appearance. If one considers ideas about creativity in historical perspective, it is possible to detect a swing of the pendulum alternating between attributing the chief value to the will, or alternatively to inspiration and passivity. Galton, for example, writing in the second half of the nineteenth century, prefaces the second edition of his book *Hereditary Genius* with the following remarks:

'At the time when the book was written (1869), the human mind was popularly thought to act independently of natural laws, and to be capable of almost any achievement, if compelled to exert itself by a will that had a power of initiation. Even those who had more philosophical habits of thought were far from looking upon the mental faculties of each individual as being limited with as much strictness as those of his body, still less was the idea of the hereditary transmission of ability clearly apprehended.'[18]

Galton, in his highly original work, was of course principally concerned to show that hereditary transmission played a major part in the endowment of gifted individuals, and succeeded in doing so. In other words, he demonstrated that a man's mental endowment was indeed both determined and limited in the same kind of way that his height might be. But, interestingly enough, Galton felt sure that, if a man's hereditary equipment was good enough, nothing could keep him down. He did not believe that social factors, for instance, could prevent a man of genius from rising to the top; and would certainly have been incredulous that neurosis could seriously interfere with success.

Galton adduces three gifts, all of which he believed to be inherited, as prerequisites for great achievement. These he named 'ability', 'zeal', and a 'capacity for hard work'.

'If a man is gifted with vast intellectual ability, eagerness to work, and power of working, I cannot comprehend how such a man should be repressed.' The will might be limited by inheritance, but hardly by anything else; and Galton is intolerant of the notion that inspiration, or anything approaching mental instability might also play a part in creative achievement.

'If genius means a sense of inspiration, or of rushes of ideas from apparently supernatural sources, or of an inordinate and burning desire to accomplish any particular end, it is perilously near to the voices heard by the insane, to their delirious tendencies or to their monomanias. It cannot in such cases be a healthy faculty nor can it be desirable to perpetuate it by inheritance.'[19]

Galton was evidently not familiar with, or reluctant to take notice of, the accounts given to us by creative people themselves who not only acknowledge the necessity of something which cannot be willed, and which we may call inspiration, but who actually demonstrate that the exercise of will may be inimical to the appearance of new ideas.

Creation is not simply a matter of a highly gifted person sitting down, thinking hard, and then writing, composing or painting something. There is an element of passivity, or dependence, even of humility in the creative process; and this element is indeed a surprising finding in the man of notable ego-strength, who is used to relying upon his will. For new ideas cannot be conjured up voluntarily: they come to people; and although it is possible to arrange life so that they are more likely to make their appearance, there can be no guarantee that they will do so.

'I can call spirits from the vasty deep,' boasts Owen Glendower, and Hotspur replies, 'Why, so can I, or so can any man; but will they come when you do call for them?'[20] Hotspur is right. Creative inspiration cannot be voluntarily summoned, even by the Welsh; it must be wooed and waited upon. Although there are well-authenticated instances of dreams giving rise to solutions to problems, or birth to new ideas, creative inspiration more usually makes its appearance during a state of reverie, intermediate between sleep and waking. Here, for example, is Wagner's account of his discovery of the orchestral introduction to *Das Rheingold*—a remarkable inspiration, indeed, since no less than the first 136 bars are based upon the major triad of E flat, which sounds throughout this long passage without interruption.

'After a night spent in fever and sleeplessness, I forced myself to take a long tramp the next day through the hilly country, which was covered with pinewoods. It all looked dreary and desolate, and I could not think what I should do there. Returning in the afternoon, I stretched myself, dead tired, on a hard couch, awaiting the long-desired hour of sleep. It did not come; but I fell into a kind of somnolent state, in which I suddenly felt as though I were sinking in swiftly flowing water. The rushing sound formed itself in my brain into a musical sound, the chord of E flat major, which continually re-echoed in broken forms; these broken forms seemed to be melodic passages of increasing motion, yet the pure triad of E flat major never changed, but seemed by its continuance to impart infinite significance to the element in which I was sinking. I awoke in sudden terror from my doze, feeling as though the waves were rushing high above my head. I at once recognized that the orchestral overture to the Rheingold, which must have long lain latent within me, though it had been unable to find definite form, had at last been revealed to me. I then quickly realized my own nature; the stream of life was not to flow to me from without, but from within.'[21]

In some instances, notably that of Coleridge, such a state of reverie, intermediate between sleeping and waking, is the product of opium or some other drug; but often it is not so, and the fact remains that creative people possess an uncommon combination of the power to act effectively, while yet retaining the ability to daydream.

The last pair of opposites we shall consider is closely related to the others which have been discussed. It is that of mental health versus neurosis or mental instability. This argument as to whether genius and 'madness' are related is a very old one, and to explore it requires a chapter on its own.

REFERENCES

1. MACKINNON, Donald W. 'Personality and the Realization of Creative Potential', in *American Psychologist*, Vol. 20, No. 4, April 1965, pp. 273-81.
2. HARTMANN, Heinz. *Essays on Ego Psychology* (London: The Hogarth Press and The Institute of Psycho-Analysis, 1964) p. 258.
3. GOUGH, Harrison G. 'Identifying the Creative Man' in *Journal of Value Engineering*, Vol. 2, No. 4, 15 August 1964, pp. 5-12.

4. HARDY, G. H. *A Mathematician's Apology* (Cambridge University Press, 1940).
5. BARRON, Frank. *Creative Person and Creative Process* (London: Holt, Rinehart & Winston, 1969).
6. KEATS, John. *The Letters of John Keats*, ed. M. B. Forman (London: Oxford University Press, 1935) Letter 32, p. 72.
7. JONES, Ernest. *Sigmund Freud. Four Centenary Addresses* (London: Tavistock Publications, 1956) p. 12.
8. JONES, Ernest. *Sigmund Freud* (London: The Hogarth Press, 1955) Vol. II, pp. 481-2.
9. BARRON, Frank. *Creative Person and Creative Process* (London: Holt, Rinehart & Winston, 1969) p. 42.
10. HILLIARD, L. T., and Kirman, Brian H. *Mental Deficiency* (London: J. & A. Churchill, 1957) p. 261 et seq.
11. MACKINNON, Donald W. 'The Nature and Nurture of Creative Talent', in *American Psychologist*, Vol. 17, No. 7, July 1962, p. 488.
12. BIDOU, Henri. *Chopin*, trans. C. A. Phillips (New York: Knopf, 1936) p. 154.
13. IBSEN, Henrik. *Hedda Gabler*, trans. Michael Meyer (London: Hart-Davis, 1962).
14. WAGNER, Richard. *Die Meistersinger* (New York: Franco Colombo) pp. 60-70.
15. JONES, Ernest. *Sigmund Freud. Four Centenary Addresses* (London: Tavistock Publications, 1956) p. 19.
16. Ibid, p. 108.
17. HEIM, Alice. *Intelligence and Personality* (Harmondsworth: Penguin Books, 1970) p. 41.
18. GALTON, Francis. *Hereditary Genius* (London: Macmillan, 1892) p. vii.
19. Ibid, p. x.
20. SHAKESPEARE, William. *Henry IV, Part I*.
21. WAGNER, Richard. *My Life* (London: Constable, 1911) Vol. II, p. 603.

16

Genius and Madness

In our explorations of creativity various types of 'psychopathology', have been outlined and the ways in which these dynamic constellations provide the motive power which activates the creator have been demonstrated. Creativity is one mode adopted by gifted people of coming to terms with, or finding symbolic solutions for, the internal tensions and dissociations from which all human beings suffer in varying degree. The less gifted find other, less obviously creative, solutions; but are equally debarred from obtaining the whole of their satisfaction in life from instinctual expression. The problem now confronting us is whether creative people can be said to have more psychopathology than those who are equally gifted, but who are not impelled to be creative. It is a popular belief that 'we all have neurotic symptoms'; and it is true that there is no sharp dividing line to be drawn between the normal, the neurotic, and the psychotic. One of the main themes of this book has been to assert the inevitability of man carrying with him into adult life from childhood, as part of his peculiar adaptation, 'pregenital' traits, 'childish' attitudes, and the dissatisfactions which are their accompaniments. Although psychopathology is therefore ubiquitous, its intensity and degree varies widely. We all suffer from our psychopathology, but some suffer more than others. As I demonstrated in earlier chapters, one kind of original genius of the first rank is almost certainly inseparable from a schizoid personality structure. If it is accepted that the creative are driven to create by their psychopathology one might argue that the average man who is not so impelled has less of it than they. On the other hand, one might also argue that the creative are less likely to suffer from their psychopathology; because they are fortunate enough to have a better way than the average of coping with their inner tensions.

In this last sentence the central issue is manifest. Creativity may be a way of coping with psychopathology, but it is not neurosis or psychosis. Indeed, it is their opposite; and there is good reason to believe that mental illness interferes with creativity.

In the early days of psychoanalysis it was much easier to make a distinction between neurotic (or psychotic) and normal. Neurotics were people who displayed neurotic symptoms. They had hysterical amnesias or paralyses; they suffered from ritual compulsions, depressions, or were plagued by perversions; they complained of phobias, or of other irrational anxieties. Since the growth of psycho-analysis, and a more profound understanding of psychopathology, the distinction between neurotic and normal has become blurred. Many psychoanalysts never see the kind of neuroses which were treated by their predecessors in the 1900s. They are concerned with 'character disorders', not with neurosis at all. That is, they are treating people who are maladjusted to life, who have 'psychopathology', and who suffer; but who may not display any clear-cut neurotic symptoms. Yet these people, because they are seeking treatment, are not really distinguished from the neurotic. Psychoanalysis, once it is under way, pays but little attention to symptoms in any case. Many of these people are unhappy; and some are helped by their analyses: but being unhappy is not the same as being neurotic. There is much to be said for a return to making this distinction clear; and indeed, for revising the whole conception of neurosis and psychosis.

When we speak of a person being neurotic or psychotic, we imply that his ego, his conscious, ratiocinating self, has been to some extent overwhelmed. As Freud wrote: 'The neuroses are, as we know, disorders of the ego.'[1] Or, as Fenichel puts it: 'All neurotic phenomena are based on insufficiencies of the normal control apparatus.'[2] In our fascination with psychopathology, this is often forgotten. To be psychotic or neurotic a man's psychopathology must be, to some extent, out of control, and showing in the form of symptoms. One of the reasons that creative people are apt to be labelled neurotic even when they are not is that their psychopathology is also showing; but it is showing in their works, and not in the form of neurotic symptoms. The work is a positive adaptation, whereas neurosis is a failure in adaptation. The fact that some psychoanalysts do not really make this distinction has already been commented upon in the first chapter. The question we are here concerned with resolves itself into asking whether creative people suffer more frequently than ordinary people from neurotic or psychotic symptoms; or whether less so; or whether the answer to this problem is not known.

It follows from what has been said that it is important to make a clear distinction between illness and character structure. A man may have a manic-depressive psychopathology without being clinically ill or having any kind of breakdown. Balzac may have killed himself with overwork, but he did not become mentally ill. Schumann, on the other hand, had well-defined depressive breakdowns in which he was unable to work, suffered from delusions, and made a suicidal attempt by throwing himself into the Rhine. Sometimes the distinction cannot be as clearly made as in these examples. Dr Johnson, with his obsessional rituals, would be accounted ill by many psychiatrists; and indeed clearly became so periodically when his obsessional defences broke down and he relapsed into depression. Nevertheless, at the descriptive and phenomenological level, it is mostly possible to distinguish between persons who are or have been psychiatrically ill and those that are not.

Throughout history, there have been two schools of thought about the relation of creativity with mental instability. One denies that there is any such association; the other alleges that the two are intimately connected. We have already quoted Galton's belief that great achievement depended upon zeal, ability and the capacity for hard work; and his opinion would be supported by Hogarth who stated: 'I know of no such thing as genius, genius is nothing but labour and diligence.'[3] Carlyle's remark that 'Genius is first of all a transcendent capacity of taking trouble'[4] is perhaps even better known. However, even Galton, intolerant as he was of any suggestion that creativity might depend upon such irrational forces as inspiration writes: 'The relation between genius in its technical sense (whatever its precise definition may be) and insanity, has been much insisted upon by Lombroso and others, whose views of the closeness of the connection between the two are so pronounced, that it would hardly be surprising if one of their more enthusiastic followers were to remark that So-and-so cannot be a genius because he has never been mad nor is there a single lunatic in his family. I cannot go nearly so far as they, nor accept a moiety of their data, on which the connection between ability of a very high order and insanity is supposed to be established. Still, there is a large residuum of evidence which points to a painfully close relation between the two, and I must add that my own later observations have tended in the same direction, for I have been surprised at finding how often insanity or idiocy has appeared among the near relatives of exceptionally able men. Those who are over-eager and extremely active in mind must often possess brains that are more excitable and peculiar than is consistent with soundness. They are

205

likely to become crazy at times, and perhaps to break down altogether.'[5]

Havelock Ellis, better known for his *Studies in the Psychology of Sex*, also wrote a book, published in 1904, called *A Study in British Genius*. This was based on the Dictionary of National Biography, from which he selected 1,030 names, of whom 975 were men and 55 women. It is with evident regret that, amongst these eminent people, he could discover only 44 (4.2%) who were demonstrably insane. He writes of this: 'It is perhaps a high proportion. I do not know the number of cases among persons of the educated classes living to a high average age in which it can be said that insanity has occurred once during life. It may be lower, but at the same time it can scarcely be so very much lower that we are entitled to say that there is a special and peculiar connection between genius and insanity. The association between genius and insanity is not, I believe, without significance, but in face of the fact that its occurrence is only demonstrable in less than five per cent cases, we must put out of court any theory as to genius being a form of insanity.'[6]

Ellis's figures are the more remarkably low since they include senile disorders. Nowadays, in Great Britain, one person in every fifteen will enter a mental hospital at some time during their lifetime. There were 50,000 males and 66,000 females resident in mental hospitals at the end of 1969 in this country; and nearly half the beds in the National Health Service are for the mentally ill. Obviously, social factors account for this high proportion. Since Ellis' day, provision of care and treatment for the mentally ill is much more extensive than it was; and the stigma attached to being admitted to a mental hospital rather less, with the result that the true incidence of mental illness in the population is becoming more obvious; although admission to mental hospital does not exactly parallel this incidence, since many people suffering mental illness remain outside hospital. Ellis' figures, if they mean anything at all, tend to show that mental illness is probably less amongst the educated and successful, a finding supported by modern research, which has shown a higher incidence of mental disorder in lower social classes and also a greater degree of severity of illness amongst them.

Terman's famous studies of gifted children, selected in 1921–2 in California, show that the physique, general health and mental stability of children with IQs of 135 and over is better than average. The incidence of insanity, delinquency, alcoholism and homosexuality is less than the rate for the population as a whole. He also showed that success in adult life, in the sense of fairly conventional achievement, is 'usually associated with emotional stability rather than instability: with the absence rather than the presence of conflicts, although intellectual ability and achievement are far from perfectly correlated'. As we have already seen, high IQ and creativity are not very highly correlated, although high IQ and conventional achievement may be; and the Terman project, although it included a few subjects with IQs of 190 and beyond, did not include anyone showing promise of 'matching the eminence of Shakespeare, Goethe, Tolstoy, Da Vinci, Newton, Galileo, Darwin or Napoleon'. Terman finds this not surprising in view of the fact that 'the entire population of America since the Jamestown settlement has not produced the like of one of these'.[7]

Amongst scientists, Cattell and Butcher state that 'the average level of ego strength and emotional stability is noticeably higher among creative geniuses than among the general population, though it is possibly lower than among men of comparable intelligence and education who go into administrative and similar positions. High anxiety and excitability appear common (e.g. Priestley, Darwin, Kepler) but full-blown neurosis is quite rare.'[8] These authors believe that creative artists show much more instability than scientists; but they produce no hard evidence. 'To digress for a moment, it is probably in this respect that creative scientists and artists diverge most markedly. Among the latter, particularly perhaps in the nineteenth and twentieth centuries, neurotic, psychotic and addictive tendencies are so frequent as hardly to need illustration. This applies least, perhaps, to composers, though from Beethoven to Ravel, Bartok and Peter Warlock (Philip Heseltine) their lives have often been stormy or unhappy. The tendency among writers, from Flaubert, Ruskin, Nietzsche and Strindberg in the nineteenth century to Proust, Eugene O'Neill and Dylan Thomas in the twentieth is clearer, and possibly clearest of all among painters (Van Gogh, Utrillo, Modigliani). Many different explanations, temperamental, sociological and economic, could be given for this greater susceptibility to nervous disorder among artistic than among scientific geniuses. In this sphere the "great wits to madness near allied" contention has most plausibility, but has little explanatory value.'[9]

Of course there are differences in personality between scientists and and other types of creative individual; but the similarities are more remarkable than the divergencies. I have already alluded to the fact that a test of aesthetic preference is the best predictor of creativity in both the physical sciences and the arts. It is not difficult to match Cattell's list of artists with some equally 'neurotic' scientists; and his contention that painters are more neurotic than other types of creative individual is not borne out by history. Indeed, Rudolf and Margot Wittkower, already quoted in Chapter 3, have demonstrated in *Born under Saturn* that painters have been of very variable personality types, and that some of the greatest geniuses amongst them have been notably stable. Rubens, for example, was temperamentally equable, and employed as a special diplomatic agent in the negotiation of peace terms between England, France, Spain and the Netherlands because of his calm persuasiveness. In spite of losing both his wife and his eldest child, and in the face of diplomatic reverses, he remained calm. 'Rubens had that admirable fortitude in the face of adversity which stems from an innate harmony, a balance between emotional engagement and intellectual detachment. Misfortune did not sap his strength, nor did success spoil his clear judgment.'[10]

Charles Lamb, in his essay 'Sanity of True Genius' writes: 'So far from the position holding true, that great wit (or genius, in our modern way of speaking) has a necessary alliance with insanity, the greatest wits, on the contrary, will ever be found to be the sanest writers. It is impossible for the mind to conceive of a mad Shakespeare. The greatness of wit, by which the poetic talent is here chiefly to be understood, manifests itself in the admirable balance of all the faculties. Madness is the disproportionate straining or excess of any one of them. "So strong a wit," says Cowley, speaking of a poetical friend, "did Nature to his frame,

As all things but his judgement overcame;
His judgement like the heavenly moon did show,
Tempering that mighty sea below."

The ground of the mistake is, that men, finding in the raptures of the higher poetry a condition of exaltation, to which they have no parallel in their own experience, besides the spurious resemblance of it in dreams and fevers, impute a state of dreaminess and fever to the poet. But the true poet dreams being awake. He is not possessed by his subject but has dominion over it.'[11]

In this statement of Lamb's is the heart of the matter. Neurotics and, still more, psychotics, do most emphatically *not* have dominion over their inner worlds. It is this which makes them suffer, and have symptoms which, by definition, are felt as alien to the conscious ego. To repeat Fenichel's definition: 'All neurotic phenomena are based on insufficiencies of the normal control apparatus.'[12] What is unusual about the creative person is that he has easy access to his inner world, and does not repress it as much as most people. When he is able to create, he certainly is not overwhelmed by it, but has dominion over it, as Lamb asserts.

At first sight, the playwright Strindberg seems an exception to the rule that madness impairs, rather than enhances, creativity. At times in his life, Strindberg seems to have exhibited most of the symptoms of paranoid schizophrenia. In the so-called 'Inferno' crisis of the nineties, he stated that his enemies penetrated the walls of his room with poison gas and electric currents, which was also invaded by an unknown species of fly exhibiting red, fiery spots. He also alleged that he suffered from auditory hallucinations. Like D. H. Lawrence, he rejected the evidence of science, and believed that the stars were optical illusions and that the earth was not a sphere. His misogyny was extreme; and his three marriages all ended in divorce. There is no doubt that, in more than one period, he came very near to being overwhelmed by psychotic symptoms; and yet it never happened. It is clear that his creative ability served him well as a defence. As F. L. Lucas writes of him: 'Strindberg illustrates also the consoling power of art. The one thing that over long periods of his later life could give him a kind of calm, even a kind of happiness, was his power to create. So he has himself recorded. And indeed without this imaginative outlet he might well have ended in a madhouse.'[13]

Strindberg was the son of a waitress and a shipping agent. His mother died when he was thirteen, and his father then married the housekeeper. His father treated him abominably; for he would beat him for offences that he was supposed to have committed but denied; and then would beat him again if he admitted them. This is a typical 'double-bind' situation of the kind supposed to be productive of schizophrenia. There is no doubt that Strindberg's inner world of phantasy was psychotic; but his exploration of it was deliberate and to some extent controlled. 'Not everyone is capable of being mad; and, of those lucky enough to be capable of madness, not many have the courage for it.'[14] So he said himself, and he was right. He also wrote: 'I write best in hallucination.'[15] Evert Sprinchorn, in his introduction to *A Madman's Defence*, has perceptively realized that

Strindberg's madness was not the madness which lands a man in a mental hospital, because his ego was never completely overthrown. He always retained a measure of control; even, perhaps, a measure of histrionic simulation. Sprinchorn writes: 'A mad genius, paranoid and Oedipal, is driven by some compulsion to set down the experiences he believes he has had—such is the usual view of the *Defence*. It seems an extraordinarily naïve view that ignores the evidence offered by Strindberg's letters and takes no account of his avowed principles as an artist. A far more sensible view is that Strindberg created his experiences in order to write about them. Interested in exploring the frontier where jealousy encroaches on madness, he set up a model of the terrain in his own home. That is the scientific method. It is also a method not unfamiliar to actors.'[16]

During the period of his most acute mental disturbance, in the years 1894–96, Strindberg was writing his autobiography; and, during the next seven years, he produced no fewer than seventeen plays. As F. L. Lucas remarks: 'His main output consisted either of fiction that was largely autobiography, or of autobiography that was largely fiction.' But, although he did not always distinguish phantasy from reality, and although the phantasies which he produced were undoubtedly psychotic, he never entirely abandoned control. His material was psychotic, but he himself was not.

Some psychological tests, of which the Minnesota Multiphasic Personality Inventory is the best known, purport to measure an individual's tendency towards neurosis and psychosis by means of a questionnaire. The questions are so framed that the individual's replies indicate whether he possesses depressive, hysterical, paranoid and other neurotic or psychotic traits or not. It will not surprise any reader who has been patient enough to follow the argument of this book so far to learn that creative persons tested in this way do actually admit to more psychopathological traits than the average population, thus confirming the popular belief that artists are 'mad' or at least neurotic. But, as I showed in the last chapter, they are also different from the general population in possessing greater ego-strength. In other words, although their psychopathology may put them under greater stress than the average person, they have a superior controlling apparatus, and are thus no more, though perhaps no less, likely to suffer from neurosis and psychosis than anyone else. These test results confirm our general hypothesis; and, especially for this reason, we must be cautious in interpreting them. It may be that creative people, because they are often so well in touch with what goes on inside themselves, answer such questionnaires with greater insight than the average person; and therefore only appear to have more neurotic traits than other people. The average are often unconscious of their neurotic propensities; tend to be self-satisfied, and often answer questions with less self-doubt than they ought.

It seems probable that the idea that genius is somehow allied to madness did not originate in observing that creative people had more neurotic or psychotic symptoms than anyone else, but in the feeling that both creative people and mad people had mental experiences which the ordinary person found incomprehensible or did not share. We have already quoted Galton's disparaging remarks about genius and inspiration. But it is surely the experience of inspiration, the feeling of being controlled by, rather than controlling, which does in fact link creativity (falsely as I maintain) with neurosis and psychosis. As Fenichel puts it: 'All symptoms give the impression of a something that seems to break in upon the personality from an unknown source—a something that disturbs the continuity of the personality and that is outside the realm of the conscious will.'[17] In Montaigne's essay on Drunkenness, he writes: 'And so that poet is often rapt in admiration of his own work, no longer recognizing the track along which he ran so fine a race: in him we also call it madness and frenzy. And as Plato says that in vain does a sober-minded man knock at the door of poetry, so Aristotle says that no mind of any eminence is free from a tinge of madness. And he is right in calling madness every transport, however admirable, that transcends our reason and judgment; seeing that wisdom is a well-ordered government of our soul, carried out with measure and proportion, for which she is responsible to herself.

'Plato argues thus: "that the power of prophecy is above us; that we must be beside ourselves when we exercise it: our sober senses must be clouded either by sleep or some malady, or lifted from its place in heavenly rapture." '[18]

There is a failure here to distinguish between creative inspiration, and the solution of problems by means other than the conscious exercise of will, which actually misrepresents what Plato probably had in mind. For the Greeks did in fact distinguish between madness and inspiration: and Aristotle's remark became misinterpreted when Seneca took it over and said: 'Nullum magnum ingenium sine mixtura dementiae fuit.'

In that invaluable work *The Origins of European Thought*, Onians shows us what the Greeks thought of inspiration, and how the Latin 'genius' derived from this: 'The genius was, I suggest, in origin the Roman analogue to the ψυχή as here explained, the life-spirit active in procreation, dissociated from and external to the conscious self that is central in the chest. This will explain many facts not hitherto accounted for. The genius was believed to assume the form of a snake, as was the ψυχή. The ψυχή was believed to be in the head.'

Later he adds: 'Not only was his genius thus apparently liable to intervene or take possession of a man but we shall also see reason to believe that it was, in the time of Plautus, thought to enjoy knowledge beyond what was enjoyed by the conscious self and to give the latter warning of impending events . . . The idea of the genius seems to have served in great part as does the twentieth-century concept of an "unconscious mind", influencing a man's life and actions apart from or even despite his conscious mind. It is now possible to trace the origin of our idiom that a man "has" or "has not" genius, meaning that he possesses or does not possess a native source of inspiration beyond ordinary intelligence.'[19]

This view of the unconscious, attributed by Onians to the twentieth century, is actually more 'Jungian' than 'Freudian'. Freudian psychoanalysis has always been reluctant to attribute any positive constructive role to the unconscious, since Freud originally conceived of it as the repository of repressed material, banished to the nether regions because it was unacceptable. This is probably because so many of his original patients, upon whom his early theories were based, were hysterics. For it is such patients who do, indeed, repress their 'nasty' sexual and aggressive impulses, who deny most fervently that their minds contain any such horrors. This is not nearly so true of other types of neurotic, and certainly not so of the creative, who tend to be well aware of what others repress. This view of the unconscious as consisting only of the unacceptable, and the id as chaotic and undifferentiated impulse, has had many unfortunate effects, among them being the failure to distinguish between the sterile rituals of the obsessional and the creative ritualistic activity of the artist or scientist. Thanks to the writings of Marion Milner, Anton Ehrenzweig, and D. W. Winnicott, psychoanalysis is shifting its ground; and this limited, negative view of the unconscious is now outmoded. I shall return to this theme in the last chapter.

Inspiration and madness have in common only the fact that the

212

ego is influenced by something emanating from a source beyond its ken, and what artists actually do is very far from being mad. Indeed, when artists become insane, they generally either cease production altogether, or else show a deterioration in their work. I showed in Chapter 7 that Schumann's depressions tended to stop him composing. There is evidence that Handel, also, was of manic-depressive temperament, although his mood-swings were never so severe as to justify calling him psychotic. During most of his life he was in a hypomanic state, in which he produced an immense amount of music; but he had phases of depression in 1737, 1743, and 1745. During 1743, at any rate, he produced very little. In Chapter 8, I described Rossini's obsessional method of composition, and also briefly touched on his depressive tendency. After his retirement from operatic composition at the age of thirty-seven, Rossini continued to have severe episodes of depression, accompanied by insomnia, loss of appetite, suicidal ideas, and self-reproach. In 1854, he announced: 'Someone else in my state would kill himself, but I . . . I am a coward and haven't the courage to do it.' In 1855, he said: 'Death is better than living this way.' But by the spring of 1857 his depression had passed; and he therefore began to compose again. What he wrote was prefaced with this touching dedication. 'I offer these modest songs to my dear wife Olympe as a simple testimonial of gratitude for the affectionate, intelligent care of which she was prodigal during my overlong and terrible illness. Shame of the (medical) faculty.'[20]

Manic-depressive psychopathology may spur a man to create: but manic-depressive illness stops him doing so, and the same is true of schizophrenia. In his interesting book on psychotic art, the Dutch psychiatrist, J. H. Plokker, writes: 'Everyone who knows anything about art sees the difference between the normal and the pathological when he looks at a series of works by one patient, and soon becomes bored on seeing psychotic creations, once the first moment of surprise has passed. The arid, stereotyped and fixed elements in the content and particularly in the shapes soon show the mental stagnation.'[21] Although, at the onset of a schizophrenic illness, the strangeness of the experience may stimulate an artist to record something of his new way of perceiving the world, rather as mescaline or LSD may do, this is generally short-lived; and the evidence points to deterioration.

'Various publications render this view probable on the basis of case histories of artists who become affected by the schizophrenic process and whose productivity—often after an initial rise—either rapidly ceased completely or showed a rapid qualitative deterioration until there finally remained nothing but senseless bungling. Intermediate stages include the appearance of stereotypes, the occurrence of rigid compositions and of decorative elements. Studies of the Swedish painters Hill and Josephson, Jasper's book on van Gogh, Strindberg and Holderlin, Verbeek's thesis on Arthur Rimbaud, Westerman Jolstijn's article on Vincent van Gogh—to mention but a few—describe this course of events in detail. It can, in general, be stated that if there were no artistic skill prior to the outbreak of the disease, there can be no question of the production of "works of art" once it has begun to reveal itself.'[22]

In the same vein, Kris says: 'For reasons not discussed here, the search for genius in the insane has become fashionable. Clinical experience, however, demonstrates that art as an aesthetic—and therefore as a social—phenomenon, is linked to the intactness of the ego. Although there are many transitions, the extremes are clear.'[23] Intactness of the ego is of course just what schizophrenics lack. Indeed, one of the characteristic symptoms of schizophrenia is what has been called 'fragmentation' of the ego, with a consequent lack of contact with both the external world and other people.

I mentioned that taking LSD, mescaline or one of the other hallucinogenic drugs might stimulate an artist by giving him a new vision of the world. There is no doubt that drugs can, very temporarily, give access to the unconscious source of inspiration. But their habitual use is inimical to creativity. Even so comparatively harmless a drug as marihuana so impairs the will that, although it may encourage the appearance of inspiration, it prevents constructive use of it. Jazz musicians appear to believe that marihuana enhances their ability for spontaneous improvisation; but playing is a different matter from writing. One composer acknowledged that, after smoking 'pot', he found that new and apparently enthralling tunes came to him without difficulty. However, he found that he was quite unable to write them down; and, when he had recovered from the drug sufficiently to do so, he was disappointed to discover that the tunes had faded from his memory. Anyone who has read Alethea Hayter's scholarly study, *Opium and the Romantic Imagination*,[24] will be convinced that any value which the visions induced by opium possessed was far outweighed by the misery consequent upon addiction. Drugs, like insanity, impair the functions of the ego. For creative work, access to the inner realm of the psyche is essential. But so is a strongly

214